GETTING
EVEN

*WHY WOMEN DON'T GET
PAID LIKE MEN —
AND WHAT TO DO ABOUT IT*

Evelyn F. Murphy
with E.J. Graff

A Touchstone Book
Published by Simon & Schuster
New York   London   Toronto   Sydney

TOUCHSTONE
Rockefeller Center
1230 Avenue of the Americas
New York, NY 10020

Designed by Jaime Putorti

For information about special discounts for bulk purchases,
please contact Simon & Schuster Special Sales at
1-800-456-6798 or business@simonandschuster.com.

Manufactured in the United States of America

10   9   8   7   6   5   4   3   2   1

Library of Congress Cataloging-in-Publication Data
Murphy, Evelyn F.
    Getting even : why women don't get paid like men—and what to do about it /
Evelyn F. Murphy, with E.J. Graff.
        p.   cm.
    "A Touchstone book."
    Includes bibliographical references and index.
    1. Sex discrimination in employment—United States—Prevention.   2. Sex
discrimination against women—United States.   3. Women in the professions—
United States—Interviews.   4. Women employees—United States—Interviews.
5. Women—Employment—United States—Anecdotes.   I. Title: Why women
don't get paid like men—and what to do about it.   II. Graff, E.J.   III. Title.
HD6060.5.U5M87   2005
305.42—dc22   005048563

ISBN-13: 978-0-7432-5466-3
ISBN-10:   0-7432-5466-X

TO JACQUE

Contents

PART 1: WHY NOT A DOLLAR?

Chapter 1: Introduction   3

Chapter 2: Why Not a Dollar?   16

Chapter 3: The Personal Cost of the Wage Gap: 22
            A Second-Class Life

PART 2: NOW ADD DISCRIMINATION

Chapter 4: Cents and Sensibilities   37

Chapter 5: Plain Old Discrimination   51

Chapter 6: Wage Discrimination by Sexual Harassment   100

Chapter 7: Women's Work   145

Chapter 8: Everyday Discrimination: Working   174
            While Female

Chapter 9: Working While Mother: The Mommy Penalty   194

PART 3: GETTING EVEN

Chapter 10: No More Excuses   217

Chapter 11: Starting to Get Even   232

Chapter 12: Women, Working from the Inside Up   266
Chapter 13: CEOs, Working from the Top Down   284
Chapter 14: All of Us, Working from the Outside In   299

Notes   309
Acknowledgments   323
Index   327

PART 1

Why Not a Dollar?

CHAPTER 1

Introduction

Are you paid as much as a man would be if he had your job?

Most working women today, if they're over thirty, would probably blurt out, "No. A man would be getting more."

Their intuitive sense is borne out by the facts. Women working full-time — not part-time, not on maternity leave, not as consultants — still earn only 77 cents for every full-time male dollar. Very few individual women can ever find out exactly what their male counterparts would be making in the same job. But that yawning gap between the *average* male and *average* female paycheck is a pretty good clue that he'd be paid more.

If you're a woman, what would *you* do with that extra 23 cents — *an increase of nearly one third on top of your current 77-cent paycheck* — a raise that got you even with men?

The wage gap has been stalled for more than a decade. It exists between women and men working at every economic level, from waitresses to corporate lawyers, from nurse's aides to CEOs. *Getting Even* tackles the questions: Why are women's paychecks still so far behind? And what do we have to do to catch up?

Let me explain how I became interested in women's pay—and why these questions are particularly urgent now. Back in the 1960s, when I started working full-time as a newly minted Ph.D. economist, women earned 59 cents for every dollar earned by men. At the time, I accepted the common explanation that the gender wage gap existed because of a "merit gap." Women, this theory went, were not as well educated as men, hadn't worked as long, or were working in low-skill, stopgap jobs until they got married while men were working at higher-end jobs as family breadwinners. But this "merit gap" was closing. Women were streaming into colleges and jobs. Like many observers, I was convinced that the wage gap would soon close.

Over my working life, I have kept my eye on that number. And for roughly the next two decades, my widely shared expectation seemed to be coming true. The gender wage gap narrowed slowly but steadily. By 1993, women were making 77 cents to a man's dollar.

Then came a shock. In 1994, despite the growing economy, the gender wage gap abruptly widened. A *wider* wage gap? That took my breath away. Worse, this reversal came at a time when the Dow Jones Industrial Average was starting its spectacular climb and the economy was chugging into a period of historically high employment, when every worker was needed, when highly qualified women had long been graduating at the same rates as men. How could that be?

Nor was this increased wage gap a statistical aberration. Over the next several years women continued to lose ground. This made no sense. More than 40 million American working women were educated, experienced, and holding full-time jobs comparable to men's. This was a fair comparison of full-time female workers to full-time male workers, apples to apples. It left out all women who worked part-time, who were on leave, or who had dropped out of the labor force to be stay-at-home moms or caretakers for elderly relatives. Like men, these women had families dependent on their earnings. Some, like some men, were furiously ambitious, working night and day to get ahead. Most, like most men, worked hard at their nine-to-five or swing-shift schedules to keep those badly needed paychecks coming in. Why, instead of catching up, were these hardworking women suddenly falling further behind? What had changed? And why weren't women alarmed by this?

Maybe it was because individual working women didn't necessarily notice that they were losing ground. In fact, many women were dumbstruck by how much more money they were making than they'd ever imagined possible. Women were comparing themselves with themselves, their income and achievements with their own expectations—and by that measure, they were doing great.

But the wage gap is not about an individual's comparison with herself. It compares the average earnings of all women with the average earnings of all men. Over the course of the decade, many women's earnings rose. Yet as the economy steamed ahead in the mid-1990s, on average, women's earnings did not go up *as much as men's did.* For instance, women in their late fifties and early sixties saw their paychecks growing as they approached retirement—but men of the same age saw their paychecks increase almost *seven times* more than women's did. And that signaled a major social injustice.

The real outrage was that precisely the *opposite* should have happened. The 1990s was the decade in which women should have *closed* the wage gap. Women had all but closed the "merit gap." But the wage gap had not only remained astonishingly wide but was going backward. The mid-1990s' widening in the wage gap was too large and too sustained to be explained by casual social theories such as time-outs for motherhood, new elder care demands, welfare moms forced to work, or a handful of high-achieving women who abandoned their careers. And the persistently wide size of the gap—almost 25 cents—required explanation. Why weren't women's earnings catching up to men's in these boom times, when the gap should have closed?

Having watched the wage gap all my working life, I couldn't get my mind off these questions. For me, the wage gap is a keenly personal issue. Neither of my parents went to college; I didn't start out aimed toward an intellectual or professional career. To put myself through college, I waited tables at an ice cream parlor, punched a desk calculator, and did general office work at a government job. I've always known I had to live on my paycheck—and that many other women must as well.

And so I began asking everyone I came across—nurses, businesspeople, politicians, journalists, academic researchers, transit authority workers, women and men, black and brown and white—how they might explain this shift. Few had noticed. But after a pause, whomever I was speaking with almost invariably started to tell a story of unfair treatment in the workplace. For instance, a top-ranking physician at a Boston teaching hospital told me that of course female doctors didn't earn as much as the male doctors: while women did the grunt work in committees, men were awarded administrative appointments that boosted their income. A veteran clerical worker in California said that, despite her college degree and twenty-five years' experience, she earned less than the newly hired, unskilled men her government department hired to pick up "ratty old sofas" abandoned on curbsides. And a laid-off computer programmer, a strong and athletic woman who tried to get temporary "light industrial" work—unskilled factory or construction labor—was told to come back on a day when they had "women's work" such as filing or telemarketing. Consider the experience of a midwestern psychiatric case manager. When her unit had an opening, she suggested a man with whom she had previously worked. "He didn't have any more experience than I did," she recounts. "They offered him the job at, like, three thousand dollars more than what I had been offered." She knew that because he told her.

The details varied. But the theme was utterly consistent: Men's jobs paid more. Men advanced more easily. And that was costing women money—real money that we needed in our everyday lives, to buy groceries or put a down payment on a house or save for retirement.

Most women harbor some such memory of unfair treatment, some irritating or infuriating moment that almost surely set back her wages: that job where colleagues treated her as incompetent, the position where the manager insisted on taking the team to Hooters each Friday until she finally left for a lower-paying spot, or the time her manager passed her over for promotion because, he said, now that she was a mom she had other responsibilities. Most women have such a story to tell.

Throughout *Getting Even*, stories will be told of women who volunteered to talk about their experiences at work. Some of these were solicited in a small-scale research project of the kind social scientists call "qualitative" rather than "quantitative." I recruited women through several public Web sites.[1] Others found their way to me informally, as the word got out about what I was doing. Still others were found because they were named plaintiffs in discrimination lawsuits or because their EEOC attorneys asked them if they would be willing to speak with me. Many asked for anonymity, out of concern that their stories might be used to set back their paychecks. These women were by no means a "random sample," as that term is used in statistics or social science. Nevertheless, they come from very different walks of life. They live in a variety of regions and work in many kinds of jobs and industries: a secretary in Hollywood, a corporate executive at a Fortune 100 manufacturing firm, a manager in the U.S. Justice Department, a midwestern insurance analyst, an independent New Hampshire carpenter, and so on.

I tell these stories to illustrate and illuminate the stark data that is *Getting Even*'s backbone. Women today are stuck making almost a quarter less than men. Why? Because of unfair treatment on the job—unfair treatment that may not always be intentional, but is so deeply ingrained that it will continue *unless we act.*

Getting Even is written for every woman—and for every man who cares about the women in his life. It's written for the woman who has seethed under such a moment of injustice—and for the man who's been furious on hearing her tale. It's written for the woman who assumes she is getting paid fairly but who has not yet considered how unfair treatment might be crippling her paycheck—and for the man who hasn't yet recognized how his wife's crimped wages are hurting their family finances. Most important, *Getting Even* is written for every woman who doesn't want to pass the wage gap on to her daughters—and for every man who cares whether his wife, girlfriend, daughters, sisters, nieces, and granddaughters are being paid fairly.

Getting Even's premises are simple. The gender wage gap is unfair. It's still with us, and it's not going away on its own. It pinches the daily lives of women throughout the country, at every economic level. It is being passed along from one decade to the next, from one generation to the next. It measures discrimination against women on the job, which comes in many forms. The most blatant barriers to women in the workforce may be down, but that just makes eliminating the "hidden" barriers—unspoken assumptions, unexamined attitudes, habitual ways of behaving—that much more urgent. In 2000, two thirds of all U.S.

working women were still crowded into twenty-one of the five hundred occupational categories. Legal changes have been helpful, but government can't do everything that's necessary to close the gap the rest of the way.

But there *is* a solution. Women (and sympathetic men) have to stop making excuses about why our wages are lower than men's. We have to look at the problem squarely, as this book will. And then we have to work together at the pragmatic solution laid out in *Getting Even*'s final section. A few visionary employers, such as MIT's former president Charles Vest, have figured out how to treat women fairly. The solution is not rocket science. It involves paying close and sustained attention to how women and men are treated and measuring progress along the way. Working women (and the men who care about them) need to stand up for ourselves on the job. We need to work together to pressure *every* boss to follow MIT's lead and to get women even. If we all work at this together, steadily and attentively, women can—and will!—be paid just like men, in just one decade.

That's why I've titled this book *Getting Even*, which is meant to be simultaneously provocative, funny, and quite serious. You've heard the saying behind it: "Don't get mad; get even." I've always taken this to mean we should be smart about how we correct wrongdoings. Anger has its place, if it prompts you to respond with thoughtfulness and care. That's this book's goal: to get you angry enough to act; to offer up an overall strategy that will fix women's wages; and to give you constructive tools so that you, as an individual, can get financially even with men. Getting you angry should, unfortunately, be easy enough. *Getting Even* will do this simply by examining how much the wage gap is costing women, each and every day. It will show you what it means to be deprived of nearly one fourth of your rightful income. It will calculate how much you—or your sisters, daughters, nieces, granddaughters— are losing over a lifetime. The wage gap has a higher cost than most women will admit to themselves. *Getting Even* will look unflinchingly at that deprivation.

The subtitle tells you a little more: *Why Women Don't Get Paid Like Men—and What to Do About It*. That word "why" is important. This book is full of stories, statistics, research, and facts—about sex discrimination, about the wage gap, about lawsuits, about women's experiences on the job—so that you can see that, when you face unfair treatment, you are not alone. We have to know why things are as they are before we can come up with an effective plan for what to do. (If you're interested in more scholarly detail about the whys and wherefores, follow the end-notes to academic studies and legal cases about how discrimination per-meates workplaces' nooks and crannies.)

Until this book, you will not have read that the wage gap is all about discrimination. Since the passage of Title VII of the Civil Rights Act of 1964, which prohibits employment discrimination based on race, color, religion, sex, or national origin, academic and media analysts have theorized that the wage gap exists because something is wrong with women. Such theories have included these: women are less edu-cated; women don't work as long or as hard as men; women haven't been in jobs for as many years; women aren't as committed to work.

Over time, as those more obvious differences between working women and men narrowed but the wage gap remained, analysts pro-posed finer-grained distinctions. For instance, you've probably heard these: Women are less skilled in negotiating; women are not strong leaders; women choose family over work. But note that the central the-ory remains the same: Women are deficient.

Here's the problem: economic and academic analysts are confined by their data's limitations. They're trying to draw conclusions based on the available nationwide statistics, which are provided by the U.S. Cen-sus Bureau and U.S. Bureau of Labor Statistics, and which describe working people by their age, race, gender, educational attainment, job earnings—and nothing more. When social scientists try to draw con-clusions about the wage gap based only on data about workers' demo-graphic characteristics, they're drawing conclusions from only part of the picture. They're not looking at behavior in the workplace—and so their theories are limited.

Alarm bells should go off when a forty-year-old theory no longer matches the facts. Working women's characteristics have essentially caught up with men's. The wage gap persists. So either the theory is in-adequate or the data are inadequate, or—as *Getting Even* will show—both are inadequate. So let's try a new theory: Women are essentially equal workers, but employers are not treating them equally. *That* would explain the wage gap. But economic analysts will not be able to measure such a theory until they *also* look at data from behind employers' doors.

Such internal employment data can be hard to get. Sometimes lawyers can get such data when a woman sues her employer, and depositions and document searches bring forth comparative wage information and other important facts about that employer's pay schedules, policies, and practices. But government does not collect from all employers information about jobs and wages that's broken down by sex. Keep that in mind while you read this book. Today's conventional wisdom about what causes the gender wage gap ignores anything that happens behind employers' doors.

That's why *Getting Even* will spend six chapters looking at exactly that. I've assembled and examined records—never before collected in one place—of recent lawsuits in which sex discrimination was so obvious and so clearly documented that courts actually awarded women money to compensate for their losses, or that employers settled and paid women to avoid the risk and expense of a court finding against them. As you'll see, women have to be treated very badly before that happens. And yet employers are paying out millions upon millions of dollars, year after year, as a tax on their ongoing misbehavior toward women. As I write this preface, in the autumn of 2004, two of the biggest recent stories have been about sex discrimination at Wal-Mart and at Merrill Lynch. Clearly discrimination transcends both class and geography. You'll be shocked—I certainly was—to read just how bad, and how widespread, that misbehavior is.

In addition, *Getting Even* examines how the very same kinds of unfair treatment crimps the worklives of women who cannot afford a lawsuit's risks and costs. This kind of insidious sex discrimination rarely hits the headlines. It's what happens when a man is promoted on his potential while a woman has to prove herself first. Or when a man who has a child is given a raise on the assumption that he now must support a family (a bump up that's so common researchers call it the "daddy bonus"), while a woman who has a child is automatically shunted off the promotion track on the assumption that she's now unreliable. Many women shove such incidents aside so that they can get on with their lives. But it's still costing them, and their families, dearly.

So who decides which actions, policies, and behaviors are discriminatory? From campaigning for public office, I learned to trust the people who talked with me in their living rooms, their offices, and on factory floors. They were the ones who best understood the conditions they faced. Journalists would capture their stories in newspaper articles. Researchers would absorb and analyze their stories in academic studies. But the people on the front lines, in their own words and with their own ways of explaining their experiences, were the ones who taught me the most vivid lessons.

Most women go through their work lives doing the best they can at their jobs; they don't sit around totting up every slight or injustice if they feel there's nothing they can do about it. But when asked to step back and examine their employers' behavior, they—and only they—are in a position to consider whether or not their workplace is fair. Women are the experts on what unfairness they encounter at work every day— whether it's as blatant as being told mothers can't be promoted or as subtle as a woman's good work being attributed to luck instead of effort. Experts all have important perspectives: lawyers, economists, sociologists, public policy analysts, social psychologists, organizational specialists, business schools, ethics experts, and all the rest. Each profession looks at wage discrimination through its own lens and adds different insights into how and why women are treated unfairly, many of which I have tried to include in this book. But in this book, working women get the last word on what happened to them on the job.

Decide for yourself, as you read these stories in combination with the rest of this book, whether this approach seems fair. Draw your own conclusions based on these lawsuits, studies, statistics, and stories. See whether other women's experiences resonate with your own. Decide for yourself whether the wage gap is women's own fault—or is due to discrimination.

The second half of *Getting Even*'s subtitle is just as important as the first: "what to do" so that women get paid fairly. Many women and men have worked on efforts to close the wage gap. And those efforts have had important results. Essential laws have been passed. Lawsuits have been, and continue to be, brought against outrageously unfair employers. Women's organizations, diversity consultants, and "work-family" specialists have pushed to make offices and factories more female-friendly. Economists have evaluated the statistical factors involved in pay equity. Social scientists have researched the mental mechanisms behind bias. And yet the wage gap persists.

It needn't persist any longer. We can get rid of the wage gap in ten years. Having academic, government, politics, *and* business experience gives me a rare 360-degree view of the wage problem—*and* of how to solve it. I'm trained as an economist, so I can slice and dice statistics and data until I've squeezed out the juice. I've held top government posts, such as Massachusetts secretary of economic affairs, secretary of environmental affairs, and lieutenant governor—where I learned intimately what government can and cannot do. Government *can* lead by setting out laws and mandates. It *can* punish those who flagrantly violate the American social consensus about what's just. But it *cannot* micromanage or even monitor how employers carry out their daily legal and moral responsibilities to be fair, whether that means paying women and men equally or ensuring a real shot at advancement for women and other historically disadvantaged groups.

Employers have to close the wage gap. I know they can. I've been a business executive and served as director on actively involved corporate boards, so I know how to see through an organizational chart and a balance sheet—and how to manage and motivate folks on the line and in the boardroom. That's important. If women are to get even, businesses will have to change their policies and practices—in ways that are not especially difficult or expensive. The boss can, and must, insist that women be paid fairly. Research, methodologies, and specialists are available to help.

So how can we persuade bosses to commit their organizations to paying women fairly? Pressure. *Getting Even* will ask every woman in this country to act on behalf of her own (and other women's) paychecks. Some of us will work individually to bring up our own wages. Some of us will work together, in a very loosely coordinated national campaign, which I will sketch out at the book's end. Whenever I speak about this subject in public, as I often do, women afterward ask what they can do to help. That's why I know it can be done. Together, we can push bosses to do the right thing.

To some, this plan may sound too ambitious; to others, it may sound too slow. But keep reading. I believe I can convince you not only that this *must* be done, but that it *can* be done.

What Exactly Is Discrimination?

What do I mean by discrimination? Each profession—economists, social scientists, lawyers, politicians, businesspeople, and so on—has a technical definition of the term. But *Getting Even* uses the broadest and most common understanding of "discrimination": treating women and men differently not because of merit but because of sex. That's the meaning in law. In Title VII of the Civil Rights Act of 1964, Congress made it illegal for employers to discriminate on the basis of sex as well as race, color, religion, and national origin. This sweeping law doesn't give employers latitude: an employer is discriminating when *any* woman at *any* time is treated unfairly based solely on her sex.

This book uses the phrases "sex discrimination" and "wage discrimination" interchangeably. While "sex discrimination" is the legal language in the 1964 Civil Rights Act's Title VII, "wage discrimination" is my phrase for reminding readers that this discrimination costs women money. Because Americans are committed to fairness, we may rail against discrimination in and of itself. But *Getting Even* focuses on the fact that discrimination is wrong morally and legally *because of its financial consequences.* When a boss denies a working mother a well-deserved promotion because he assumes she doesn't want more responsibilities and then gives a less qualified man the chance to move up in her place, she loses money. Her paycheck is less than what it could and should be. When a woman is so sexually intimidated she cannot do her best work in the office or on the plant floor, that costs her money, too.

Sex discrimination is not some abstract principle. Sex discrimination costs women money—money we can ill afford to lose. One of this book's goals is to get you to think instinctively of that cost whenever you face, or hear about, unfair treatment. Sex discrimination, wage discrimination, sexual harassment discrimination, occupational segregation, being "mommy-tracked": that's money being taken out of your wallet.

Are women always right when they claim discrimination? Of course not. Sometimes human beings make mistakes, or distort, or even lie. But in my experience, most women step back and try to assess a situation impartially—even when it's happening to them. Women will often bend over backward to be fair. For the purposes of this book, it doesn't matter whether that's because of nature, nurture, or culture. Here's what matters: few women make formal discrimination charges lightly. As you'll see, most women realize that charging or suing for discrimination is a daunting prospect, likely to permanently set back a career.

Who Is Affected by the Gender Wage Gap?

The wage gap does *not* affect all women equally. The appalling fact is that on average African-American and Hispanic women earn much less than Caucasian women. African-American women earn only 70 cents for every dollar an average man earns, whereas Hispanic women earn only 58 cents to the average male dollar.[2] As a result, many of these women live even more dangerously close to, and in, poverty, simply because they are not men *and* not white.

Similarly, discrimination's knife cuts more painfully into the wallets of women at the economy's bottom than in its upper reaches. When a female marketing executive faces wage discrimination, she loses an important chunk of earning power. When a female janitor faces wage discrimination, she may lose the ability to keep a roof over her children's heads.

Getting Even focuses on how the wage gap bites into *all* these women's budgets. Women higher on the income scale lose more money. Women lower on the income scale teeter more dangerously toward disaster. *All women lose.* All women—rich or poor, whatever their race, color, native language—are being cheated by wage discrimination, which is far more entrenched in the American economy than most people realize. None of us will catch up unless, with the help of one another and sympathetic men, women act—not only by turning to the government but also by proving to American employers that we will not accept the depth and breadth of wage discrimination within our own workplaces.

Working together, we can wipe out wage discrimination within the next ten years. But before I show you how, let me show you why.

CHAPTER 2

Why Not a Dollar?

Sometimes I ask people, "What should women be earning today compared with men?" I don't ask what women *are* earning, which hardly anyone can answer with certainty, but what women *should* be earning. Most people shrug and say they have no idea, or guess that it should be about eighty cents to a man's dollar.

No one says "One dollar." That is the correct answer. There should be no gender wage gap at all.

Is that an exaggeration? Statisticians point out that women do not yet have quite as many years' experience in the workforce as men have. It's true that for the generation that began working in the 1960s, fewer women than men have a steady forty or fifty years of on-the-job experience. So maybe there should be a gap of a few pennies—at most!—to reflect that slight disadvantage. But not 23 cents' worth. Social scientists hedge their conclusions about what causes that broad gap with disclaimers. They acknowledge that biases exist in their measurements. They admit that they cannot say for sure that differences between women and men in what's called "merit"—education, experience, and other personal capital—add up to 23 cents. But despite the absence of rock-hard proof, this explanation has been accepted. Instead of demanding an immediate end to the wage gap, most Americans believe that it's closing slowly, at an evolutionary pace, moving women penny by penny toward equality.

But that's just not so. If the explanations heard forty years ago were correct—if the reason for the wage gap was indeed that there was a "merit gap" and that in 1965 women had inferior qualifications, little experience, and less career commitment—that gap would have disappeared by now. The wage gap should have closed more than a decade ago. Instead, for several years during the 1990s, it actually widened.[1] It should have disappeared at every rung, from entry level to executive suite. Women have closed the education, career time, and commitment gap. So why hasn't the wage gap closed as well?

Some commentators answer this question by pulling out little slivers of data—comparing, say, male and female engineering graduates' starting salaries in a particular year—to announce that women are already even. Their claim is that young women and young men (in that job category, at least, for that year) made just about the same amount when they got their first jobs. Therefore, the claim goes, the gender wage gap is over: the very newest generation of adults has gotten even.

But that's just plain wrong. The only way to reach such a conclusion is to cherry-pick the most equal job category during its most equal year (ignoring the vast majority of working women, who are far from equal)—and then to ignore how those young women fare as the years go by. Otherwise, here's what you find: women start out behind, and the longer they work, the further behind they fall. One former bank clerk (now an administrator) told me that when she and her husband entered the job market in the 1970s, doing the same work, they "started off at the same range of pay and he just completely left me behind. His salary just kept going up and up every year, and mine just went up incrementally."

That experience has continued for every generation since. We have heard in recent years that young women have caught up within high school and college, matching or surpassing young men as valedictorians, school newspaper editors, and the like. But that's no longer true once women and men start competing not for grades and accolades but for dollars. No matter how *nearly* equal some are at that first job, the wage gap between men and women in their age group keeps widening throughout their lives.

Take those new graduates just entering the job market, the data sliver sometimes held up as proof of emerging equality. For a brief shining moment in 1991, young women and young men in their first postcollege jobs did get much closer to even: the women earned $20,556 while the men earned $22,479, just (just!) a 9 percent difference. That sounds terrific: 9 percent, when only thirty years before it had been 41 percent. Had that apparent trend continued, women and men might be even by now. But it did not—not for that generation of women, who rapidly fell farther behind, and not for their little sisters, for whom even the *entering* wage gap widened. The young women and men who entered the job market in 2003 were actually *farther* apart than their counterparts in 1991.[2] When these women started working, they earned 16 percent less than young men college grads. So much for the optimistic belief that the gender wage gap is steadily declining with each successive generation of workers.

Why have so many of us held that belief? Because most people thought that the wage gap was narrowing over the last forty years because women were catching up on "merit." A close analysis of the data proves that it's not so. The largest drop in the wage gap—a hefty 8 cents during the 1980s—came not because women were catching up, but because men's real wages were declining, as manufacturing left the United States. Women caught up at men's expense. That's much of the story in the post–World War II American economy: in bad economic times, men's wages flatten, even decline; women catch up only by comparison, not because they're actually gaining more equal treatment on the job. Look at that unpleasant *increase* in the starting wage gap between female and male college graduates in 1991 and 2003. American women's hard work, increasing skills, and improving qualifications do *not* put us on an inevitable course toward equal pay.

If You Graduated in 1991, Your Raises Have Not Kept Pace with Men's

Let's illustrate that more fully by looking at what's happened to a single generation of women and men—a generation whose mothers worked, whose entire lives had been spent under the assumption that they could and would be equal on the job.

What happened to your wages if you graduated from college and entered the job market in 1991? Over the decade, *their raises did not keep pace with men's*. At the beginning of the decade, they were making 91 cents to a man's dollar. By the end of the decade, these very same women were making only 89 cents to a man's dollar. These women fell behind. They lost money. Their wage gap widened.

Let me repeat that: Their wage gap expanded during the nation's biggest economic expansion since the 1950s. It expanded for the generation of women and men *most equally prepared* for the job market in history. The wage gap widened. In 2003, the 25-to-34-year-old women who had graduated from college were making, on average, $47,364—and the men who had graduated alongside them were making, on average, $53,271. Women's real wages had grown by 130 percent—while men's real wages had grown by 137 percent.

Remember, these are no longer baby boomers, the ones who were just breaking open the doors to women's employment, fighting male chauvinist attitudes and general social resistance, and who may have aimed too low, considering that often their mothers didn't work. These young adults grew up with mothers who were just as educated, qualified, employed, and employable as their fathers. These young men and women didn't simply grow up believing that women *could* work, if given the chance; they actually knew women who were bus drivers and doctors, heavy-metal guitarists and helicopter pilots, corporate managers and professional tennis players, state senators and Supreme Court justices. These aren't the trailblazers. These are the trail followers.

Remember, too, that most of these college-educated women could not afford to drop out of work for a couple of years to be stay-at-home moms. These women took their maternity leave (and some husbands even took paternity leave) to have a child—and then had to go right back to full-time work. Those families needed both paychecks—the wife's *and* the husband's—just to keep up their standard of living.[3]

These full-time, year-round working women hadn't even hit their thirty-fifth birthdays, and they were already behind by $6,000 a year—when they had started only $2,000 a year behind. That's a lot of tamales, diapers, or movies. Add that up for a few years, and that's a Ford F150 SuperCrew instead of a Chevy Cavalier. That's a renovated kitchen, a year's college tuition, a time-share in Florida, a significant retirement fund contribution.

Young women with only a high school diploma fell even further behind during these years. When between the ages of 18 to 24 these women entered the job market in 1991, working year-round and full-time, they were earning an average of $13,558—while men with their age, education, and experience earned $16,559. That was a nasty 18 percent gap.[4] By 2003, these women earned 22 cents less for every dollar their male counterparts took home. Having started out earning $3,000 a year less than their male peers, these women were now earning $7,000 a year less—an enormous bite out of a low-wage paycheck.

Women who graduated from professional schools and started their working careers in 1991 fared a little better than these other working women. When between the ages of 25 and 34 these women entered the job market, working year-round and full-time, they were earning an average of $43,429—while men with their age, credentials, and experience earned $61,038. That was a nasty 29 percent gap for a group of people with the same qualifications. By the year 2003, female J.D.s, M.B.A.s, and M.D.s between the ages of 35 and 44 were making an average of $97,756 each year while men their age, with the same credentials, made $113,805, outearning them by only—*only!*—14 percent.

Except for that small number of high-earning women with professional degrees, this recent generation of women starting their working careers followed that same old trend: the longer they worked, the more they fell behind.

Women Fall Farther Behind Men over a Lifetime

The wage gap is an expanding bullet in a woman's finances, tearing away at her checkbook more and more each year. Perhaps that's why, for so many women, the creeping suspicion that things are unfair transforms into a smoldering sense of outrage somewhere between the ages of 35 and 45. Having expected that by working hard they would earn the appropriate rewards, they look around in some shock—and reluctantly realize that the men they graduated with or were hired alongside are far-ther along in their finances and careers. They come to the distressing conclusion that either they've utterly bungled their careers — or they've been cheated out of their rightful earnings.

Heidi Hartmann, president of the Institute for Women's Policy Re-search, who's been tracking the shifts in men's and women's wages for decades, says that when times are good, men advance more than women do. Nobody knows why. But understanding why is important. For that brief moment between 1993 and 2000, women should have gotten even. These were the most promising set of circumstances since the mid-1960s, which saw the Equal Pay Act passed in 1963; Title VII of the Civil Rights Act, which banned gender discrimination at work, passed in 1964; and an Executive Order banning discrimination by fed-eral employees and federal contractors, issued in 1965. That's when we as a nation started paying attention to the idea that women deserve equal pay.

In the 1990s, more than a generation later, women were as qualified as men in just about every particular. This was the decade in which the economy's transformation from brawn to brains, from a manufacturing to a service- and information-based economy, seemed complete. And that's where women are just as well equipped as men: in human rela-tions, in verbal and numeric skills (if you look at the SATs or GREs), in solving problems and creating ideas. America's commitment to reach-ing wage equality for women — and all that meant for women and men becoming socially equal as well — had failed.

If women's earnings could not catch up to men's in a time of nearly unreal prosperity, at a time when women's qualifications had caught up, what was holding them back?

The answer is simple: discrimination.

CHAPTER 3

The Personal Cost of the Wage Gap: A Second-Class Life

My ex-husband moved out. I have purchased the house that we moved into, and it is pretty expensive for my salary. I am trying not to be too attached to it, in case we can't afford it.

—50-year-old civil service employee, Maryland

I could not support myself on a woman's wage. Women cannot. That's why they depend on men. This is why—if you don't make enough to keep yourself off the streets, to put a roof over your head, to eat, to pay for a car, to pay for insurance—if you don't make enough on a normal wage to pay for all that, you're going to have to depend on another income.

—45-year-old worker, Washington

I used to worry about [retirement], a lot. I did. Because I had nothing, when I was a single parent, other than Social Security. And everybody knows that that's kind of iffy. All those years raising my kids by myself, I could put nothing towards my retirement, nothing.

—50-year-old carpenter, New Hampshire

This book's goal is to add up the personal and social costs of wage discrimination, and to show how it can be eliminated. That 23-cent gender wage gap is a *personal* gap in each woman's life: vacations not taken, dental work put off, or lessons her children are denied.

Few women think about it this way. Women don't talk about what they *should* have earned, or how each year's missing lump of money—whether one thousand, ten thousand, or fifty thousand dollars—would have added up over her lifetime. Most women know they have not been paid as much as equally qualified men. But I've never heard a woman let herself dwell on how much that meant she was deprived of overall—or how much more her male coworker could afford that she could not.

Surely that attitude is *personally* sensible: no sane person wants to dwell on what she believes she can't have. Immersed in the relentless current of day-to-day life, few women have the time, energy, or fury to step back and count up what that missing pay has subtracted from their daily lives—let alone how they have been deprived over a lifetime. But you can hear the costs in their conversations, if you listen closely: the missing retirement fund, the nonexistent car, the precarious mortgage, the clothes worn past their expiration dates. Maybe an unexpected change in financial circumstances—especially the loss of a husband's income through layoff, divorce, or death—cut the shoestring on which a woman has been hanging financially, so that she and her children were faced with sharp and sometimes drastic financial choices from week to week or day to day.

Consider the stark case of a New York City middle manager[1] whose boss—noting that she had an hour-and-a-half commute to work each day—one day suggested that she should get a car. "I said, 'You should pay me more. I am not against getting a car in principle. It's just that I can't afford it on what you pay me.' He chuckled. He thought that was amusing." Her office employed sixteen people, eight men and eight women. "The men are making substantially more," she noted without bitterness, just commenting on the way things were. Then she said something quite interesting—something that, I suspect, she hadn't fully added up. "When I first took this job, they paid me $32,000 a year. I saw the time cards and pay scale of the guy who worked there ahead of me."

Her predecessor, she discovered, hadn't worked the standard forty-hour workweek. "He would come and go at will; he worked as many hours as he felt like." For working less than full time, he had been paid $36,500—$4,500, or roughly 14 percent more than she was paid—a smaller-than-average wage gap. Over five years, even without any raises, that would have added up to $22,500. That's her missing car.

In the minds of economists or social scientists, such stories are merely "anecdotal." They prove nothing. But try finding a woman who doesn't have one. Most women know that they are earning less than men doing comparable work. Through their stories runs an undercurrent of frustration and anger, an undercurrent that rarely surfaces. But they don't add up how much that unfair pay is costing them.

American women know they're not being paid fairly. In a recent AFL-CIO survey of working women,[2] 92 percent listed "equal pay" as their top legislative priority, ranking that subject higher in their collective concerns than health insurance, pensions or Social Security, family leave, child care, or any other topic. But in daily life and in conversations with me, women shrugged off the inequity as simply the way things were. "I just accepted that women don't always get a fair shake, we have to work harder," as an engineer in Minneapolis put it. Or they were grateful to have enough to live on, like one woman who was a secretary at a large Hollywood firm. While married to an alcoholic, this woman had been evicted and had had to declare bankruptcy. Now widowed, she was relieved that her financial life was at least stable. She made tart observations about how, in both her current and her previous jobs, women were being paid less than men in comparable jobs. Yet she had clearly decided to be content. "I have my own apartment," she said. "I just bought a new car. I have what I need."

Sometimes women believed that challenging wage discrimination—or even thinking of it by such a confrontational name—would be futile or self-destructive, perhaps even costing them a badly needed job. A property manager told a fairly common story. "I was the most effective person they had. My staff had very little turnover. I always met budget," she explained. But even though she knew she was expected to dress better, she couldn't afford high-end clothes on what she was paid—and still feed her kids. Nor did she feel, in her region's economy, that she had the luxury of making a stink about her salary. "My compensation was always a tad below everybody else's. I was a single parent, and they knew I had to have that job."

Accepting life's limitations, being grateful for what you have, refusing to dwell on what you lack: these may be admirable strategies for emotional stability. American women are pragmatic. We simply make do with less.

But we're not going to close the gender wage gap until women realize how much it's costing us and our families. When you earn 23 cents less on the dollar, you have 23 cents less to spend. You are missing a very large chunk of money, money that is crucial to your well-being. Let's add up exactly what you have been deprived of—in dollars, in economic security and peace of mind, in opportunities for your children, in quality of life.

Before we do, let me first explain some decisions I've made about the numbers. First, throughout the book, I will round off estimates of earnings and expenditures, numbers that would be worked out to the precise penny if this were an economics article. Second, wherever possible, the numbers for women's and men's average income are worked out using statistics about median weekly wages, rather than annual wages. Let me explain why. When you hear about the wage gap, you are usually hearing about a number that has been calculated using weekly wages. That's where we get the figure of 23 cents. For technical reasons, if it is calculated using annual wages, the earnings gap is actually wider: 27 cents. Switching back and forth in this book between a 23-cent gap and a 27-cent gap would be confusing, to no purpose. Talking about the 23-cent gap throughout the book is both more consistent and more conservative, and illustrates just as well the gender wage gap's practical cost to women.

I Want My Million Dollars

What *does* it mean to be deprived of 23 percent of what you earned? Let's add it up over a lifetime. The numbers below rely on the calculations of lifetime earnings losses developed by the Institute for Women's Policy Research using U.S. Census Bureau data ("Current Population Survey," March 1997), which compare lifetime annual earnings of women with men by age and education level, using a forty-seven-year adult life span for working full-time and year-round.[3]

- A *high school graduate loses $700,000.* A young woman graduates from high school this year and goes straight to work at $20,000 a year. Over her lifetime, she will make $700,000 less than the young man graduating right behind her.
- A *college graduate loses $1.2 million.* A young woman graduates from college into a $30,000 starting salary. Over her lifetime, she will make $1.2 million less than the young man getting his diploma next to her.
- A *professional school graduate loses $2 million.* A young woman gets a degree in business, medicine, or law and graduates into a $70,000 starting salary (along with staggering student loan debts). Over her lifetime, she will make $2 *million less* than the young man at her side.

That graduate may be you. Or she may be your daughter, niece, granddaughter, or young friend. Whoever she is, the wage gap will take a heavy toll. What would *you* do with another $700,000, $1,200,000, or $2,000,000 over your lifetime?

Those numbers are conservative. They assume that a woman works for forty-seven years without pausing. If instead she stopped, as many women do, for a year or two or five to raise children or take care of elderly parents, her losses accelerate. Journalist Ann Crittenden calculated that by leaving her newspaper job to spend more time at home with her child, she lost from $600,000 to $700,000 (at a conservative estimate), not counting her pension rights. When she made the decision to take time off, she never considered the cost. She just took for granted that she'd catch up later. That wasn't possible. Instead, she writes, she sacrificed "more than half my lifetime earnings" to raise her child.[4] If you're not earning at Crittenden's prestigious level, you may not lose as much—but the *percentage* lost from your lifetime earnings will be just as devastating.

That's also true if you stop out to care for anyone other than a child. A first-ever study of midcareer women who paused to care for elderly parents or grandparents found that, on average, they lost $659,000 in combined earnings, Social Security benefits, and pension benefits. Women who had thought the caregiving would last only six months spent more than a year at it; those who had expected a one- to two-year stint ended up spending four years or more. Coming at a time in women's work lives when their earnings should have peaked—45 years and older—these duties cost them dearly.[5]

Few women subject themselves to such a cold calculus: child rearing and caretaking can be profoundly rewarding, satisfying in ways that can't be measured in dollar figures. At the same time, for reasons I'll examine in depth in chapter 9, "Working While Mother," the "choice" to stop out or go part-time for child rearing or caretaking isn't always as free a decision as it's portrayed. As you'll see, many women "choose" that option because once they have children, they're treated unfairly on the job—in ways that employers could stop but do not.

But in this chapter, we're not asking why it happens; we're simply asking how much it costs. Whatever the reason they're taken, the amount a woman loses during caretaking and mothering pauses can't simply be added onto the amount she loses to the wage gap. No one has yet studied or calculated those combined financial effects. But anyone with a gap in his or her résumé knows that potential employers look askance at those missing years. As chapter 9 will examine, saying you spent those unaccounted-for years as a "mother" almost certainly means you'll get hit with the "mommy penalty," treated as less competent and remunerated at a lower rate than when you left, as if you had checked your ambition and skills at the maternity ward door. But again, whatever the reason, here's the bottom line: When women who've stopped working to care for their families come back into the workforce, their earnings are unlikely to catch up.[6]

Once, when I laid out these numbers to a small audience, a senior corporate manager exclaimed, "I want my million dollars!" As do we all.

A 77 Percent Life

No one, of course, would see that money in a single lump sum. Instead, it's subtracted from our lives bit by bit: food we couldn't buy, homes we couldn't afford, credit cards we couldn't pay off. With 77 cents to a man's dollar, women have less money to buy basics. Yet prices are the same whether you are female or male, rich or poor. Which means that once a woman buys one staple, she has less money left over for the next.

Let's make that a little more particular. According to the 2000 census, the median income for a single dad was $42,000.[7] If you assume (as many budgets do) that 15 percent of that goes for food and groceries, our single dad can spend $120 a week on food. But transform that single dad into a single mom, and suddenly there's only $95 a week for food. That missing 23 percent comes directly out of the mouths of her family. Each woman would spend that money differently: on fresh fruit and vegetables, a splurge night at the local taco house, or barbecue instead of rice and beans. What would you do with an extra $25 a week for food?

Many women expect to be financially sheltered by marriage. And yes, male earnings will lift most women for some, possibly even most, of their working years. But those years aren't guaranteed to be continuous—and, odds are, won't last as long as the woman herself will. Statistically speaking, at any given moment, four of every ten American women between the ages of 20 and 64 years old are living on their own.[8] And husbands do unexpectedly lose their jobs, leaving the family to depend on the wife's wages. No woman can count on having that male paycheck to lean on every day of her adulthood.

Let's look at what that means financially through an average working woman's life cycle, starting with her young-adult years. Once upon a time, single American women lived with their families before marrying in their twenties. For a brief period in the 1950s, they married right out of college. But today, those young women are supporting themselves for a good decade before marrying a mate. That's at least one decade of scrimping by on less.

Nine out of ten American women do marry at least once in their lives. But one in two marriages ends in divorce.[9] That's a large percentage of adult women who are supporting themselves for some unpredictable number of years. What's more, women usually get custody of the children. In 2001, 30 million women were solely responsible for their children. Now here comes the bad news: Single moms are actually *worse* off than other women, making only 69 percent of a single dad's dollar (even counting the average $3,000 a year that half of them manage to collect in child support). Any time there are unexpected expenses—new school shoes, asthma inhalers, scout uniforms, swimming lessons, costumes for the school play, higher gas prices or bus fares or electricity bills—the money must come from *her* 69 percent paycheck. Her children get used to thrift store clothes, to wearing heavy sweaters in the house, to not having friends over for food-costly sleepovers. She will probably remarry, possibly a good earner who will relieve the family of poverty. But no woman can budget for that. Her new husband may arrive in two years or ten years or never. And even when our single mom does remarry, she will never make up for those missing 31 cents on the dollar during her single-mom years.

If we base that 31 percent on a single dad's annual income of $42,000, our single mom is missing $14,000 each year. That money is missing from a down payment she could make on a house. It's missing from her savings for her children's college tuition. It's missing from her retirement fund. That missing money is never made up.

And that missing money takes a harsh toll on single mothers. If that single mom with two children is living and working in a city such as Memphis, Chicago, or Salt Lake City, she simply cannot afford everything her family needs. Her 69 percent paycheck just will not stretch to cover it all—housing, food, utilities, transportation, child care, doctors' visits, medicines, and other essentials. That missing money forces her into escalating credit card debt, into overcrowded and unsafe housing, into skipping meals so her children can eat. On $28,000 a year, she may not be officially poor, at least according to the government's definition of poverty. But every day is a financial battle—and she is constantly losing.[10]

Because of the wage gap, a woman's everyday life is unnecessarily precarious, leaving her teetering just on the edge of financial disaster and sometimes plunging in—far more often than is true for the average working man.

Above-Average Earnings, Above-Average Losses

By definition, of course, some women have an income above the median. But her income is never as much as her male counterpart's would be. No matter what the income bracket, the average man can always afford more than the average woman. He can afford higher-quality necessities such as child care, home ownership, food, and health insurance. He can afford higher-quality extras than she can, such as a new bicycle instead of a used one or personal tennis lessons instead of group lessons at the Y. He can afford a new car when she has to keep repairing her used one. He can put money away for the future when she can't. If she has three dollars, he has four.

Remember, these aren't hangovers from a prefeminist era whose earnings still lag. These are women who always assumed that women could get an advanced education, who launched their careers early in the Reagan era, a good sixteen years after the Civil Rights Act outlawed sex discrimination at work. These women took it for granted that by working hard, they would pull even with men. Instead, they're almost as far behind as their mothers were.

For instance, one woman I spoke with was an auditor who preferred to remain anonymous lest she jeopardize her job. This auditor explained that of all the auditors and financial supervisors in her agency, she was the only one with a CPA. "I am still the best-qualified person in my department," she said. "I have a CPA, an MBA, a bachelor's in accounting, and a CMA, a certified management accountant. My boss has a master's but no certification. His boss has a CFE [Certified Fraud Examiner], but that is not as good as a CPA. None of the other people I work with has any certification. They are being paid more: they are Analysts 3, and I am an Analyst 2. They are guys." This auditor was making $40,000 a year. Had she been a man, she would have been making $52,000. This auditor was missing $12,000 a year—enough, in her area, to put a down payment on a new three-bedroom house.

But that particular woman was closer to her male counterpart than usual. On average, a female midcareer college graduate—age 42, working full-time—is making $48,000 annually. The man who graduated right behind her in line—age 42, working full-time—is making

$72,000. What would you do with another $24,000 a year: replace an aging car, pay off credit card debts, put money away toward retirement?

And it's still worse for the 42-year-old professional woman—lawyer, physician, M.B.A. graduate—who's making 60 cents for every dollar made by the man who graduated beside her. If she were a man, she would have still another $55,000 a year.

So wouldn't that single mother and her son have been better off financially had she stayed married? That suggestion often comes up in today's public discussions. For the moment, let's leave aside the potential toll taken by a bad or abusive marriage, whether physical, emotional, or moral. Let's imagine that she makes a purely financial decision to stay married. What happens when the economy takes a downturn—and her husband loses his job? For six months, or a year, or two, all three are now scraping by on her 77 percent paycheck.

Double or Nothing: Aging with Less

Even happy marriages end eventually—if not in divorce, then in death. Most women marry men older than themselves, and men's life expectancy is five years less than women's. Because of that demographic double whammy, more women outlive their husbands than vice versa—and so, in later years, widows outnumber widowers by more than four to one.[11] As a result, most women will be widows, which will bring them another spate of years—maybe a decade or more—in which they must live without leaning on a man's earnings or his pension, which usually dies with him. If a woman has been married for a long time, the drop in her standard of living may be startling—and push her into poverty.

Our culture takes it for granted that many more women than men will live out their senior years in poverty. Scratch a well-off professional woman, and you're likely to find a person with a recurring fear of a lonely and impoverished old age. That gut-level fear is accurate. Eleven million older American women (and only 4 million older men) make do with less than $8,300 a year, the federal definition of poverty. Nearly three times as many women as men live at subsistence level in their old age.

What does that mean, day to day? Once again let's take the theoretical case of a widow, now a 65-year-old living alone, and of a widower who's her demographic counterpart. On average, the widow, like her younger self, lives on just 77 cents of what she would have if she were a he. And it's no easier to live on less when you're older. Her expenses don't go away; they shift—from paying for child care to physical therapy, from recreation to medication, from work clothes to warm clothes.

Our widow and widower each have a median annual income and pay average costs for everything. She's living on $996 a month. He's living on $1,319 a month.[12] Neither has much wiggle room. But what happens to her when she has to repair her car's brakes or pay the heating bill for an especially cold February? He has a slight cushion. She has none.

Why are widows so much poorer than widowers, since they've inherited the house, most of their husband's property, and a share of his Social Security income? Here's the answer: the wage gap.

She earned less in her working lifetime, and so, if she was lucky enough to get a pension, hers is only about half of what a man's pension would be. If she saved, she saved less. She continues to earn less when she decides she has to keep bringing money in past retirement age; older women make only 58 *percent* of what male retirees bring in.

Less money in pensions, earnings, and savings income: all that means that many more retired women than men are living in poverty or teetering at its edge. One in four of now-single older women— widowed, separated, divorced, or never married—lives poor.

But aren't women in today's workforce—with better educations and richer earnings histories—going to be in a better position later on? No. Home ownership, accrued pensions, savings, earnings in future years: as long as a woman earns 23 percent less *now*, she will have 23 percent less *later*. She will become more financially vulnerable, not less. No wonder women fear growing old.

Will We Pass It On?

Everything that women—single or married, young or middle-aged— *don't* earn accrues. Many of us have seen those investment charts that show how much $1,000 invested today would turn into over ten or twenty or thirty years. That's what happens to the money women *weren't* paid: it doesn't just add up, it multiplies over time.

If we are to "get even," every working woman must calculate for herself just how much the wage gap costs her now and throughout her life. Every woman needs to add it up, to see just how much money she's losing. Do it. You'll see that you're missing a lot of money. That's painful. But without facing up to that loss, we will not press for the pay we deserve—and need.

Women may be uncomfortable adding up what a lifetime of wage inequity has meant for ourselves. But ask women if they want their *daughters* to face the same financially strained lives, and they snap to attention. As one 65-year-old accountant in Tucson, Arizona, said, "I have many granddaughters coming up who are now in the workforce. It would be nice to know that everything we've done through these years will help the next generations."

The wage gap makes almost every woman fear poverty—and ensures that many struggle with it. Will we pass it on?

PART **2**

Now Add Discrimination

CHAPTER 4

Cents and Sensibilities

Does the wage gap measure discrimination? Many of the people I spoke to seemed to hold that theory, although they did not articulate it so clearly. Every time I mentioned my shock that women's wages had fallen further behind men's for several years during the booming 1990s, someone told me a story of women who had been underpaid, passed over, or otherwise treated unfairly.

A nurse said that, at her hospital, men—even when they had few skills and far less training than her own—quickly moved up in the hospital pay ranks, while harder-working women stayed in place, year after year. A graphic designer said that, throughout her career, she'd seen advertising firms lay off new moms (though not equally sleep-deprived new dads) within a year of a child's birth—as if fatherhood was a temporary setback, while motherhood was a permanent disability. Men said that they had watched their highly qualified, high-achiever wives take years longer than male colleagues to make partner or be promoted to manager.

Everyone I met had a story. Although they might not have said so outright, clearly they strongly suspected that unfair incidents like these explained why women still made less than men. But I had no way of knowing whether these experiences were common. Was I hearing unusual anecdotes that meant little except to the individuals involved, stories from the perennially disgruntled or oversensitive—or were these everyday occurrences, a pervasive workplace pattern that might explain the persistence of the wage gap? And if so, how could such a pattern be quantified or measured?

While the government releases comprehensive data about all workers' demographic characteristics, it issues no comparable data about all employers' behavior. So social scientists have drawn conclusions from those one-sided data—data that are about workers, rather than employers. I wanted to look at the other side, at the data that reveal employers' behavior. At the same time, I wanted to make sure not to jump to conclusions from stories alone. I'm an economist and a businessperson. Before I draw conclusions, I want to see the data. Implicitly, discrimination was being proposed as a theory that could explain the wage gap. Where could I find data that would disprove or confirm such a theory?

After I gave it some thought and did some research, I came up with an answer: those data exist in lawsuit settlements and awards.

For good or for bad, in the United States, the legal system is the way in which formal discrimination charges are leveled, explained, investigated, rebutted, examined, and either upheld or rejected. Any working woman who believes she has been mistreated just because of her sex, and who is not satisfied with her employer's response, can go to her local, state, or federal equal employment opportunity commission and bring formal charges. By law, these commissions are responsible for investigating those charges. If the investigators conclude that the woman has indeed been discriminated against illegally, it can mediate or bring a lawsuit, or give her an official go-ahead to bring her own private lawsuit. (Federal employees—postal workers and the like—can't bring lawsuits against the U.S. government and so must use a slightly different process, but the idea is the same.)

Discrimination lawsuits, in other words, could serve as my data source about how much employer misbehavior existed toward women. If a discrimination charge could survive the harsh examination of a lawsuit—if a judge, jury, or administrative board awarded money to punish and correct wrongdoing—then I could count that as hard evidence of discrimination. And if an employer "voluntarily" settled by offering money to women who had brought discrimination charges—which, as a businessperson, I knew meant that that employer fully expected some judge or jury to recoil from its behavior or data, ordering it to pay up—I could count that as potential evidence of discrimination as well. And if the dollar award was especially large—if a judge or jury awarded, say, a few million dollars—I could be pretty sure there had been outrage at a woman's mistreatment. Americans believe in fairness. They know that no employer is perfect, and that people can't be blamed for messing up a little bit here or there. So a large number means that judge or jury was shocked and wanted to send a strong message that such behavior was so appalling that it could not and would not be tolerated in a fair society.

That would be my data. And in order to measure recent discrimination, I wanted only incidents concluded in the last ten years.

Is it fair to conclude that settlements measure discrimination? That's an important question, since many of the cases you'll read about here did settle before going to trial. Of course it's true that employers settle cases for any number of reasons. Sometimes they settle because they realize (or their lawyers have advised them) that their egregious misconduct will almost surely be punished by a judge or jury. Sometimes they settle even though they believe they've done nothing wrong—simply to avoid risking a loss or spending huge sums on attorneys' fees and other court costs. But of course, employers will almost always claim that they've done nothing wrong, and are just avoiding risk and expense. So judge for yourself. Whenever you see a discrimination case that has been settled, in which the employer admits no wrongdoing and says it is settling to avoid the risk and expense of a protracted lawsuit, examine that disclaimer closely. Weigh it against how much money was paid out and against the woman's claims. Does the employer's denial seem accurate—or does it smell a little fishy?

Despite my best efforts at scouring government and media sources for six years,[1] my data set is only partial. I could not read every local newspaper or trial court record in the country. As a result, I managed to gather only a small fraction of the known successfully settled or adjudi-

cated sex discrimination claims in the United States between 1994 and
the end of 2004. But what you'll see in the tables in this book does give
you a fair idea of how widely spread sex discrimination is throughout
the United States, eroding women's wages in every part of the country,
in employers large and small, and in every job title, industry, and economic sector.

I was staggered by this evidence. Most of us hear about discrimination occasionally, one anecdote or newspaper story at a time. One
month, you might hear that Merrill Lynch, say, has had to pay out $54
million to its female bond traders. A few months later, you might catch
a glimpse of an article about a local office worker who was paid $15,000
because she was illegally fired when she got pregnant or a waitress who
was paid a few thousand dollars because, after a coworker assaulted her
in the kitchen, her manager fired *her*.

But it's entirely different to assemble *all* those cases and examine
them as a group. When you do, here's what you see: sex discrimination
is far more widespread and vastly more entrenched than anyone has recognized. Month after month, year after year, employers are paying out
tens of millions of dollars because of sex discrimination. Sex discrimination isn't an occasional event, an aberration that's quickly found and
mopped up. Quite the opposite. Severe sex discrimination is being
charged, proven—*and paid for*—month after month, year after year.
Treating a female worker differently just because of sex may have been
illegal for forty years. And yet it continues—regularly, persistently, and
in every corner of the economy.

For the year 2002 alone, a fairly typical year, I was able to assemble
records of employer payouts that added up to at least $263 million,
which are listed in the table on pages 43–48. That's a stunning amount
of money.

Take a look at this painstakingly assembled and verified list. This
single year's data give you a clue to how deep and how widespread sex
discrimination is, how profoundly embedded in the workplaces of
America. It's happening to women in every industry and economic sector, in nonprofits and for-profits, at public and private employers. Den-
tists' offices, public schools, restaurants, transit authorities, financial
industries, grocery stores, hospitals, DVD manufacturers, clothes retail-

ers, police departments, truck dispatchers, universities, finance companies, phone companies, hotels, jails, temp agencies: they've all discriminated against women so severely that they've had to pay up.

As you look over this list, keep in mind that each one of these cases represents a ferocious fight by one or more women. Sex discrimination is hard to prove; for a woman to win her case, the misbehavior had to be egregious. And as you'll see later in this book, a woman loses an enormous amount when she decides to go to court. These women chose to engage in exhausting battles that tested their sanity, knowing that doing so would probably cost them their jobs, careers, and a few years of their lives. A court fight almost always means a financial setback for the woman who brings charges: the award or settlement money, if it ever comes, will never make up for the money lost while being underpaid or fighting mistreatment.

Nor have these steady payouts changed employers' behavior for the better. They merely represent the cost of doing business. In fact, considering how impossible it would be for the perennially underfunded Equal Employment Opportunity Commission (EEOC) or any other antidiscrimination agency to actively look for misbehavior, considering how few women bring charges, and considering how hard those charges are to prove, employers could make a sensible economic calculation that it would cost more to *fix* sex discrimination than to ignore it, gambling that they'll never be held accountable—and that even if they are, paying for their misbehavior after the fact is less expensive than treating women fairly in advance.

Some discrimination keeps employers' costs down. Paying women less—by keeping their wages lower than their male peers' in the same job or slotting them into lower-paying jobs or career tracks—holds down not only the payroll but also all the additional costs calculated based on wages, such as benefits, retirement payments, and so on. Some other discrimination unfairly redistributes wealth toward men. If an employer promotes a man instead of a more qualified woman, he's making money at *her* expense. Either way, this redistribution of wealth—toward the employer or toward the male employee—is un-American.

I am not suggesting that employers sit down and calculate all this coldly. They don't have to. Sex discrimination is often default behavior, business as usual. Social scientists have come to understand how bias is ingrained in our social dynamics. It's self-perpetuating. I'll back up this claim with more information and analysis later in this book. But the headline is this: unless an employer makes a deliberate and conscious effort to *prevent* sex discrimination, it will continue. That's why the wage gap is not going away. You can't undo the status quo through good intentions alone. Active steps must be taken to make change.

But that's jumping ahead of the story. Before we look into the whys and what-thens, let's look at the raw data. Is sex discrimination widespread in the United States? Decide for yourself by looking at the sample statistics for a single year.

Most of these cases are hidden from public view. Some surface for a day or two. Buried in local newspapers, local courts, and local hearings is a steady drumbeat of discrimination against women. American businesses are steadily paying out hundreds of millions of dollars every year to compensate for their gross injustices. Don't automatically believe it when companies say they're settling just to avoid the expense of a lawsuit. Too often, they pay when they want to avoid the expense of the jury's award *and* the stigma of being proven to be cheating working women out of their rightful wages. In effect, such companies are writing discrimination off as the cost of doing business, letting this very expensive habit of undervaluing and mistreating working women continue.

And remember, these cases are just the tip of the iceberg. Many cases are settled with confidentiality clauses. Other cases are never reported, even in local newspapers. Even the EEOC data are incomplete: the commission doesn't publicly report specific information about all its successfully settled or litigated cases. Rather, it reports top-line statistics, including the fact that the agency resolves or settles thousands of cases each year — cases in which an employer had to pay its employees. But in its full listing, it reports only a few *hundred* of those cases, making public the names, charges, and awards from perhaps ten percent of the employers that the EEOC forced to pay up because they had discriminated based on sex. Which means that this list — as disturbing as it is — is illustrative rather than comprehensive.

Looking this list over, you will quickly see an enormous amount of variety. Some of the payouts are major class action lawsuits that showed

EMPLOYERS THAT HAD TO PAY FOR SEX DISCRIMINATION IN 2002[2]

These are the sex discrimination payouts found for the year 2002. If you know of any others, please inform WAGE at www.wageproject.org.

Employer	Discrimination Charged	Award	Type of Action
Advantage Staffing, Inc. Detroit, Mich.	Failure to hire based on sex, race, ability, religion, and national origin	$60,000	Settlement
American Express Financial Advisors, Inc., Minneapolis, Minn.	4,000-person class action, age and sex discrimination	$31 million	Settlement
Anthony Allega Cement Contractor, Inc., Ohio	Failure to rehire worker after seasonal layoff because of her sex	$50,000	Settlement
Dr. Avery Beall, Jr., LaGrange, Ga.	Sexual harassment	$135,000	Jury award
Bean Lumber Co., Glenwood, Ark.	Refused to promote pregnant woman, then fired her	$45,000	Settlement
Boies, Schiller & Flexner, Armonk, N.Y.	Failure to promote	$75,000	Settlement
Brink's, Inc., Phoenix, Ariz.	Failed to promote woman to assistant branch manager; instead promoted less-qualified man	$58,750	Settlement
BMW, North Carolina	Unequal pay, retaliation	$530,000	Jury award
Casa del Sol, Las Cruces, N.M.	Owner sexually harassed and assaulted employee	$225,000	Settlement
Case Western Reserve University, Cleveland, Ohio	Biology professor twice denied tenure	Undisclosed	Settlement
Chesrown Chevrolet, Denver, Colo.	Sexual harassment of and retaliation against business development manager	$1 million, reduced by judge to $550,000	Jury award
Church's Chicken, Wichita, Kans.	14-year-old employee subjected to hostile environment and sexually assaulted by store manager	$150,000	Settlement
Cook County Forest Preserve District, Illinois	Police officer charges sex discrimination, harassment, and retaliation	$3 million, later reduced to $300,000	Jury award, reduced by judge
Country Kitchen Family Restaurants, Globe, Ariz.	Sexual harassment	$75,000	Settlement
Danka Office Imaging, St. Petersburg, Fla.	Sex and race harassment of, and retaliation against, African-American women	$375,000	Settlement

(continued on next page)

Employer	Discrimination Charged	Award	Type of Action
DeCoster Farms, Wright County, Iowa	Sexual harassment	$1.525 million	Settlement
Delta Airlines, Atlanta, Ga.	Two ramp agents discriminated against because pregnant: one fired, other forced to take unpaid leave	$150,000	Settlement
Delta Faucet, Chickasha, Okla.	Sexual harassment	$50,000	Settlement
Denny's, Carbondale, Ill.	Sexual harassment and retaliation	$135,000	Settlement
Dixie Stampede Dinner Attractions, Inc., Tennessee	Female trick riders paid less than male riders	$135,000	Settlement
Double T Diner, Baltimore, Md.	Sexual harassment of 12 female food servers	$300,000	Settlement
Eagle Tannery, Waterloo, Ohio	Sexual harassment	Confidential	Settlement
Fort Dodge Animal Health and Fort Dodge Laboratories, Inc., Overland Park, Kans.	Six women sexually harassed; two human resources employees fired for reporting harassment	$487,500	Settlement
Ford Motor Co., Dearborn, Mich.	Sexual harassment	Undisclosed	Settlement
Ford Motor Co., Norfolk, Va.	Sexual harassment	Undisclosed	Settlement
Golf Galaxy, Inc., Chicago, Ill.	Customer service manager sexually harassed by general sales manager; company retaliation for charges	$80,000	Settlement
Good Samaritan Surgery Center, Puyallup, Wash.	Nurses subjected to sexually hostile environment and retaliation	$170,000	Settlement
Hanson Motors, Inc., Olympia, Wash.	General manager and supervisors sexually harassed, threatened, and physically assaulted three saleswomen	$670,000	Settlement
Heil Trailer International, Chattanooga, Tenn.	Did not hire women, segregated other women in lower-paying positions with limited opportunities	$250,000	Settlement
Jack in the Box, Arizona	Sexual harassment	$92,500	Settlement
John Elway AutoNation, Boulder, Colo.	Sexual harassment by general manager and five sales managers, retaliation for reporting	$1 million	Jury award
Key Energy Services, Inc. Midland, Tex.	Female controller paid less than predecessor	$25,000 plus $80,000 raise	Settlement
L & L Wings, Inc., Myrtle Beach, S.C.	Manager and assistant manager sexually harassed two teenage summer workers	$115,000	Settlement

Little America Hotel, Salt Lake City, Utah	Laundry worker sexually harassed by supervisor	$88,000	Jury award
Los Angeles County Police Department, Calif.	Race and sex discrimination	$100 million in back pay and $140 million in future raises	Jury award
Lowell Public High School, Lowell, Mass.	Housemaster charged with sex discrimination	Undisclosed	Settlement
marchFIRST, Inc., Chicago, Ill.	Demoted executive assistant because of pregnancy	$120,000	Settlement
Massachusetts Department of State Police	Pregnancy discrimination against four female troopers	$1.347 million	Jury award
Medical Center Brace & Limb, Houston, Tex.	Sexual harassment by owner/CEO	$200,000	Settlement
Milwaukee, Wis., Mayor's Office	Sexual harassment of aide	$375,000	Settlement
The National State Bank (Corestates), New Jersey	Two branch managers fired because of sex	$4 million reduced to $2,083,324	Jury award reduced by judge, upheld on appeal.
New Boston Select Staffing, Massachussetts	Sexual harassment and retaliation	$2.166 million	Jury award
New England Serum, Topsfield, Mass.	Six Honduran women sexually harassed by two managers	$150,000	Settlement
New York City Police Department, New York	Police officer retaliated against by supervisor for charging sex discrimination	$470,159	Jury award
New York City Police Department, New York	Sexual harassment and retaliation by six fellow officers	$1.85 million	Jury award
Nielsen & Bainbridge, Illinois	Race and sex harassment	$155,000	Settlement
Norstan Apparel Shops, Tampa, Fla.	Female store manager fired when she complained about sexual harassment of women employees by male manager	$250,000	Settlement
Optical Cable Corporation, Roanoke, Va.	Race and sex discrimination; assigned women to lower paying jobs than similar men	$1 million	Settlement
Owosso Country Club, Mich.	Female clubhouse manager lost job because directors wanted an all-male management team	$209,000	Arbitration award
Phoenix Management Limited Co., St. Louis, Mo.	Female controller paid less than predecessor and successor	$120,000	Settlement

(continued on next page)

Employer	Discrimination Charged	Award	Type of Action
Piazza Trucking, Pollock Pines, Calif.	After her husband resigned, leaving her to work solo rather than as part of a team, truck driver fired because of her sex	$80,000	Settlement
Portsmouth, Va., Police Department	Sexual harassment	$300,000	Settlement
Project Development Group, Inc., Pittsburgh, Penn.	Two women fired as asbestos abatement workers because of their sex	$47,000	Settlement
Ralph's Grocery, San Diego, Calif.	Sexual harassment and retaliation	$30 million reduced to $8.5 million	Jury award reduced by judge
Rent-A-Center, Plano, Tex.	5,000-person class action: refusal to hire, unequal pay, refusal to promote, sexual harassment, pregnancy discrimination, unlawful firing	$47 million	Settlement
Roquemore, Pringle & Moore, Los Angeles, Calif.	Two Hispanic paralegals fired for complaining about sexual and racial harassment by managing partners	$135,000	Settlement
Royal Air Maroc, New York	Failure to promote	$903,017	Jury award
Sacramento Kings, Sacramento, Calif.	Sexual harassment and retaliation	Confidential	Settlement
Sacramento Regional Transit District, Calif.	Unequal pay, hiring, training, and promotion	$2.5 million	Settlement
Salomon Smith Barney, Los Angeles, Calif.	Sexual harassment and sex discrimination	$3.2 million	Arbitration panel award
San Diego County, California	County treasurer/tax collector sexually harassed	$100,000	Settlement
San Francisco Municipal Railway, California	When custodian reported that she was being sexually harassed by coworkers, supervisors retaliated against her	$450,000	Settlement
San Joachin County, Calif., Office of Substance Abuse	Supervisors sexually harassed and racially discriminated against three women	$562,000	Jury award
Santa Barbara, Calif., Police Department	Refusal to promote women	$3.2 million	Jury award
Santa Clara County Medical Association, California	Manager sexually harassed three female employees	$73,000	Settlement
Sears, Greensboro, N.C.	Employees sexually harassed by coworker	$20,000	Settlement

Seattle, Wash., public schools	Sexual harassment	$90,000	Settlement
Select Appointments North America, Wakefield, Mass.	Division president sexually harassed by CEO and fired for complaining	$2.1 million	Jury award
Sodexho Marriott Services, Inc., Owings Mill, Md.	Discharged a day porter because of pregnancy	$50,000	Settlement
South Beach Beverage Company (division of PepsiCo), Norwalk, Conn.	Sexual harassment and retaliation at a sales and distribution facility	$1.79 million	Settlement
Star Concrete, San Jose, Calif.	Employee harassed and retaliated against by owner's son	$250,000	Jury award
State Adjustment, Inc., Salem, Oreg.	CEO sexually harassed clerk	$10,000	State commissioner order
Dr. George Stewart, Anchorage, Ala.	Serial sexual harassment	$3,000	Alaska state medical board fine
SuperValu Holdings, Inc., Minneapolis, Minn.	22 women paid less than men doing similar work	$400,000	Jury award
Swift Transportation, Kansas City, Mo.	6 female driver managers paid less than men with same jobs	$450,000	Jury award
Teaneck, N.J., Police Department	Police chief and coworkers sexually harassed and retaliated against first female police officer	$1.1 million	Jury award upheld on appeal
Technicolor Videocassette, Inc., Camarillo, Calif.	18 women sexually harassed and retaliated against after complaining	$875,000	Settlement
Timber Ridge University Medical Center, United States	Race and sex discrimination	$60,000	Settlement
UNICCO, Newton, Mass.	Seven women sexually harassed and retaliated against after complaining	$1.54 million	Settlement
U.S. Department of the Navy	Sexual harassment	$5,000	Administrative law judge
U.S. Postal Service	Sexual harassment	$50,000	Administrative law judge
University of Arkansas	Hostile work environment and retaliation against female professor	$353,000	Jury award
University of California Regents (LLNL)	Retaliation against computer technician at Lawrence Livermore National Labs who charged unequal pay	$1 million	Jury award

(continued on next page)

Employer	Discrimination Charged	Award	Type of Action
University of Houston Health Sciences Center, Tex.	Retaliation after charging discrimination	$396,000	Jury award
University of Texas, San Antonio, Medical School	Unequal pay	$400,000	Jury award
Verizon (formerly Bell Atlantic and NYNEX), thirteen states and Washington, D.C.	12,500 women denied benefits related to pregnancy and maternity leave	$25 million (estimated)	Settlement
Virginia Speaker of the House, Amherst County, Va.	Sexual harassment of file clerk	More than $100,000 (exact amount confidential)	Private payment
Wal-Mart, Phoenix, Ariz.	Failed to hire pregnant woman	$220,000	Settlement
Washington, D.C., Department of Corrections	Sexual harassment, widespread hostile environment	$9.6 million	Settlement
Whitley County, Ky.	Jailer and son harassed two women employees	$598,000	Jury award

an ongoing, proven pattern of outrageously blatant misbehavior. For instance, while it denied wrongdoing, Rent-A-Center settled its class action lawsuit for $47 million for such behavior as demoting, firing, and forcing out women through such measures as throwing away women's job applications, getting rid of female job classifications, adding weight-lifting requirements unrelated to the job, and harassing women until they quit. Other judgments or settlements gave a few thousand dollars to individual women who were mistreated in some way, whether by being fired for getting pregnant, demoted because they refused to be groped, or simply left behind while men were steadily promoted. For instance, until two police officers brought a lawsuit against the Santa Barbara Police Department, no woman had been promoted—ever—in the department's 102-year history.

What you *don't* see in this list is that many of these employers made it onto the charts over and over again:

- Ford Motor Company, for instance, settled a small sexual harassment lawsuit in 2002. But that was just the latest tax on Ford's ongoing mistreatment of women. Ford had already paid, in 2001, a $10.6 million settlement in an age and sex discrimination lawsuit; and in 1999, settled for $8 million in damages and pledged $10 million in training for the very same offenses. That's a total of $30 million for just three years. And that doesn't even count the confidential settlements Ford made at its Dearborn and Norfolk plants in 2002.

- Salomon Smith Barney made the 2002 list with a $3.2 million payment to one woman who, four years earlier, had refused a class action settlement and had instead taken her claim to arbitration—with another 91 women waiting in line to have their claims arbitrated as well. Exactly how much Salomon Smith Barney paid in 1998 to the other 1,900 women in the class action hasn't been publicly disclosed, but the company did announce its agreement to put another $15 million into diversity programs.

- Wal-Mart is on this list for a small $220,000 pregnancy discrimination settlement. But in 1996, a Missouri jury ordered Sam Walton's creation to pay $50 million for sexual harassment on appeal to $385,000. In 1997, an Iowa jury ordered Wal-Mart to pay $28,000 for sexual harassment, which was upheld on appeal. And it looks like there's more to come: Wal-Mart now faces the biggest discrimination class action lawsuit ever, representing 1.5 million women complaining of ongoing bias in pay and promotion.

Beyond the Numbers: Facts on the Ground

As important as it is to add up the plain data about discrimination—the sheer numbers that give an overview of sex discrimination's scope—it's not enough. Exactly what was happening at all those employers that drove women to sue? What kind of employer actions are keeping women's paychecks down? How bad is it, really, out there on the factory floors and in the office cubicles where women are trying to make a fair living?

I found five categories of discrimination—each costly in a different way. Each chapter in this section of *Getting Even* will examine one of these five forms of discrimination in detail—what it looks like, how widespread and pernicious it is, and how it subtracts from women's earnings. The first two chapters look at those moments of discrimination that have been egregious enough that some employer had to pay money. But not every incident of sex discrimination makes it into the courts. The next three chapters look into forms of discrimination that, for very valid reasons, women may not pursue in court—perhaps they need the job too much to put it at risk—but that nonetheless subtract money from their paychecks. These are the five categories: blatant sex discrimination, sexual harassment, workplace sex segregation, everyday discrimination, and discrimination against mothers. In each of the coming chapters, we'll look more closely at how one of these five categories of discrimination eats away steadily at women's pay.

CHAPTER 5

Plain Old Discrimination

Her supervisor told her that no woman would be promoted into management in the security department and that she had better get out of there.

> —Lawyer for Lori David, a Caterpillar security guard in Peoria, Illinois; in 2001, David's $850,000 jury award for retaliation was reduced to $300,000 under federal law.[1]

Why should someone have to leave an industry just because of their age, just because of their sex? They shouldn't have to, not if they're good.

> —Janet Peckinpaugh, news anchor, who in 1999 won a $8.3 million sex discrimination lawsuit when WFSB-TV in Hartford, Connecticut, replaced her with a much younger woman while male anchors were allowed to age on the job.

Most people think that "sex discrimination" means refusing to hire, promote, or fairly pay women who have the same qualifications as men. Many of us imagine that if this still happens, it's because some ancient employer hasn't quite shaken off his hangover from the bad old days of the 1950s and 1960s, when newspapers' classified ads still had separate listings for "men's work" and "women's work." In our era of powerhouse women—such as Senator Hillary Rodham Clinton, media mogul Oprah Winfrey, and nationally renowned breast surgeon Dr. Susan Love, to name just three—it's hard to believe that anyone could still behave as if most women are less capable than most men. And surely every American employer knows by now that sex discrimination is flatly illegal—under the Equal Pay Act of 1963, Title VII of the Civil Rights Act of 1964, the Civil Rights Act of 1991, and an arm's-length list of Supreme Court rulings.

And yet plain old sex discrimination still happens—much more than most of us suspect. Employers still refuse to hire, promote, or equally pay women for no other reason than that they're women. It happens all the time, in every kind of organization, throughout the country: in restaurants and government agencies, supermarkets and stockbrokerages, newspapers and car manufacturers, hospitals and universities. It happens to women at every economic level, from minimum-wage workers to million-dollar M.B.A.s. Sometimes it happens openly; sometimes it happens subtly. Sometimes it's done with malice aforethought; sometimes it happens because employers are not really paying attention to mindless bias.

But whatever the motives or means, sex discrimination always costs women money. Every time a woman doesn't get hired (or promoted or equally paid) just because of her sex, that's one extra week she's missing a paycheck or stuck on a lower-paying rung of the wage ladder. That's true even if she does get hired elsewhere (or promoted or given a raise) just a week or month or year later. Each job she doesn't get, each raise that is delayed, holds down all her future earnings as well. Every missing dollar now multiplies into many missing dollars later. Those incremental delays keep subtracting from her income over her lifetime, slowly siphoning hundreds of thousands of dollars from her wallet.

Many employers have been coasting unchallenged for a long time. They've been able to remain blind, sometimes willfully so, to their company's background pattern of treating women as less competent than men. When they see more men climbing the ladder, they say that women just aren't trying hard enough or that they're perfectly willing to promote a woman *if she's qualified.* You'll read about employers like that in this chapter—and you'll see how impatient the courts were with such feeble reasoning. Explanations like that should flash a big warning signal to a company's female employees: such an employer is taking no responsibility for shaping its managers' behavior.

Unless trained to do otherwise, managers are probably acting on ingrained cultural assumptions that rate men's capabilities just a little bit higher than women's, as we'll see later on. And those assumptions become self-perpetuating. Whether formally or informally, most employees quickly learn "how things are done around here." That's called socialization. If all the cashiers are women and all the managers are men, that sends a message. If the boss gets annoyed at seeing an all-male slate of promotional candidates and insists that it's impossible that *no* female employees are qualified to move up, that sends a very different message. Either way, your coworkers and colleagues know by now what's acceptable. Overcoming the gravitational force called "corporate culture" requires effort. The effort needn't be a lawsuit; in fact, as you'll see in this chapter and the ones to come, lawsuits should probably be the option of last resort, since they can have such devastating effects on both a woman's pocketbook and her career.

In the previous chapter, we looked at the magnitude of sex discrimination in a single postmillennial year. This chapter takes an entire decade's worth of sex discrimination data and breaks it down into various categories, in order to show *what kinds* of discrimination regularly hit the courts' windshields. How common is it, say, for employers to simply refuse to hire women, or to dismiss women because they get pregnant?

Then we'll look beyond the data into the stories behind the numbers. How bad does employer misbehavior have to be for women to sue the hand that feeds them—and to win? Much of the appalling discrimination you'll read about in this chapter went on for many years before a woman (or class of women) brought formal charges. Reading about this long-standing and egregious mistreatment, I had to wonder how many American workplaces are simmering with discrimination that may be illegal but that's just not bad enough to drive a woman into a lawyer's office. I had to wonder how much *more* discrimination is taking place every day, under the radar, never making it into court.

You may also notice, as I did, a disproportionate number of lawsuits at certain frontiers, where the battle for women's equality remains especially difficult. Various theories could explain this. Some observers suggest that when those who have power are genuinely challenged, their behavior gets especially bad: rather than ceding money or power, they fight back. Others believe that women who grew up expecting to be equal on the job are shocked when, say, they're demoted for getting pregnant, and are outraged enough to sue. Whatever the reason, you'll see more lawsuits in certain jobs or professions that have managed to remain male bastions longer, such as financial services. You'll also see more lawsuits wherever the standards for pay or promotion have remained especially subjective, as in the retail industry or in academia. And you'll see more lawsuits at career junctures—pregnancy and motherhood—where women and men are not exactly the same and where workplace practices and policies don't yet treat those differences fairly.

You may notice that very few lawsuits are being brought in the trades. This doesn't mean that women finally make up 50 percent of all electricians, plumbers, forklift drivers, and so on. Rather, as we'll see in chapter 7, "Women's Work," lawsuits brought long ago did not produce changes, and so women have more or less given up trying to break in via lawsuits and are trying more individual approaches—admittedly without much success.

But here's the main point: Discrimination is costing women far more money than the lawsuits are costing employers. And that money is being taken out of women's pockets every single day of our lives. Even low-wage women, as you'll quickly see, lose hundreds of thousands of dollars because employers refuse to treat them fairly. Nor, as you'll see, do these women ever get even through lawsuits, which merely serve as a kind of ongoing levy or import duty on the underpayment of women and don't make up for it. Keep your eye on how much discrimination is costing women. Sometimes it costs a lot all at once. Sometimes it drains money away a little at a time. But every time you read about sex discrimination, remember: it means that much-needed money is being subtracted from women's wages.

Many women have a habit of blaming themselves for underearning—chastising themselves for making the wrong career choice or being too shy to insist on credit for the project that got a male coworker a promotion. And perhaps you *should* learn to stand up for yourself as an individual; this book will look into that idea in the final section. But lay aside that habit of self-blame while you're reading this chapter. Instead, consider this possibility: Am I making less than a man not because of my own mistakes, but because there's a societal pattern of discriminating against women on the job?

But I'm getting ahead of myself. Before looking any further into how sex discrimination gets perpetuated on the job or what we have to do to stop it, I want you to see for yourself how widely it's spread across the economy. Each of the next five short sections will examine discrimination at different junctures of the workplace lifecycle: hiring, pay, promotion, pregnancy, and firing (or driving someone out). Breaking it down that way is a little misleading; discriminatory employers often treat women unequally in more than one way. Nevertheless, let's break it down for clarity's sake—so we can get a glimpse of how widespread discrimination trims women's paychecks at every stage.

Hiring: No Women Need Apply

Just a few decades ago, the idea that women could do some kinds of jobs and men were better than others was widely accepted. Let a woman apply for a job as, say, a lawyer, and she would be told that the firm didn't hire female lawyers and offered a job as a secretary instead—as happened to Sandra Day O'Connor after she graduated third out of 102 students in her 1952 Stanford Law class.

But a lawsuit by women's organizations, led by the National Organization for Women, outlawed sex-segregated help-wanted ads in the 1970s. During that decade, many barriers to women's employment, both real and symbolic, fell down. But while blatant segregation is now widely known to be illegal, some employers still openly refuse to hire women.

Consider what happened at Rent-A-Center, perhaps the most egregious case of open employer sex discrimination of the past decade. In 1998, Ernest Talley's Renters Choice chain of rent-to-own stores acquired Rent-A-Center (RAC), another such chain, and adopted the RAC name. Immediately, Talley and his senior vice presidents fanned out across the country to explain to the newly acquired managers that there would be no women at RAC. The weight-lifting requirement for the job had been fifty pounds; Talley raised it to seventy-five pounds because, he explained—as many managers later testified—it "would keep women from applying." [2]

A few men tried to stand up against the policy—and lost. For instance, Michael Karraker of Illinois tried to hire the most experienced and qualified job applicant—but his manager told him that he couldn't hire that person because she was a woman and to keep looking until he found a qualified man. Instead, like a handful of other store managers, Karraker quit. But most who tried to resist the female-free juggernaut quickly decided it wasn't worth their jobs—especially not in the face of executives' and senior managers' statements. In the later lawsuit, literally dozens of midlevel managers from across the country, in separate and uncoordinated depositions, testified that the top executives and senior managers who were their direct reports had said such things as "In case you didn't notice, we do not employ women" and "I regularly throw away women's applications" and "The day I hire a woman will be a cold day in Hell" and "Mr. Talley does not like women working in his stores" and "This is how they run the company. They don't hire women" and "This isn't a woman's kind of job." [3]

Dozens upon dozens of employees, such as Michele Conley of Memphis, Tennessee, testified that their managers told them to throw women's applications in the trash. Laquinta Benn of Detroit, Michigan, was told that a woman who was scheduled to be interviewed "would not be hired because she was a woman." Dan Eddy of Plainfield, Illinois, testified that "small and weak men were hired but women were shut out. . . . I do not believe the company ever gave a lifting test, but just said they had it." And if women did somehow squeak by the ban, they (and not men) were required to take a psychological test, which many described as offensively and inappropriately sexual. Lisa Adams of Coffeyville, Kansas, for instance, testified that the test was "extremely personal, asked about my feelings towards my mother, inquired as to how many bowel movements I had in a day."[4]

RAC's Talley was caught in part because he took over an existing company and tried to retrofit it with his no-woman policy, shocking many employees. As a result, after a few years of legal skirmishing, in 2002 RAC agreed to pay out $47 million, revamp its personnel policies and procedures, and submit to EEOC oversight for four years. But while the few named plaintiffs got lump sums of either $100,000 or $55,000, taxable as a single year's income, the rest of that money had to be spread out over thousands of women, who, on average, received a lump-sum payment of less than $10,000 each—not enough to make up for their three years of lost wages, much less the strain and exhaustion of being disparaged and hounded daily. Those women did not get even.

Here's what's most disturbing about this strange story: it's not unique. As can be seen in the following table, over the past decade a number of employers have been accused of refusing to hire women (and often minority men as well)—and have had to pay up.

In this table, you can see that far too many employers kept women out of traditionally male jobs, such as truckdriving, groundskeeping, and machine operating, or out of male-dominated businesses, such as trailer hauling and cement contracting. But you can also see that other employers kept women out of jobs that relied on women's stereotypical skills.

For instance, wouldn't you think that women could easily get hired to wait tables? It's not so. In a 2003 study,[5] 25 percent of New York City and Philadelphia's seventy-five most expensive and elite restaurants had no women waiting tables; the more expensive the restaurant, the lower the percentage of female servers—and in cities with no dearth of experienced waitresses looking for a better job. A 1996 study found that, in the more expensive Philadelphia restaurants, women were 40 percent *less* likely than men to be hired to wait tables—but 30 percent *more* likely to get table-waiting jobs at the lowest-end eateries.[6] Many high-end restaurants contend that male waiters are *haute*-ier than females, flattering wealthy diners with the sense that they're important and powerful enough to be served by men. Only a few establishments get caught. For instance, in 1998, one of New York City's most prestigious caterers, Glo-

COMPANIES THAT HAD TO PAY UP
FOR REFUSING TO HIRE WOMEN

Employer	Charges	Type of Action	Award Year	Amount
Abercrombie & Fitch, United States	Refusal or failure to hire and promote: s, r, n.o.	Consent decree	2004	$50 million
Advantage Staffing, Inc., Detroit, Mich.	Failure to hire: s, r, d, re, and n.o.	Consent decree	2002	$60,000
Anthony Allega Cement Contractor, Inc., Ohio	Failure to rehire: s	Settlement	2002	$50,000
Ashtabula County Sheriff's Office, Ohio	Refusal or failure to hire	Consent decree	2000	Court oversight
Baton Rouge, La., Schools Department	Refusal to hire female janitors	Judicial award	1997	$95,000
Ben E. Keith Co., Fort Worth, Tex.	Systematic refusal to hire: s	Department of Labor	2004	$131,508
Carl Budding & Co., Homewood, Ill.	Refusal to hire or promote: s, r	Class action settlement	2004	$2.5 million
Cipriani Restaurants, New York, N.Y.	Refusal to hire women as servers	State attorney general settlement	2000	Establishment of hiring goals for women
Eagle Global Logistics f/k/a Eagle USA, Houston, Tex.	Failure to hire women into warehouse, delivery and truck driver positions*	Settlement	2001	$9 million
EaglePicher Filtration & Minerals, Nev.	Failure to hire:* s	OFCCP settlement	1999	$92,471
EGW Temporaries, Buffalo, N.Y.	Refusal to refer: s, r	Settlement	2003	$335,000
Glorious Food, New York, N.Y.	Refusal to hire:* s	Settlement	1998	$425,000
Heil Trailer International, Chattanooga, Tenn.	Failure to hire:* s	Settlement	2002	$250,000
Hyundai Semiconductor, Eugene, Oreg.	Refusal to hire: s, r	Jury award, reduced after appeals to undisclosed settlement	1999	$2 million
Joe's Stone Crab, Miami, Fla.	Refusal to hire female servers	Settlement	1998	$150,000
Langeloth Metalurgical Company, Washington County, Pa.	Refusal to hire for entry-level production and maintenance	Class action settlement	2003	$500,000 and consent decree with court oversight

Mike Shannon's Restaurants, St. Louis, Mo.	Refusal to hire female servers	Settlement	1997	$45,000
Palm Restaurants, United States	Failure to hire (as servers): s	Class action settlement	2003	$500,000
Phoenix Suns Limited Partnership and Sports Magic Team, Inc., Phoenix, Ariz.	Refusal to hire women to Zoo Crew	Settlement and consent decree	2003	$104,500 and consent decree with court oversight
PJAX, Md.	200 women employees refused jobs as truckers and dockworkers*	Settlement	2003	$2 million
SKF USA, Inc.	Failed to hire women as entry-level machine operators	OFCCP consent order, administrative law judge	1999	Back pay, required to hire 12 members of class
STI Holdings, Inc., f/k/a Stoughton Trailers, Wis.	Disparate impact hiring test: r, s	Settlement	2003	Consent decree with court oversight
SYSCO Food Services of Portland, Inc., Portland, Oreg.	Failure to consider qualified female applicants for warehouse jobs	OFCCP consent decree	1998	$55,000
Toyota Logistics Services, Port Newark, N.J.	Failure to hire: s, r	Settlement	2000	Consent decree
Utah State University College of Engineering, Utah	Refusal to hire female dean	Settlement	2004	$25,000
Village of Rochdale, N.Y.	Refusal to hire for groundskeepers and maintenance workers	Settlement	2004	$90,000
Voice of America, U.S. Information Agency	Failure to hire or promote women	Settlement	2000	$543 million
Winn-Dixie, Jacksonville, Fla.	Failure to hire and promote women, minorities	Class action settlement	1999	$33 million

* Indicates one or more additional charges, such as lack of equal pay, demotions, refusal to promote, firings, hostile working environment, or sexual harassment.

Codes: s = sex; r = race; re = religion; a = age; d = disability, n.o. = national origin.

OFCCP: Office of Federal Contract Compliance Programs, U.S. Department of Labor.

rious Food, had to pay its female waiters a settlement of $425,000, after they charged that the company had allowed only male waiters to work its most exclusive (read: highest-tipping) corporate parties.[7] Ditto for Mike Shannon's Restaurants in St. Louis, Missouri, which in 1997 settled by paying $45,000 after women charged they were kept out of the higher-tipping dining room. And when four women sued the elite restaurant Joe's Stone Crab, one of the highest-paying service gigs in Miami, Florida, for having hired 108 men to wait tables and not a single woman, Joe's argued in court that it offered customers a "classier" dining experience with male waiters. Would any restaurant today dare make such a public claim about either black or white waiters? It was a losing argument: in 2001, a federal judge ordered Joe's to pay $154,205.

Why does this matter? Because upscale restaurants bring in much higher tips. Because women are disproportionately shoved down into the lower-earning eateries; waitresses, on average, make less money than waiters. In 2002, a full-time waitress made 87 percent of a full-time waiter's dollar—but that's just in official wages, without counting tips. Tips in high-priced restaurants can add up to two and a half times wages.[8] So while those waiting tables *officially* bring in $15,000 a year, men waiting tables at expensive restaurants can earn another $45,000 a year, for an annual income of $63,500, while women waiting tables in low-priced restaurants add only $18,750, for an annual income of $35,000.[9] So look around next time you eat at a restaurant. See whether the proportion of male to female waiters varies according to how expensive the meal is. If you're paying more money and you're being served only (or almost entirely) by men, some qualified woman was probably denied the job.

Some companies have enough sense not to be so obvious about refusing to hire women. Instead, they hire intermediaries—and instruct or expect those hiring firms to keep the women away. For instance, when Detroit employers asked Advantage Staffing to send only women or only men, Advantage went along. "MALES ONLY!" read one open work order assignment for a warehouse job; "NO FEMALES" read another. Meanwhile, clerical supervisors insisted that they wanted only women. One appalled Advantage Staffing employee, Tammie Manor, refused such illegal instructions. But she was repeatedly overridden. When she tried to send qualified women to fill the warehouse jobs, her boss sent a man instead. When she sent a qualified man for an office job, her boss sent e-mails insisting that "males get bored too easy" and "I explained to you once before that [the clerical supervisor] does not want men there. They never work out." Disgusted, Tammie Manor quit and called the EEOC. Manor's supervisor had told her that if Advantage Staffing wanted to stay in business it had to please its customers, explained EEOC Detroit Regional Attorney Adele Rapport; since every other employment agency did it, Advantage had no choice but to comply.

When Hyundai Semiconductor America, Inc.'s, human resources manager told the company's recruiting firm to stop sending along the résumés of women and blacks, that recruiter balked, took Hyundai to court, and won. But that became a cautionary tale: Hyundai kept appealing until the recruiter was nearly bankrupted by the legal fees and settled for much less than the jury award. Folks willing to risk their income on principle are surely rare. Although Tammie Manor's supervisor at Advantage Staffing couldn't have been correct in asserting that "everybody does this," many recruiters, headhunters, and temp firms surely go along when asked and help to bar women from well-paying jobs from the start.

So look around next time you walk into an office, warehouse, construction site, or manufacturing plant — or any kind of employer. Where are the women? Where are the men? If they're in different jobs, it didn't just happen. Someone is deciding who to hire based on sex — not on qualifications, skills, experience, aptitude, or ability. We'll look more deeply into why this happens in chapter 7, "Women's Work."

Promotion: Dead-End Jobs Only (Or Can You Say "Glass Ceiling"?)

> I believe I would have been promoted if I was a man.
> —Carol Atkins, one of the named plaintiffs in a class action lawsuit against Publix Super Markets, Inc. Atkins filed charges after fourteen years on the job, having watched several less experienced men move ahead of her into management.[10]

When I met with my superiors to discuss my interest in an assistant store manager position, they tried to discourage me by asking questions about my child care arrangements, and emphasizing the long hours that I'd have to work and the difficulty of the jobs that I'd have to learn.[11]

—Pennie Weddington, plaintiff in lawsuit against Ingles Markets

Discrimination comes in more guises than actively malicious and intentional policies to keep women out. It can be just as devastating and illegal for a company to passively let managers do business as they always have, relying on their own unexamined assumptions—which are so ingrained that they're called "gut instinct"—that men are more capable than women. Many folks who make hiring, pay, and promotion decisions truly think that they're being open-minded and fair. But that doesn't necessarily mean women have an equal chance at the better-paying jobs.

Here's how it works. Two job applications, two résumés, or two bios look equally impressive. After interviewing the applicants, the hiring manager must decide on "gut instinct" which one will work harder and fit in better. If the employer ends up with far more men than women, he usually doesn't notice, or believes it's an accident. But he usually concludes that the men who applied just *happened* to be better qualified for the jobs. And he (or, occasionally, she) honestly means it.

It doesn't occur to this manager that his "gut instinct" might be biased in a way he hasn't examined. He might not realize that his "gut instinct" relies on an assumption that men can handle things (whether those things are power tools, bond trades, a meat counter, or employees)—but that he won't believe women are competent until he's seen them prove it. He might mindlessly slot women into one kind of job, which just *happens* to pay less, and men into another kind of job, which just *happens* to pay more, without seriously considering individual credentials and capacities. Social scientists have studied the mental processes that make these thoughts feel like second nature. They've also documented that it is fully possible to correct and override these ingrained cultural assumptions. "Gut instinct" is really a set of thoughts that happen so quickly they're experienced less as thoughts than as *facts*, as truths.

Sex discrimination doesn't happen only because a manager *intends* to underpay women or hold them back, laughing maliciously, like a cartoon villain. It also happens when that manager just goes with the flow, shunting women into lower-paid work. That puts a lid on women's pay just as effectively as RAC President Ernest Talley's openly declared insistence on keeping women out.

Consider what happened at Home Depot, one of the much-touted business successes of the 1990s. In 1978, Arthur Blank and Bernard Marcus started Home Depot, as the company's Web site announces, "with a vision of warehouse stores filled from floor to ceiling with a wide assortment of products at the lowest prices with trained associates giving absolutely the best customer service in the industry." As Home Depot grew, it rapidly hired from the obvious feeder industries: plumbing, contracting, construction, electrical, and similar trades. During the 1990s, Home Depot was opening a new store, on average, every forty-three hours—which meant a lot of seat-of-the-pants hiring.[12] And in this case, hiring quickly meant hiring thousands of people without carefully examining their *actual* qualifications, as opposed to the managers' unexamined cultural *assumptions* about men's and women's qualifications. Maybe that wouldn't have mattered—except that part of those assumptions included how much each job should be paid.

And so women were hired to be cashiers or to work in the back office—which just *happened* to be low-wage jobs with no promotion track. Men were hired as sales associates in the company's premier aisles—staffing and selling electrical parts, plumbing, lumber, hardware, and other home improvement and construction goods—which just *happened* to pay more and to lead to promotions into management. Men moved up. Women didn't. Men got well-paying jobs. Women didn't. By 1996, more than 80 percent of HD's cashiers and computer workers were women—while more than 90 percent of the sales associates in the more highly paid sales aisles were men. A cashier's average hourly wage was $8.75—while a sales associate's average hourly wage was $11.25. Women's entry-level job (cashier) paid 78 percent of men's entry-level job (sales associate). That's pretty close to the national wage gap. And that was just at entry level: Home Depot's overall wage gap would have been wider, however, since the higher-paid management jobs were overwhelmingly male.[13]

Paying women less than men was part of Home Depot's corporate culture. And somebody was responsible for creating and perpetuating the attitudes by which that culture hired, promoted, and paid women and men.

Nevertheless, faced with a class action lawsuit in 1996, Home Depot's founders were outraged. They said that they were fair people. They said that their company was fair. No one wants to believe that he's a villain; even if his actions are wrong, he will find good motives underneath. Here's how Blank and Marcus put it in their 1999 book, *Built from Scratch*:

> [T]he accusations in the suit were so 180 degrees opposed to our personal philosophy that, in that sense, it was a shock. . . . We recruit in the construction trades; it is no secret that the construction trades are predominantly male. In fact, a scant 2.6 percent of the people working in these trades are female. . . .
>
> [T]here is a good reason that that statistical disparity exists. And that reason is *not* discrimination. It is due to the qualifications and choices of the applicants and candidates for the positions at The Home Depot—not a deliberate policy of exclusion or discrimination.

In the minds of Blank and Marcus, in other words, the disparity had just *happened*. Women were choosing to be cashiers, while men were qualified to sell lumber. And that's what their human resources managers and store managers believed, too—to the detriment of the women who applied, no matter what their qualifications.

Was that what women really wanted—or was it what the hiring managers wanted or believed women *should* want? Listen to what the male managers said, and see if it doesn't reveal an underlying set of ideas about women and men. Various (male) senior managers testified that women "feel comfortable being in a cashier position"; that "the male gender is not necessarily equipped" for computer work; that women are less capable of handling the physical demands of merchandising jobs (since lifting garden hoses is much harder than, say, lifting toddlers); that women do not want to "mix it up with customers," "throw freight," "get dirty," or climb ladders; that women "like the office environment"; that "cashiers should be women and they're better with their fingers." You can hear in those comments that hiring women for lower-paid jobs didn't just *happen*: managers were allowed to think and say that men and women had fundamentally different skills. At Home Depot, you didn't have to examine an individual woman's skills: you could get away with assuming that because she was a woman she wouldn't want to get dirty. You could get away with putting her in a lower-paying job, just because she was a woman.

Home Depot's female employees wanted to make more money. They knew why they weren't: the managers ran the stores based on their own ingrained beliefs that women couldn't—and shouldn't—be qualified to hold better-paying jobs. They heard those beliefs every day, in the ways that managers talked down to women. The female employees testified that managers called them "girls," while males were "men"; that women were told to fetch lunch and coffee because "it's a woman's job"; that assistant managers were told to bring their "wives" to company events, which made it clear that they were supposed to be men; that there are "jobs women aren't going to do as good as guys"; that "men produce more. They work harder. Men work harder than women"; and that "you need to have balls to succeed in this company."[14]

In other words, Home Depot managers thought they knew what (all) men and (all) women could and couldn't do well—and so they didn't check the actual qualifications and capabilities of *individual* women and men. As a result, a woman who applied for "any job" was considered only for cashier—even if (as was actually true for some plaintiffs) she had spent years in the lumber business, had worked through her adolescence helping her uncle in his construction business, or had sold big-ticket items elsewhere. And once she was ringing up and bagging, there she stayed. Promotions were completely subjective. There were no public job postings. Managers sized up and promoted candidates based on "gut instinct"—read: unexamined bias—and familiarity. It wasn't that all men were all more capable than all women, which would be one possible conclusion from those jobs' statistical skew. The managers themselves were just more comfortable with other guys and so barely looked at the women's qualifications and abilities.

All of which raised questions. If a company hired 105,000 new people, as Home Depot did in 1999,[15] was every man who applied really an expert in plumbing or lawn mowers—or did he just think he was, because he was a guy? Did driving a forklift really require (male) hand-eye coordination skills that were radically different from those (females) used while driving a pickup or an SUV? Was there really something inherently masculine about selling industrial-strength floor detergent, wet-dry shop vacuums, gas grills, or floor tile—or could women conceivably learn to understand the basics of cleaning, cooking, and spackle?

Faced with overwhelming evidence that men made much more than women and that women almost never had a chance to move up, in 1997 Home Depot settled for $87.5 million, with the customary denial of wrongdoing. Just as important, Home Depot agreed to transform its hiring, pay, training, and promotion processes and to be overseen by court-appointed monitors for four years. No longer were Home Depot managers allowed to tap their favorite candidate and create a new job, a process easily influenced by bias. Whenever managers have openings, they must post the job, complete questions about its requirements, and then interview applicants that a new computer system has sorted and selected by experience, training, and skills. That at least puts women (and not coincidentally, people of various racial, religious, and national backgrounds) into the running. Interestingly enough, Home Depot now celebrates its more diverse hiring and promotion policy as a real boon to the company—especially given that half its customers are women.

Here's the point: statistics matter. There's a reason that Home Depot's numbers pushed it into settling the lawsuit, literally on the courthouse steps, right on the brink of juror selection. The reason is this: Home Depot's advisers thought the company could well have lost in court. Here's what Black and Marcus wrote in their book:

> Bernie and I—as well as the entire board of directors and senior management of the company—were sickened by the eventual settlement, both in terms of the dollar figure we gave out and the concession it implied. But even I must concede now that it was

absolutely the right decision. Because we concluded two key things were against us: the judge and the jury.[16]

And Home Depot *should* have lost in court. When women show a policy or practice that leads to them overwhelmingly filling an employer's lower-paid jobs while men overwhelmingly fill its better-paid jobs, that's illegal on its face. It means that managers are making promotion decisions based on sex, that women have to be *much* better than men to get ahead. It means that *their* managers are allowing it to continue. It means that the company has an unwritten policy of discriminating against women, a policy that permeates its day-to-day corporate culture.

It would be easy to think of Home Depot's tilt toward men as an aberration, something understandable in a hardware store that's akin to a glorified toy store for guys. But many retail chains are cut from the same template as the old Home Depot. By doing nothing—essentially, by ignoring the fact that women cluster in low-end jobs while men keep rising—these employers are illegally letting managers' gut biases sort women and men by sex. Women end up as bottom-of-the-barrel hourly workers, as if being female makes it impossible to write up work schedules, oversee inventory, or count daily receipts. And that unfairly costs women money.

Employers always come up with a line of reasoning to "explain" why women are ending up in the lower-paying jobs. When examined, however, that reasoning sounds just a little ridiculous—and turns out to be just an excuse for letting managers do things the same old way. Take Publix Super Markets, which in 1997 agreed to pay $81.5 million and to have its promotion and pay processes monitored until 2001.[17] Home Depot had at least been able to argue that its male applicants had more experience with its products. Publix (and the other supermarkets) couldn't use that line; it's hard to say that men are naturally more interested than women in displaying broccoli or arranging cupcakes. So they were a little more creative and argued that women didn't really *want* to make more money. Here's how Publix's attorney, R. Lawrence Ashe, Jr., put it in 1996: "No one has figured out a way for men to have babies. That is a matter of choice of those families. We don't seek to plumb all the reasons that a woman might not want to move long distances

to seek a promotion." Apparently, childbirth—or even its potential—
permanently frees *all* women from wanting to move up and make more
money to support themselves and their families.

The truth was that, as at Home Depot, women at Publix (as at other
grocery chains) couldn't turn down promotions and raises—because
they were not offered. Women were running the cash registers; men
were stocking the shelves or slicing the meat. Just as at Home Depot,
cashiers were paid less and almost never promoted. Instead of posting
jobs and promotion opportunities, store managers (who were 98 percent male) would pick out someone in the stocking aisles and ask if he
wanted to move up to one of the three highest-paying departments: produce, bakery, and meat. It just *happened* that more than 98 percent of
those offers went to men, who just *happened* to be more qualified to
order vegetables, bake large quantities of cookies, display cuts of meats.
They were using the infamous tap-on-the-shoulder method, by which
they didn't have to explain or articulate their biases. Translation: managers were promoting based not on qualifications but on sex, whether
that's how they explained it or not. And sometimes they *did* say so out
loud. When one woman, Genevieve Oney, complained that she had no
chance to move up, she was actually told, "You're making good money
for a woman." [18]

What *is* "good money for a woman"? Before the lawsuit, men working at Publix full-time made, on average, 35 percent more than women
working there full-time. Apparently "good money for a woman" is 65
cents to a man's dollar.

But Home Depot and Publix were scarcely alone in preventing
women from having a fair shot at better-paying work. For many
women—not all, but a great many—these patterns will seem painfully
familiar. All you have to do is glance at your corporate organizational
chart. Or stand up and see who's in the cubicles and who's in the corner
offices. Or look around the factory or store to see who's standing and
who's sitting where. That, too, is "gut instinct."

Many women have been told that their subjective impression that
it's harder for women to get ahead is merely anecdotal, not factually
true—despite the statistical evidence. But in fact, the two-track promotion system—upward for men, slower or never for women—has been so

obvious that, over a decade, a wide range of industries and employers has lost in court or agreed to settle, as can be seen in the following table.

What you can't see in a chart like this are the astonishing stories and eyebrow-raising details. Reading the cases themselves, you wonder what these employers could have been *thinking*. You don't see that an independent commission ranked the Atlanta Fire Department's Lieutenant Liz Summers as its *top* candidate for two open jobs—and that the department nevertheless ignored that ranking and awarded both jobs to less-experienced men. You don't see that when Raytheon was closing a Virginia office, it transferred that office's nine male employees to higher-paying posts in Moscow—but refused to transfer the three women who also applied. Juries, judges, and arbitrators balked at such stories and agreed that women's careers had been illegally and offensively stalled, just because they were women.

As I mentioned in chapter 4, the biggest such award in American history may soon hit the headlines. As this book is going to press, the largest discrimination class action lawsuit ever is under way against Wal-Mart, which employs more women than any other private company in the United States. In *Dukes v. Wal-Mart*, the named plaintiffs represent 1.5 million women. The plaintiff lawyers' data show that although more than two thirds of the company's hourly employees are female, women hold less than 15 percent of store manager positions. Further, women have made less than men with the same seniority and position in every year since 1997, even though the female employees on average have higher performance ratings and less turnover than men. Those statistics are damning. They suggest exactly the kind of unwritten but widely accepted policy that held women back at Home Depot and Publix Super Markets. Is there a reasonable explanation? Did this just *happen* because women didn't want to work late or weren't interested in moving up? Or will Wal-Mart soon appear in the headlines with the largest sex discrimination payout in history—becoming one more employer for whom such penalties are just the cost of doing business?

The point of these lists is to prompt you to ask: Where are the women? Are they clustered in the lower-paying jobs? Or are they fanned out across all positions, including the most responsible? Keep this question in mind every time you walk into a store, bank, office, fac-

COMPANIES THAT HAD TO PAY UP AFTER BEING CHARGED WITH REFUSING TO PROMOTE WOMEN

Employer	Charges	Type of Action	Payout Year	Amount
American Express Financial Advisors, Inc., Minneapolis, Minn.	Denied promotions, account assignments, mentoring, training, equal pay*	Settlement and consent decree	2002	$31 million and court oversight
Arkansas Department of Correction	Refusal to promote and hire	Settlement	1997	$20 million
Atlanta, Ga., Fire Department	Denied promotion	Federal jury award	2003	$1 million
Boeing Corporation, Seattle, Wash.	Sex discrimination in promotions, pay	Settlement	2004	Between $40.6 and $72.5 million
Boies, Schiller & Flexner, Armonk, N.Y.	Relegated to nonpartnership tracks*	Settlement	2002	$75,000
Brink's, Inc., Phoenix, Ariz.	Promotion denied	Settlement	2002	$58,750
Calcasieu Parish School Board, Louisiana	Failure to promote	Settlement	2000	$80,000
CBS Broadcasting, Inc., New York, N.Y.	Denied promotions, training, assignments, overtime*	Settlement	2000	$8 million
Chevron Corporation, United States	Discrimination in promotions, jobs	Settlement	1996	$8.5 million
Chicago Police Department, Illinois	Failure to promote female lieutenant	Federal jury award	2004	$550,000
Clarke County, Ga., School District	School principals; discrimination in evaluations: s, r	Settlement	2004	$170,000
Diamond Offshore Drilling, Houston, Tex.	Refusal to assign to higher-paying job	Settlement	2001	$60,000
Federal Law Enforcement Training Center, Brunswick, Ga.	Refusal to promote*	Federal jury award	1997	$672,000
Frederick Transport, Inc., and GJHSRT, Inc., United States	Promotion denied, unequal pay, retaliation	Settlement	1998	$70,000
City of Gardena, California	Failure to promote, retaliation	Jury award	2001	$1.65 million

Home Depot, Texas	Female sales clerk denied promotion	Settlement and consent decree	2003	$125,000
Home Depot, Western states	Denied training, promotions	Settlement	1997	$87.5 million
Ingles Markets, United States	Denied promotions	Settlement	1999	$16.5 million
International Association of Machinists and Aerospace Workers District Lodge 160, Wash.	Denied promotions	Jury award	2001	$637,000
Kentucky Department of Corrections	Failure to promote*	Jury award	2003	$730,000
Landis Plastics, Inc., Solvay, N.Y.	Failure to hire or promote	Settlement	2000	$782,000
Merrill Lynch, New York, N.Y.	Refusal to train, support, promote	Settlement	1998	$600,000 and individual mediation awards
Morgan Stanley, New York, N.Y.	Failure to promote, unequal pay	Settlement	2004	$54 million
Nob Hill Foods, San Francisco, Calif.	Failure to promote	Settlement	1998	$1.3 million and court oversight
Optical Cable Corporation, Roanoke, Va.	Assigned to lower-paying jobs: s, r	Settlement	2002	$1 million
Publix Super Markets, Florida	Failure to promote	Settlement with consent decree	1997	$81.5 million and court oversight
Raytheon, Massachusetts	Promotion denial	Jury award	1997	$500,000
Raytheon, Virginia	Denied higher-paying assignment	Federal arbitrator award	2000	$870,000
Royal Air Maroc, New York	Failure to promote	State jury award	2002	$903,017
Sacramento Regional Transit District, Calif.	Systematic training and promotion denials	Class action settlement	2002	$2.5 million court oversight
Santa Barbara, Calif., Police Department	Promotion denials	Jury award	2002	$3.2 million
Sealy Corp., Madison, Wis.	Promotion denied to sales representative	Jury award	2003	$1.102 million; judge reduced to $401,500
Sunnyvale, Calif., Police Department	Failure to promote, retaliation	Settlement	2004	$2 million
Svenska Handelsbanken, New York	Failure to promote banker	Jury award reduced by federal judge	1997	$1.57 million, later reduced to $370,000

(continued on next page)

Employer	Charges	Type of Action	Payout Year	Amount
Trendwest Resorts, Inc., Oreg.	Failure to promote	Settlement	2004	$475,000
United Airlines, United States	Discriminatory weight policy	Judicial reinstatement of award	2004	$36.5 million
University of Wisconsin, Platteville, Wis.	Refusal to renew employment contract	Federal jury award	2004	$400,000
Wellesley College, Wellesley, Mass.	Refusal to promote female security guard	Settlement	1996	Undisclosed

* Indicates one or more additional charges, such as refusal to hire, unequal pay, demotions, firings, retaliation, hostile working environment, or sexual harassment.

Codes: s = sex; r = race; n.o. = national origin.

EEOC: Equal Employment Opportunity Commission.

tory, government agency, restaurant, university, rental car service, and anywhere else your life takes you. Later in the book, I'll talk about what we should be doing about all this. But we can't make effective change unless we can see what needs to be changed. For now, the important thing is to train yourself to recognize whether and where discrimination exists. So wherever you go, keep asking: Are women being treated fairly on this job?

Unequal Pay for Equal Work

I kept believing they would recognize the job performance as it really was and the right thing would be done.

> —Lilly M. Ledbetter, Goodyear Tire & Rubber [19]

My salary over [the past twenty-five years] has ranged from 40 percent to 20 percent less than the salaries of men in the same department where I work. On the average, my salary has been 26 percent less than male professors. The meaning of the comparison is easy to see. I have been working for . . . six of my twenty-five years without pay.

> —Professor Norma Sadler, Boise State University [20]

If you do the same day's work, you should earn the same day's pay. That's a fundamental American idea. But many employers flatly refuse. And that refusal happens at *every* economic level, in *every* kind of job. No industry or sector is immune. Consider Theresa Siler-Khodr, M.D., Ph.D. During the 1990s, Dr. Siler-Khodr, a specialist in reproductive endocrinology at the University of Texas Health Science Center at San Antonio, found out that she was making $20,000 less than her male colleague Dr. Sidney Shain. Each doctor had a medical degree; advanced training in obstetrics and gynecology; and a Ph.D. in biochemistry. They had exactly the same job duties. She had more seniority, having been there since 1976. Yet he made $83,000, while she made $63,000. That's a wage gap of 24 percent, even without figuring in how much less she had accrued in her pension fund during the previous twenty years. She sued and won—and, along the way, found that as far back as 1992, the school had finished an internal study that showed that every other female professor there could have made the same complaint, since on average, the school's male professors made 26 percent more than female professors.

For many of us, it's startling to think that women in academia and the professions would not be paid equally. Universities have a public reputation as strongholds of liberal thought, political correctness, diversity and justice for all. You can see, in the data, that women and men are (at the very least) equally qualified: women today earn 57 percent of all bachelor's degrees and 58 percent of all master's degrees in the United States alone.[21] In certain fields, women seem to be *more* qualified: in literature, for instance, women have earned by far more B.A.s, M.A.s, and Ph.D.s than men in every year since 1979.

Yet even here, women are not hired, promoted, or paid at the same rate as men.

Why? Because many colleges and universities hire, promote, and pay based on informal judgments, on managers' "gut instincts"—the very same biased system that kept women down at Home Depot or Publix Super Markets. Hiring, promotion, and pay decisions are made by department chairs, who rarely have to explain those decisions to anyone higher up. These managers often have enormous power to decide such questions as: Whose research is seen as important and promising, and whose is marginal or run of the mill? Who's given enough lab space or research assistance or new computers to shine or pulled into informal conversations where new ideas are swapped? Who's given money to give presentations at conferences or allowed to take a few extra months doing archival research instead of teaching? Which brilliant graduate student gets talked up when recruiters call? In too many academic settings, all those questions are answered on—you guessed it—gut instinct. And being free to make such decisions based on your gut instinct means this: your ingrained cultural biases never need to be examined, explained, or justified.

Department chairs, deans, provosts, and presidents approve or deny hiring, promotion, tenure, and pay decisions based on their own sense of who needs or deserves a big raise and who can get by with a cost-of-living raise. Because private universities' salary scales can be as jealously guarded as a CIA roster, it can be nearly impossible for a woman to find out whether or not she's paid as much as her peers—and if not, whether she alone has sunk to the barrel's bottom or whether female professors are usually paid less, suggesting not failure but discrimination.

One former history professor talked to me about her experience at one of the nation's foremost private universities.[22] She had top credentials: degrees and fellowships from the country's most famous universities, highly placed publications, and good book reviews. At the end of the 1990s, her department unanimously approved her for tenure. But the school's dean turned her down. The reason: she was not good enough. "It's a tremendously subjective process," this history professor explained with great composure. "It's very, very easy for anybody to say, 'We just don't see the promise.' And that's what they said to me."

Since she was a historian, she checked her department's tenure record. There she learned that in the previous twenty years, nineteen of the nineteen men who had applied for tenure had been approved, one after a delay. Five out of nine women had been approved, one after a delay; another had been approved, with a demotion; and *three out of nine* women had been denied. "That raised a red flag," she said dryly. Researching the rest of the university, she discovered that her department's record of hiring, paying, and promoting women was actually *better* than those of other departments.

This former history professor is a slight, soft-spoken woman. She doesn't look or sound like someone who would challenge a politically powerful institution, a major employer and job engine in its region. She recognized that challenging her elite university would be all or nothing: if she didn't get tenure, she'd never teach again. With hundreds more new Ph.D.s falling off the assembly line each June, what other institution would hire a fiery historian notorious for challenging and suing her first, and famous, employer? But injustice made her stubborn. She appealed her tenure denial. Her dean again turned her down. She took it up to the provost, who also turned her down. Next stop was an elected faculty advisory committee, complete with a formal hearing, with lawyers and cross-examination. She won: the faculty committee declared that her dean's decision to deny tenure had been wrong.

Nevertheless, the university president, who had the final say, decided against giving her tenure. He declared that the history professor could keep working in her department for another two years and then try for tenure all over again.

This history professor was more than exhausted; she was a marked woman, and she knew it. Because she had been willing to go public, other female professors had joined her in filing claims with the EEOC; the Office of Federal Contract Compliance Programs (OFCCP) had begun to examine the university's hiring, promotion, and pay records, which hadn't been filed for years, although filing was required by law. Her case was regularly discussed in the regional papers and in *The Chronicle of Higher Education*, the trade journal for academics. Further, a presidential election was coming up; she feared losing EEOC support if a new administration cut that agency's budget for lawsuits like her own. Most important, it was too awful to contemplate another two or three years of living in the fishbowl as the university's most infamous professor, a lightning rod whom some avoided and others sought out not for her professional insight but as a symbol—only *then* to go through the whole tenure circus again. So the history professor went back to graduate school and learned a different trade, letting her lawyers negotiate with her university and prepare for a lawsuit. As that fall's presidential elections approached, the professor was afraid that a new administration's EEOC would be less aggressive in enforcing the law. She and the university settled the case for a significant—but not overwhelming—sum, enough to pay for her new professional training.

But did the ex–history professor get even—or did she lose money during her crusade for justice? Let's add it up. As an assistant professor, she had been making roughly $50,000 a year with generous benefits. Immediate tenure should have boosted that to $60,000, with incremental raises. Instead, she spent another year at $50,000, for a loss of $10,000. She took a year off at almost no pay on a fellowship to recuperate from battle; she then spent three years in graduate school, for a loss of another $200,000 in income. In addition, she lost her generous benefits and any accrued retirement contributions. That adds up to a loss of at least $210,000—even without counting the emotional toll of having spent several years as a campus pariah.

But that strain turned out to be financially costly as well. Six years later, the ex-professor hadn't yet caught back up to what she would have been earning had she gotten tenure. She had been too worn out to search hard for a new job, taking the first one offered. "The [tenure] thing was more of a drain than I realized at the time," she said. "I didn't have the energy to just dive back into the competition. I had to lay back for a while." As a result, in 2003 she was earning $60,000 a year, with almost no benefits and no pension plan. That was roughly $15,000 less per year than she would have been earning had she gotten tenure and received even the most minimal raises since.

This history professor did not get even. Nor did she win justice for women. As she said, "In my own former department, there are fewer women than there were when I left." The bad guys won all around.

Dr. Theresa Siler-Khodr and the ex–history professor are just two of many women who have sued universities for equal pay and won awards or settlements, as you can see in the previous chart. All these women—and more—charged, at great emotional and financial cost, that their universities paid them less than their male peers, even though they were equally qualified. And these are just the women who challenged the academy *publicly*. What you can't see in that chart is the vast number of

UNIVERSITIES THAT HAD TO PAY IN
EQUAL PAY AND TENURE DENIAL LAWSUITS

University	Department	Unequal Pay Charges	Type of Action	Payout Year	Amount
Boise State University, Idaho	Education	On average, females' salaries were 26 percent less than males' salary	Jury award	1997	$146,000
Case Western Reserve University, Cleveland, Ohio	Biology	Tenure denial	Settlement	2002	Undisclosed
Eastern Michigan University, Michigan	Industrial technology	Most qualified; second-lowest paid	Settlement	2000	$100,000 and pay raise
Kettering University, Detroit, Mich.	Communications	More qualified, paid less than comparable male	Settlement	2003	$55,000
Lawrence Livermore Labs (UC Regents), Calif.	3,200 women	Unequal pay	Settlement	2003	$18 million
Lehigh University, Bethlehem, Penn.	Chemistry	Tenure denial	Settlement	2004	Undisclosed
Saint Cloud State University, Minnesota	250 women faculty	Unequal pay	Settlement	2000	$830,786
Santa Clara University, Calif.	Religious studies	Tenure denial	Mediation	2000	$87,500
Southern West Virginia Community and Technical College	Art	Unequal pay, retaliation	Jury award	2000	$325,000
Trinity College, Conn.	Chemistry	Tenure denied	Jury award	1999	$12.7 million
UC Berkeley, Calif.	Art history	Tenure denied	Settlement	1997	$113,000
UC Davis, Calif.	English	Tenure denied	Settlement	1999	$600,000
University of Oregon, Eugene, Oreg.	Dance	Tenure denied because of pregnancy leaves	Settlement	2000	$495,000
University of South Florida, Tampa, Fla.	Five departments	Denied pay increases, promotions	Settlement	1998	$900,000
University of Texas Health Science Center, San Antonio, Tex.	Reproductive endocrinology	Unequal pay	Jury award	2002	$400,000
University of Wisconsin, Madison, Wis.	English (writing)	Female salary, $71,000; comparable male salaries, $93,000 and $110,000	Settlement	2001	$127,500

university women who settle under a confidentiality clause. Often, universities know they're going to lose. But their statistics on hiring, promoting, and paying women are *so* bad that they don't want to make them public; they'd rather pay off the squeaky wheel than fix the entire university pay-and-promotion machinery.

As a result, other university women keep losing money. And smart, ambitious female graduate students and professors continue to have less chance of moving up in academia—fewer job offers, lower pay, fewer shots at the top—depriving society not just of equal wages and equal role models for women and men, not just of fair pay for those women and their families, but also of whatever different intellectual insights those women might have offered to our collective understanding of the world.

You can find the same story in every socioeconomic, geographic, and industry niche: leaving managers to make subjective hiring, pay, and promotion decisions results in women earning less than what lawyers call "similarly situated" men. Women who clean, for instance, are paid less than men who clean—even when they're both lifting the same fifty pounds of trash and swabbing, mopping, and scrubbing the very same tables, floors, and toilets. At the U.S. Capitol, those women were called "custodians" and paid roughly $10 per hour; the men who performed precisely the same tasks were called "laborers" and paid roughly $11 per hour. In the Lynn (Massachusetts) Public Schools, the women were called house workers and paid $11.58 per hour; the men were called custodians and paid $13.08 per hour. In Baton Rouge, women were hired into the lower-paying Janitor I slot, while men were hired to be Janitors II and III. In 2002, 2001, and 1997, these employers had to pay out $2.5 million, $400,000, and $95,000 in settlements, respectively—a high cost for ignoring a wage gap.

Janitors and professors might seem to be at different ends of the socioeconomic spectrum, but they have this in common: the women are systematically paid less than the men. Discrimination doesn't get any more basic than that: less pay for exactly the same work, for no other reason than sex. They unfortunately have this in common with women in many other occupations as well. In the table on pages 58–59, we saw that women aren't *hired* at the same rate as men. In the table on pages 70–72, we saw that women aren't *promoted* at the same rate as men. In the table

EMPLOYERS THAT HAD TO PAY AFTER
BEING CHARGED WITH PAYING WOMEN LESS THAN
MEN DOING SIMILAR OR COMPARABLE WORK

Employer	Employee	Unequal Pay Charges	Type of Action	Payout Year	Amount
Bass Cabinet Manufacturing, Inc., Mesa, Ariz.	Assistant foreman	Paid less than comparable men	EEOC settlement	2003	$25,000
BMW, North Carolina	Controller	Unequal pay, retaliation	Federal jury	2002	$530,000
Boeing Company, Seattle, Wash.	Women and minority salaried and executive employees	Unequal pay	OFCCP settlement	1999	$4.5 million
Cabot Corporation, Massachusetts	In-house attorney	Unequal pay	Massachusetts Commission Against Discrimination order	1999	$377,748
Chesapeake Operating Co., Inc., and Sanders Trucking Co., United States	2 female dispatchers	Unequal pay	Settlement	1996	$43,000
Dixie Stampede Dinner Attractions Inc., Tennessee	Female rodeo riders	Unequal pay	Settlement	2002	$135,000
East Baton Rouge Parish School Board, Louisiana	Female janitors	Unequal pay	Settlement	1997	$95,000
Fifth Third Bank, Ohio	26 professional and managerial women	Unequal pay:* s, r	OFCCP Settlement	2000	$440,000
Flint Ink Corporation, Flint, Mich.	2 laboratory employees	Unequal pay	Settlement	2003	$120,000
George Junior Republic, Pittsburgh, Pa.	Counselors	Unequal pay, retaliation*	Settlement	2000	$280,000
Goodyear Tire & Rubber, Alabama	Female employee	Unequal pay	Federal jury award	2003	$3.8 million
Highmark (Blue Cross Blue Shield), Pennsylvania	Middle managers	Unequal pay	OFCCP settlement	1998	$200,000
Ingersoll Milling Machine Company, Illinois	64 employees	Unequal pay:* s, r	Settlement	2001	$1.8 million

(continued on next page)

Employer	Employee	Unequal Pay Charges	Type of Action	Payout Year	Amount
Jersey Community Unit School District, Illinois	5 female custodians	Unequal pay	Settlement	2000	$10,700
Kash n' Karry, Florida	All female employees	Unequal pay	Class action settlement	2004	$3.1 million
Key Energy Services, Inc., Midland, Tex.	Controller	Unequal pay	Settlement	2002	$25,000, plus pay raise
Los Angeles County, Calif., Police Department	5,000 female officers	Unequal pay	Class action jury award	2002	$240 million in back pay, pensions, and raises
Lynn, Mass., public schools	23 houseworkers	Paid less than junior building custodians	Settlement	2000	$400,000 and hired permanently
McDonnell Douglas Travel Co., St. Louis, Mo.	Operations administration manager	Unequal pay	Settlement	1997	$95,000
NYNEX Meridian Systems, Connecticut	Employee	Unequal pay	Settlement	1997	$95,000
Outback Steakhouse, Tampa, Fla.	Site development assistant	Unequal pay, retaliation	Jury award	2001	$2.2 million, reduced to $414,000 under federal cap on damages awards
Penn Corporation, United States	Production	Unequal pay	Settlement	1996	$20,000
Phoenix Management Ltd. Co., St. Louis County, Mo.	Comptroller	Unequal pay	Settlement	2002	$120,000
R. E. Michel Co., Maryland	Purchasing agent	Unequal pay	Settlement	1999	$200,000
St. Paul Metalcraft, Inc., St. Paul, Minn.	10 female machine operators	Unequal pay, less favorable training opportunities	Settlement	1998	$73,684
City of Sauk Rapids, Minn.	Account clerk, secretary/office clerk, city assessor	Paid less than comparable men	Minnesota Department of Human Rights settlement	2004	$133,145
Sunoco, Philadelphia, Pa.	15 female finance and sales employees	Unequal pay	OFCCP settlement	2000	$250,000
Super Valu Holdings, United States	Grocery warehousing	Unequal pay	Jury award	2002	$400,000

Swift Transportation, Kansas City, Mo.	6 female dispatchers	Unequal pay	Jury award	2002	$450,000
Temco Service Industries and SEIU Local 54, New York, N.Y.	Cleaning personnel	Unequal duties/pay	Administrative law award	1996	$30,445.60
Texaco, United States	186 female administrators	Unequal pay	OFCCP review	1999	$3.1 million
US Airways, United States	30 female managers and professionals	Unequal pay	OFCCP review	1998	$400,000
U.S. Capitol, Washington, D.C.	300 female custodians	Unequal pay	Settlement	2001	$2.5 million

*Indicates one or more additional charges, such as refusal to hire, train, or promote, demotions, firings, retaliation, hostile working environment, or sexual harassment.

Codes: s = sex; r = race.

EEOC: Equal Employment Opportunity Commission.

OFCCP: Office of Federal Contract Compliance Programs, U.S. Department of Labor.

just presented, we saw that academic institutions don't pay women the same amount that they pay men in the same jobs. In the next table, we will see how many different kinds of employers have, over the past decade, had to fork over awards and settlements for that very basic injustice.

The Pregnancy Penalty

They told me, "Come back after you have the baby.". . . I didn't know it was illegal. I just thought it was immoral.
　　　　—Jamey Stearn, who won a $220,000 EEOC settlement
　　　　　　from Wal-Mart for pregnancy discrimination
　　　　　　　(The Arizona Republic, January 24, 2003)

"This hopefully won't happen again. I think pregnancy is one of the coolest things a person can ever experience, and for someone to say you can't [work] while you're pregnant is ridiculous. I just don't understand it."
　　　　—Marylyn Pickler, after winning a $70,000 settlement from
　　　　Berge Ford, which fired her when she announced her pregnancy
　　　　　(quote from East Valley Tribune.com, June 16, 2004)

Many commentators believe that women's wages are lower than men's because of maternity. Here's the theory: once women become mothers, they step out of the workforce for a few years, work part-time, or voluntarily step onto a lower-pressure, lower-earning "mommy track" so that they can put their kids first. As we've already seen, the first two concepts don't affect the wage gap, since nonworkers and part-timers aren't included in the average; only full-time workers are counted. And chapter 9, "Working While Mother," will look more carefully at the theory that mothers "choose" to earn less money.

But even before becoming mothers, thousands of women each year are penalized just for getting pregnant. They're fired. Or they're put on immediate unpaid leave. Or they're put on lesser duties—and lesser pay. Or they're demoted until further notice. Nor is any of this subtle. One manager at (prelawsuit) Home Depot put this attitude succinctly: "You women, you get knocked up and then you're worthless."

Consider the story of a particularly ambitious young cop. After graduating from the police academy, she was assigned to one of the hardest, most demanding stations, just as she'd hoped. She did well on the job, bringing in so many arrests, drug busts, and weapons violations that she was frequently mentioned in the newspaper. "My father used to save the articles, he was so proud," this police officer explained. She worked a great deal of overtime, making more money than either of her hardworking parents had ever made. She loved the job and worked ambitiously to do it well. Even though she was relatively slight, she said proudly, word went out on the police grapevine "that I could hold my own, that I was aggressive, that I was not afraid."[23]

This hardworking cop married another cop. After a couple of transfers, she got a detective job, landing at a station where her fellow detectives and her new lieutenant treated her well. When she got pregnant, she and her lieutenant figured out which assignments made sense and which didn't.

She was just as successful as a detective as she'd been as a street cop: she interrogated suspects, questioned witnesses, and testified in murder cases, and had a good, solid record. Thinking back later, she realized that, in the background, some subtle discrimination had been going on;

occasionally she wondered why a small circle of guys, the lieutenants' buddies, had been thrown all the really big and prestigious cases. Even after several years on the job, she was never the sole lead investigator on a homicide case. That cut down on the amount of overtime she earned. But she refused to dwell on it and brushed the annoyances aside.

Then she got pregnant again. And this time, like thousands of women each year, she was docked for it.

One day, upon coming to work, the young cop learned that her police force had a new—unwritten, but enforced—off-the-job injuries policy that included pregnancy: "lesser duties," a designation that stripped them of their cruisers, banned them from official contact with the public, changed their shift immediately to nine to five, and banned them from doing overtime.

The officer was outraged. She knew that under federal law—the Pregnancy Discrimination Act of 1978, which declared this to be discrimination under Title VII of the Civil Rights Act of 1964—this was illegal. Several other women on this large force were pregnant while this policy was in effect. These women were two, three, four, five, six months pregnant, women who hadn't even complained of morning sickness or discomfort, women with no special health needs. They weren't sick. These women were sidelined only because of someone else's discomfort with their not-yet-visible tummies.

Some local radio talk show hosts thought the new policy was reasonable. They said that pregnant women shouldn't be out tackling wrongdoers, breaking down doors, and throwing themselves in front of armed drug dealers. But these women weren't doing any of that. They weren't using their unmarked police cars to race after bad guys like Gene Hackman in *The French Connection*; they used them to drive to and from work and to travel to and from investigations. Or they drove them to and from courts to testify or to interview witnesses around the state. And yet their company cars—aka "unmarked cruisers"—were taken away. Often the family had only one other car, leaving the pregnant woman stranded, scrambling to get to work. They were no longer paid overtime, which can add one third or one half to a cop's income. They couldn't take a lead role in investigations, since they couldn't drive far. They couldn't go to or

EMPLOYERS THAT HAD TO PAY UP
AFTER BEING CHARGED WITH PREGNANCY DISCRIMINATION

Employer	Employee	Pregnancy Discrimination Charged	Type of Action	Payout Year	Amount
Bean Lumber, Glenwood, Ark.	Employee	Discharge; refusal to promote; mandatory unpaid leave after fourth month	Settlement	2002	$45,000
Berge Ford, Mesa, Ariz.	Shuttle driver	Fired for pregnancy	Settlement	2004	$70,000
Center for Coastal Studies, Provincetown, Mass.	Researcher	Forced from job because of pregnancy	MCAD (state discrimination commission) settlement	1998	$69,000
Cincinnati Bell, Ohio	More than 500	Denied retirement credits while on maternity leave	Class action settlement	2000	More than $1 million (estimated)
Creative Fabricators, Inc., Dayton, Ohio	Employee	Fired when refused to have abortion	Jury award	1997	$146,000
Delta Air Lines, Atlanta, Ga.	2 ramp agents	One fired, one told to take unpaid medical leave	Settlement	2002	$150,000
Granny's Grainery, Lebanon, Oreg.	Bartender	Hours reduced, forced to quit	Administrative law judge order	2000	$12,568
The Imagine Group, Inc., New York, N.Y.	Employee	Pregnancy discrimination and sex harassment	Mediated agreement not honored; settlement	2003	$45,000
Johnson Financial Group, SC Johnson, Racine, Wis.	Applicant for executive vice president	Job offer withdrawn because of pregnancy	Settlement	2004	$450,000
marchFIRST, Inc., Chicago, Ill.	Executive secretary	Demoted, then discharged	Settlement	2002	$120,000
Massachusetts State Troopers	4 state troopers	Demoted, benefits reduced, denied overtime	Jury award	2002	$1.556 million
Pacific Bell, Nevada Bell, United States	10,000 employees	Denied pension credit during pregnancy or maternity leave	Settlement	1999	$25 million
P&O Nedlloyd, Ltd., United States	Accountant	Denied benefits in layoff because of pregnancy, race	Settlement	2003	$125,000
Ralston Drug & Discount Liquor, Texas	Clerk	Fired because of pregnancy	Settlement	2000	$15,000

Rustic Inn Crabhouse, Fort Lauderdale, Fla.	Waitresses	Demotions after fifth month	Jury award	1998	$786,000
Sodexho Marriott Services, Inc., United States	Day porter	Discharged	Settlement	2002	$50,000
Spelling Entertainment Group and Spelling Television, Inc., California	Actress	Fired for pregnancy	Jury award	1997	$4.89 million
University of New Mexico, Health Sciences Center	3 female employees	Fired for pregnancy; refused to temporarily transfer to less physically dangerous work; retaliation	Settlement	2004	$135,382
Verizon (formerly Bell Atlantic and NYNEX), United States	12,500 workers	Denied pension credit during pregnancy or maternity leave	Settlement	2002	$25 million (estimated)
Wal-Mart, Bentonville, Ark.	Job applicant	Refusal to hire: "Come back after you have the baby."	Settlement	2002	$220,000

EEOC: *Equal Employment Opportunity Commission*

stay late for follow-up questioning, unless they were willing to work pro bono. And when one refused to accept these conditions, she was sent out on unpaid leave, stripped of her paycheck entirely.

These pregnant officers took the department to court—and won. In that, they're like thousands of other women each year. Illegal though it may be, *many* employers reward expectant women with demotion, downgrade, and firing, as is visible in the table above.

Rarely are such cases subtle. Women often win pregnancy discrimination cases because their employers say, point-blank, that they can't do the job if they're pregnant or because the company has an explicit policy that women must leave the job after a certain month. And women at every socioeconomic level have had to pay the pregnancy penalty of demotion, docked pay, or a lost job. Hundreds of them have proved it, winning settlements or lawsuits that didn't quite compensate them for what they lost. The pregnant police officer, for instance, was profoundly shaken by some of her fellow cops' refusal to publicly respect or support her. "Oh my God, there were some people that were so mad," she said at the fact that she had broken the cop code of silent loyalty to the force. Some of her male fellow officers were baffled, asking, "Why don't you just stay home and take care of your kids? Why are you doing this to yourself?" She was angry that they didn't understand how illegal and unfair the policy was. She was angry that her husband's family resented her for hurting *his* police career; the strain got so bad that during the lawsuit, she got divorced.

When we spoke, this police officer still wasn't fully emotionally back on her feet. "The job meant everything to me—it was the biggest accomplishment of my family of that generation. I was the only one to go to college and the only one to get a job like that. It was just—it was one of the family's proudest moments. And now I wake up every day and I'm like 'I've got to convince myself that it's still worth going to work and not doing something else.' "

Worse, the lawsuit did not get this police officer's paycheck even with what it should have been. In the end, this particular cop received $401,361 as part of her group's jury award. Of her portion, $137,000 went to her lawyers. Another $132,000 went directly to state and federal taxes. That left her with $132,361—some of which had to be used to cover debts she had incurred while being unable to work overtime during the lawsuit.

Reading that four women had won a multimillion-dollar lawsuit award, you might think they'd each had a windfall. That's not what it seemed like to this cop, who didn't get the money until her children were in grade school. "Was it really worth it?" she mused months after receiving the money. The money wasn't worth it, she concluded. Had she known how little she would end up with after five years of legal turmoil—resulting in a divorce, her colleagues' resentment, and her own emotional strain—she wouldn't have done it just for that. Working overtime would have been a more productive way to earn the same amount. Rather, she said, what had made the lawsuit worth it was this: "Having the policy changed to what it should have been all along."

Neither this police officer nor any of the women in this table *chose* a lower-paying "mommy track." They hadn't altered their work habits one iota. They hadn't even yet stepped off the job to give birth. They went to court because, as they reported, simply for revealing (either verbally or physically) that they *were going to* have a child, their earnings were slashed.

Four out of five American women get pregnant at least once in their lifetime. The pregnancy penalty is essentially a tax on being female.

Driven Out: Harsher Conditions

> I felt like I had been hit with a brick, I just couldn't believe that after all that had been talked about, they were asking me to go back into the control room.
>   —Testimony of Sharon Pollard[24]

The worst of these lawsuits might well be the ones in which a woman was actively driven off the job—for no other reason than that she was female. Maybe the boss didn't want her there but didn't want to fire her outright. Maybe the boss didn't mind her, but didn't care if her coworkers wanted to drive her away. Read the next story, and ask yourself how long you'd last under the conditions this woman endured.

Sharon Pollard: "She Must Be Silent"

Sharon Pollard worked in a DuPont chemical plant in Memphis, Tennessee, from 1977 to 1995. In 1987 she was promoted, becoming an "operator" in charge of the peroxide department's control room, overseeing two or three assistant operators. Not long after she took that job, one of her assistants refused to do what she asked, saying that he couldn't take orders from a woman. As explanation, he put a New Testament on her desk and opened it to these verses: "A woman should learn in quietness and full submission. I do not permit a woman to teach or have authority over a man, she must be silent." (1 Timothy 2:11–12)

He was transferred to another shift. Not long afterward, he was promoted.

In 1992, Pollard was put on a shift that, as everyone in the plant knew, was full of men who didn't believe women belonged there. These guys called themselves "an extended family": they cooked meals together, ate together, socialized. But they openly called women "bitches," "cunts," "heifers," and "split tails," even to Sharon Pollard's face. Still, Sharon managed—until, in February 1994, the plant's management asked her to give a talk to some girls for Take Your Daughters to Work Day.

The guys on her shift were appalled at the very idea. One of them sent out a plantwide e-mail ranting against Daughters Day, saying women shouldn't even think about working there. And they shunned Pollard for being involved. "If I came into the lunchroom," Pollard testified in court, "nobody would sit down at the table with me. If I sat down at a table that someone was already sitting at, they would get up and leave. . . . I heard a lot of under-your-breath kind of things . . . and snickering." This shunning went on for nearly eighteen months.

According to the trial judge's summary of the testimony,[25] the ringleader was one man. According to that summary, the ringleader told Pollard's assistants not to take her orders unless they checked with him first. He started setting off false alarms—alarms that meant that Pollard had to search the plant, which took up three city blocks, checking for a nonexistent problem. If he set off the alarm when she was cooking her dinner, the other guys would turn up the heat and burn her food while she was searching. Worse, when a real alarm went off in her area, the ringleader wouldn't tell her, leaving her in potential danger. He and the other guys repeatedly sabotaged her peroxide production, trying to drive her away with bad evaluations.

Pollard complained to her boss, who did nothing. Her bicycle tires were slashed; nothing. She said that the ringleader had tried to run her off the road in his truck; there was no investigation. One male coworker did think the ringleader was going too far and asked for a shift meeting. But when the ringleader yelled at Pollard that no one liked her, that it was all her own fault, the boss simply stopped the meeting: no reprimand for her tormentor, no change at all.

At the DuPont plant's women's group, Pollard told the others that she was constantly anxious, that she could go for hours on that night shift without hearing another human voice, that she was afraid that there'd be a dangerous accident and no one would tell her, that they'd leave her to be injured or killed. One of those women was her boss's boss: she did nothing. Pollard complained to a DuPont diversity manager who came through the plant, who passed her story on to several people in management. Nothing happened. No investigation, no reprimand, no demotion for the ringleader. The harassment kept on.

By July 1995, Pollard had had it. She begged her boss to "just get me off this shift, nothing's changed and I can't take it." He offered her a job on another shift—a shift where she'd be working with the man who'd left her those Timothy 2:11–12 verses. She refused. Next day, those New Testament verses mysteriously appeared in her locker.

Finally Sharon Pollard cracked. She left on medical leave. The ringleader and the other guys on her shift—including her boss—held a victory party, a fish fry, complete with party balloons. According to trial testimony, the ringleader declared that they were "glad the bitch is gone, glad the bitch is not coming back."

By then, unfortunately, Pollard was more than qualified for the medical leave. Living for so many months in such a hostile environment had resulted in a severe case of posttraumatic stress disorder. The long-term campaign of harassment, intimidation, isolation, and actual danger meant she had it bad: nightmares, fear of crowds, nausea, anxiety, sleeplessness. DuPont threw a barrage of psychologists and psychiatrists at her, investigating her contention that she could no longer work. DuPont's doctors all agreed: Pollard could not and should not go back to work.

Nevertheless, despite its own doctors' appraisals, six months later DuPont ordered her back to work: same shift, same department, same coworkers. She refused. DuPont fired her. She sued. She won.

"This situation was reprehensible," wrote the trial court judge in the 1998 decision. "This is a case of wretched indifference to an employee who was slowly drowning in an environment that was completely unacceptable, while her employer sat by and watched." DuPont appealed all the way to the Supreme Court. In 2001, former EEOC chairman Justice Clarence Thomas wrote the opinion that upheld Pollard's award. As this book is being written, however, DuPont is again appealing, putting off Sharon Pollard's payment and dragging her back into court.

EMPLOYERS THAT HAD TO PAY AFTER BEING CHARGED WITH RETALIATION OR DRIVING WOMEN OFF THE JOB

Employer	Employee	Charges	Type of Action	Payout Year	Amount
A&P Supermarket, Paterson, N.J.	Female employee	Fired in retaliation for sexual harassment complaint	Jury award	2000	$900,000
Anderson County, Tennessee	4 female employees	Fired by new mayor, replaced by higher-paid men	Settlement	2004	$707,700
Baltimore Cable Access Corporation, Maryland	Executive director	Retaliation for unequal pay charges	Settlement	2000	$45,000
Bon Secours DePaul Medical Center, Inc., Virginia	Female employee	Forced out in retaliation for trying to protect against sexual harassment	Jury award	2003	$4.05 million
Camden County Sheriff's Office, New Jersey	Police officer	Forced out in retaliation for discrimination complaint	Jury award	2003	$15,000
Caterpillar, Inc., East Peoria, Ill.	Security guard	Retaliation for sex discrimination charges	Jury award	2001	$850,000, reduced to cap of $300,000
Consolidated Freightways, Kansas City, Mo.	Salesperson	Demotion, harassment	Jury award	2001	$1.1 million
Danka Office Imaging, St. Petersburg, Fla.	Employee	Harassment, discrimination, retaliation: s, r	Settlement	2002	$375,000
DuPont Corporation, Memphis, Tenn.	Peroxide department operator	Driven out because of sex	Jury award	1998	$3.53 million
EaglePicher, United States	Employee	Discharge after failure to train, sexual harassment, discriminatory evaluations	Settlement	2003	$200,000
Emergency Medical Associates, Inc., Florida	Employee	Discharge after sexual harassment, failure to promote, unequal pay	Settlement	2003	$500,000
Environmental Health Department, Minneapolis, Minn.	Female employee	Lost promotion in retaliation for sexual harassment complaint	Minnesota Department of Human Rights settlement	2004	$25,000

Geologistics Americas, Inc., Florida	Female employee	Fired in retaliation for complaints of being denied comparable training and certification	Settlement	2003	$100,000
Hawkeye Community College, Iowa	Employee	Firing: s, r	Settlement	2001	$205,000
Hendrickson Trailer Suspension Systems, Clarksville, Tenn.	Female employee	Discharged after unequal terms and conditions of employment	Settlement	2003	$200,000
Home Depot, Colorado	Female employees	Hostile environment and retaliation: s, r, n.o.	Settlement	2004	$5.5 million
InteliOffice, LLC, and Intelitouch.com, Georgia	Area sales manager	Demoted, then fired in retaliation for sexual harassment complaint	Settlement	2003	$112,000
Knox County Public schools, Tennessee	Cafeteria worker	Fired in retaliation for harassment charges	Jury award	2001	$210,413
Lawrence Livermore National Laboratory, Calif.	Computer technician	Discharged in retaliation for unequal pay complaint	Jury award	2002	$1 million
Marine Bank of the Florida Keys, Fla.	2 female employees	Fired after sexual harassment complaints	Settlement	2003	$220,000
Maryland attorney general's office, Montgomery County, Md.	Employee	Fired in retaliation for discrimination complaint	Settlement	1999	$320,000
Massachusetts Bay Transit Authority, Boston, Mass.	Top administrator	Fired in retaliation for discrimination charges: s, r	Jury award	2001	$7.6 million
National State Bank, (CoreStates), New Jersey	Branch manager, Perth Amboy	Fired for age and sex	Jury award reduced by judge, upheld on appeal	2002	$4.283 million, reduced to $2.083 million
New York City Police Department, New York	Police officer	Forced out in retaliation for sexual harassment complaint	Jury award	2002	$1.85 million, reduced to $470,159
Norstan Apparel Shops, Inc., Florida	Female store manager	Fired in retaliation for complaining that her employees were being sexually harassed by a male manager	Settlement	2002	$250,000

(continued on next page)

Employer	Employee	Charges	Type of Action	Payout Year	Amount
Olsten Corp., Melville, N.Y.	Assistant vice president	Demotions, harassment, deprived of clients, income cut	Jury award	1997	$5.18 million
Oregon Department of Agriculture	Lab services administrator	Quit after being demoted based on sex and race	Jury award	2003	$1.032 million
Owosso Country Club, Owosso, Mich.	Nineteen-year employee	Fired because board wanted an all-male management team	Arbitrator's award	2002	$209,000
Pennsylvania State Police Department	Female employee	Fired in retaliation for sex discrimination complaint	Federal judge and jury award	2003	$277,000
Piazza Trucking, South Gate, Calif.	Truck driver	Fired based on sex	Settlement	2002	$80,000
Project Development Group, Pittsburgh, Pa.	2 asbestos handlers	Fired based on sex	Settlement	2002	$47,000
Rent-A-Center, United States	Every position	Driven out for being female*	Settlement	2002	$47 million
Saint-Gobain/Norton Industries Ceramics Corp., Newbury, Ohio	4 female employees	Laid off in retaliation for unequal pay charges	Jury award, affirmed by Ohio Supreme Court	2000	$1.135 million
San Francisco Fire Department, Calif.	Emergency medical director	Fired for being female	Jury award	1997	$600,000
Stanford University, Palo Alto, Calif.	Female employee	Retaliation for sex discrimination charge	Jury award	2004	$1 million
Suffolk County Police Department, N.Y.	Police officer	Fired in retaliation for discrimination charges: s, r	Jury award	2004	$229,500
Unicom Corporation, Los Angeles, Calif.	10 female employees	Driven out through s, r, n.o. harassment	Settlement	2004	$350,000
Unisys Corporation, Bluebell, Pa.	Truck driver	Fired in retaliation for discrimination charges	Settlement	1999	$80,000
Unisys Corporation, Bluebell, Pa.	Employee	Fired in retaliation for discrimination charges	Jury award	2000	$5.5 million
United Airlines, United States	Asbestos abatement worker	Firing	Settlement	1999	$47,000
University of California, San Francisco, Calif.	Medical professor	Fired in retaliation for discrimination charge	Jury award	1997	$2.4 million
University of Houston, Texas	Assistant general counsel	Retaliation for charging hostile environment and promotion denial	Jury award	2002	$396,000

University of Pittsburgh Medical Center, Pa.	Employee	Unfairly discharged	Jury award	2001	$570,891
University of Washington, Seattle, Wash.	Heart transplant surgeon	Forced out via demotions, referral refusals, annual income cut by more than half	Arbitration/mediation settlement	2000	$750,000
WFSB-TV, Hartford, Conn.	News anchor	Demoted, fired	Jury award	1999	$8.3 million

*Indicates one or more additional charges, such as refusal to hire, unequal pay, demotions, firings, retaliation, hostile working environment, or sexual harassment.

Codes: s = sex; r = race.

EEOC: Equal Employment Opportunity Commission.

OFCCP: Office of Federal Contract Compliance Programs, U.S. Department of Labor.

Here's what Pollard won: $407,364, plus attorney's fees. In the Civil Rights Act of 1991, Congress had capped damage awards in sex discrimination cases—"allowing employers to budget for damage awards in discrimination cases [and] making discrimination a predictable business expense," according to a resolution passed in 1994 by the American Federation of State, County, and Municipal Employees (AFSCME). In Pollard's case, the trial judge wrote that this amount was "insufficient to compensate plaintiff for the psychological damage, pain, and humiliation she has suffered, in addition to the loss of a lucrative career and secure retirement." Is $400,000—all taxable in a single year, at the highest rate—enough when you've been so broken you will probably never work again? Is it a windfall—or a crumb?

Sharon Pollard did not get even. Nor have the many other women in this table who charged that they were harassed or demoted until they were driven out of their jobs or fired outright, simply because they were female.

Nobody Loves a Lawsuit

I feel I've really done right by all women, not just myself and the other girls.

—Barbara Nuesse, fired from waitressing at
Rustic Inn Crabhouse for pregnancy[26]

I'm just happy I took a stand. Because I was a single mom, they thought they could take advantage of me and do whatever they wanted.
—Robin Lawrence, who won a $1.1 million federal jury award from Consolidated Freightways after she was demoted and paid less than her male peers

This suit was about fairness and changing a system that stigmatized women; it was never about money.
—Bonnie Porter, a lawyer who settled for $37,500 with Boies, Schiller & Flexner after charging she was paid much less than male lawyers doing the same work

Women don't bring these suits frivolously. They'd rather do their jobs, be paid fairly, and be rewarded for their hard work, creativity, reliability, and skills. They don't jump into lawsuits in the hopes of winning the lottery and never having to work again. Most realize that, by bringing charges, they're alienating themselves from their colleagues, disrupting their careers, tainting their reputations, straining friendships and marriages, and putting their lives on hold for two years or more. They know they'll be treated as whiners and malcontents, their motives and integrity questioned, their lives dragged unpleasantly into the spotlight. They know that there is no guarantee of justice at the end.

Despite these risks, each year, thousands of women get angry enough to file charges. After years of mistreatment, their fury and frustration push them to disrupt their lives and careers to go to court. Or something happens that's so outrageous, and their employer's indifference to it is so inexcusable, that they feel they have nothing left to lose. They become consumed with the pursuit of justice.

According to employment discrimination lawyers, women are much less likely than men to bring such lawsuits. Larry Schaeffer of Chicago-based Sprenger + Lang, the employment discrimination law firm that handled such sex discrimination lawsuits as a female workers' class action against CBS and another against American Express Financial Advisors, believes from his own observations that women bring charges or join a class action lawsuit more reluctantly than any other minority. "I

think women are very litigation-averse and conflict-averse," Schaeffer
says. "In our experience—and I don't mean to indulge a stereotype at
all—in our practice it's harder to get women to step up and take the risk
of being class representatives." Why? One might speculate that women
are more likely to blame themselves, or to think it's only their problem, or
to fear retribution. Barry Goldstein of Goldstein, Demchak, Baller, Bor-
gen & Dardarian, the California employment discrimination law firm
that won sex discrimination lawsuits against such firms as Home Depot,
Publix, and Ingles, began his career as an NAACP lawyer, working on
race discrimination. "Especially in the South," he comments, "there had
been a real tradition of working for change and civil rights through collective action and the courts. That didn't exist among female workers."

But when women do bring charges, many win. In court, women
from every field prove exactly the same complaints, again and again, at
one employer after another. Whether the job is called "janitor" or "senior vice president"; whether the promotion is to "store manager" or
"tenured professor"; whether the raise would be another dollar an hour
or another $100,000 a year, the patterns are the same. Women are de-
nied the basic rewards of doing good work: promotions, raises, bonuses,
training, social networking, rewarding assignments. Women are marginalized, shoved aside, overlooked, held back—and underpaid.

No one gets rich from these lawsuits. Class action lawsuits bring individual women anything from $5,000 to $50,000, taxable as a lump
sum—not enough to make up for years of being harassed and underpaid and not enough to make up for the financial and emotional drain
of litigation or the destruction of one's career. "You're never going to
fully address the economic harm caused by being essentially branded,"
says Schaeffer.

Many companies would rather settle with an individual woman than
face a class action lawsuit brought by one of the well-known plaintiffs'
firms. When approached with an individual offer that would bring
them more money than they'd get as part of a class, do women accept?
"No, they don't," Goldstein said. "They don't. It's amazing." These
women are in it for justice. Over and over, they say that their *real* satisfaction comes from making change not just for themselves, but for
other women. They refuse to settle until changes are made to the orga-

nizational pay, training, and promotion structures that had been holding them back.

No amount of money can repay the career time a woman has lost—either while working for less than she was worth or while struggling to undo and correct unfair, illegal treatment on the job. These women have lost significant amounts of money in their prime working years, years they can never get back. They can never establish the earnings record on which their future promotions and pensions should be based. They've tarred themselves as malcontents, as litigious employees, causing other potential employers to beware. That earnings bite becomes a permanent scar. So does the experience of litigation, which damages many women's mental health, reputations, and families. Their satisfaction comes in making life better for other working women. But those moral victories are not reflected in the wage gap: women who sue do not get even.

Why Don't Employers Just Fix the Problem— and Pay Women Fairly?

Year after year, corporations are charged with discrimination that's so egregious that they have to pay out millions—by my count, more than $1.2 *billion* between 2000 and 2004. That money isn't being put productively into the economy. It's not reimbursing women appropriately for time, money, and mental health lost. Companies are writing that money off as the cost of doing business as usual, of continuing to treat women the same old discriminatory way. How much more must employers be profiting from sex discrimination, if they're willing to risk those occasional payouts rather than change their cultures?

This chapter's tables of employer payouts give us some data about how widespread discrimination is. In these tables, you can see documentation that thousands of women are cheated out of their earnings by plain, blatant discrimination. And you can see that it happens throughout the country and throughout the economy, in private companies, government agencies, and nonprofit organizations.

Why don't employers make changes instead? One woman who sued her major corporation is still wondering about that. "To me what was the most horrifying was the reaction of the corporation," she said. "There was no reason to have a lawsuit. There was no reason to have me lose my career. All they had to do was say, 'Okay, we have a problem, let's fix it!' And they refused to do that. They refused to make a better workplace for women. I still don't understand that."[27]

Let's think about why. No *individual* manager ever has the incentive to change things under his or her purview. If he (or she) acknowledges that there's sex discrimination in his department, that acknowledgment might cost the employer a lot of money—money spent settling not just with that one woman but with all the women in jobs like hers. The manager knows that he will be blamed. That blame could cost him a raise, a promotion, or even his job. For his own safety, it's best just to keep quiet.

Besides, it's hard for an individual man to recognize or acknowledge that the woman working alongside or underneath him isn't being treated fairly. That's a threat to his self-esteem—and to his wallet. If she gets a raise, he may believe that it will come out of his pocket. If she gets a promotion, he may believe it should have been his. He doesn't want to believe that he's been treated a little better than fairly because he's male; it's easier to believe that he's simply *better* than she is, by nature. It's easier to believe that *she* is the problem, that all her whining about fairness is really a request for special treatment. We'll look a little more into how this works later in the book. But thinking about the injustices *she* faces won't get him anywhere.

If individual managers and workers have a lot to lose and nothing to gain by "fixing the problem," who *can* actually make change? Only the top boss—the CEO. And he likes to think of himself as enlightened and fair. He treats his wife well. He believes that women and men are fully equal. His subordinates aren't going to tell him that he's wrong and that things are systematically out of whack throughout the workplace. So he simply refuses to believe that his women employees are being treated unfairly. Sure, *other* employers may mistreat women—or so he might be thinking when he reads about discrimination awards within his industry. But he would *never* countenance such immoral and illegal misbehavior. And so he doesn't go looking for any information that might suggest otherwise. He doesn't realize that *unless he's acting to fix it,* women are almost certainly being stopped by sex discrimination on his watch.

Sometimes, faced with overwhelming evidence of workplace misbehavior, employers do in fact make systematic changes—and get their female employees closer to even. We'll look at the handful of those heroes in the final section of this book.

But most don't. And here's the main reason why: they don't have to. No one is holding employers accountable for systematically underpaying women. No government agency can check up on every employer's behavior every day of the week. Women bring lawsuits rarely—and even when they win, the costs aren't enough to force lasting change. Right now, most employers easily get away with explaining that they're advancing more women every year. They can point to the fact that, for instance, the number of women in senior positions has doubled in the past ten years (from one to two) or that three times as many women are on track to make partner as was the case ten years ago.

That's not good enough. Employers have had forty years to absorb women into the culture. If an employer has only a few token women here and there in the financially rewarding jobs, it means that a woman has to be *much* better than a man to be treated as equal.

So what can change the ingrained, habitual patterns of behavior that are keeping women back? Conscious, sustained effort (as we'll see in more detail in the book's final part). And that's hard. Most people want to keep doing things the way they have always done them. So long as the company is still profitable, the transportation agency is still making the trains run, or the university is still attracting paying students, then most employers will be more interested in silencing the squeaky wheel than in shaking up the corporate culture. They will keep doing things the way they've always been done—unless they face ongoing public scrutiny, or a real threat to their reputation and self-respect.

And in the United States today, no such sustained attention to women's wages exists. In the 1970s, sex discrimination lawsuits and enormous social pressure were forcing employers to hire women in male-dominated jobs. But once public attention moved on, those women and their handful of female colleagues were left alone to battle their male colleagues' resistance and disrespect, day in and day out.

They had no public backup, no outsiders outraged on their behalf. By the time they brought lawsuits, there was no longer a social movement or public outrage to hold their employers accountable—not just for paying what the court said the corporation must, but for making ongoing change in how women were treated on the job. And so even when these women won their lawsuits, they lost the war.

Here's the lesson for those of us who want women to be paid fairly: Pay attention. Look at how women are being treated on the job. But before we look at what we have to *do* about what we see, let's look a little further into how discrimination is holding women back.

CHAPTER 6

Wage Discrimination by Sexual Harassment

Another senior vice president held company meetings in strip clubs, and suggested that others do the same in order to discourage female employees from attending. . . .

[Another senior executive] told a female employee in the company's corporate benefits department, "If you would just sleep with me, I could see to it that you move up in the company." He asked another woman if she would go into the restroom with another woman so he could watch. . . . He told another female employee about a nasty dream he had about her. When she complained about [his] sexually inappropriate behavior, [he] retaliated against her by giving her a poor performance evaluation and threatening to withhold her pay raise.

— From "Plaintiffs' Brief in Support of Their Motion for Class Certification," *Wilfong et al., and EEOC v. Rent-a-Center, Inc.*, 2001, in the United States District Court for the Southern District of Illinois, citing sworn deposition testimony

A 2001 survey released by the non-profit group Catalyst indicated that one-third of women working in the seven top Wall Street securities firms reported a hostile work environment, where they faced unwanted sexual attention, crude remarks, or unequal treatment.

— "Salomon Sex Discrimination Settlement:
Arbitration Panel Awards Employee for First Time,"
www.feminist.org, December 27, 2002

Most people think of sexual harassment as exactly that: sexual, albeit in an ugly, demeaning, or menacing form. It includes supervisors' and employees' demands for sexual favors, repeated groping, stalking (including murder threats), and groups of men obscenely threatening, taunting, fondling, gesturing, slandering, grabbing, raping, and otherwise provoking their female colleagues not just once but day after day. Sexual harassment is terrorism on the job.

But distracted by the graphic details, we can easily forget that sexual harassment also drains off women's wages. After long and repeated sexual harassment, women leave or lose their jobs, potential raises, promotions, opportunities, emotional stability, ability to work, and sometimes lives. In this chapter we'll look at the *financial* costs of discrimination by sexual harassment, which can include not just those years of wages stalled while fending off harassment but also the costs of disability leave, joblessness, psychiatric fees, and being unable to work steadily and confidently again.

Exactly what is sexual harassment? Sexual harassment, like rape, is a charge that's often vehemently disputed. Some anxious employees or dismissive commentators accuse sensitive women of getting jumpy about *anything* that hints of sex in the workplace: a boorish joke, an unwelcome request for a date, an accidental bump in the hall. But courts have been quite clear that, under Title VII of the Civil Rights Act of 1964, sexual harassment isn't just men acting stupidly. Legal liability is quite specific: an employer can be sued for sexual harassment only if it involved either, first, quid pro quo demands for sexual favors in exchange for a job, raise, or promotion; or, second, a "hostile work environment," in which a job site was so saturated with sexual taunts and threats that any sensible woman would quit.

Plenty of organizations know this perfectly well. Harmful sexual behavior is simply not tolerated. Human resources practices and programs immediately investigate any suspected harassment, dealing with it promptly. In chapter 11, you'll read about one particular employer that managed to change its sexual harassment policies from notorious to noteworthy.

But too many employers still ignore or deny everyday sexual harassment. To try to get a sense of how much sexual harassment women are enduring—and therefore paying for—I gathered public records to see how often, and how much, employers had been forced to pay for it. The numbers were staggering. Just between January 1, 2000, and December 31, 2004, employers large and small paid women more than $127 million for charges that, in order to earn each day's pay, those women had had to face taunting, touching, and fears of assault. Many more women than I had imagined had successfully sued over such circumstances. In fact, the pervasiveness of sexual harassment has surprised many civil rights lawyers. "Nobody anticipated it," said Barry Goldstein, longtime plaintiffs' attorney. "The sheer amount of it is just extraordinary for those of us who were involved at the beginning."

Most of us forget that the idea of "sexual harassment" as a workplace crime was only recently articulated—and that it grew out of laws against sex discrimination. Only fifty years ago, magazines regularly ran cartoons featuring a foolish old man chasing a wide-eyed maiden around a desk. The implicit message of this common joke setup was that the boss's lust and the secretary's desperate attempts to defend herself were as inevitable as marital spats—and, to the neutral observer, every bit as funny. That changed during the 1970s and early 1980s, as women flooded the workplace—where they discovered in droves that men used sexual threats, touching, and coercion as one of many battering rams to intimidate them and keep them from gaining money or power. For a decade the women's movement, and in particular feminist legal scholars, argued in court that this experience—which they named "sexual harassment"—was anything but funny. In fact, it wasn't about sex at all. It wasn't harmless flirting or voluntary intimacy. Rather, it was a one-sided use of power that was illegal *because* it affected a woman's ability to earn her paycheck. It made her working conditions more difficult, solely because she was female.

Sexual harassment, in other words, was illegal *because* it was a tool to keep women off the job. That principle was firmly ensconced in federal case law by 1986, when the U.S. Supreme Court issued its opinion in *Meritor Savings Bank v. Vinson.* As the Supreme Court wrote in Meritor, "Title VII of the Civil Rights Act of 1964 makes it 'an unlawful employment practice for an employer . . . to discriminate against any individual with respect to his compensation, terms, conditions, or privileges of employment, because of such individual's race, color, religion, sex, or national origin.' " Read that bureaucratic sentence closely. Compensation is mentioned. Employment is mentioned. If you can't bear to go to work because your supervisor is trying to grope you every day, you're being discriminated against in the "terms and conditions of employment." Sexual harassment isn't wrong because it's sexual; it's wrong *because it deprives a woman of her money.*

Just because it's been clearly illegal for twenty years doesn't mean sexual harassment has gone away. In fact, as I collected the records that you'll see in this chapter, I was shocked to realize how widespread and truly vicious sexual harassment remains. From the public record of lawsuits I've found, there's as much discrimination by sexual harassment as *all other kinds of sex discrimination combined.* Men might find this hard to believe. But women may be less surprised, once they consider their own experiences. Almost every woman I've spoken to can recall at least one such incident in her own past. And even if sexual harassment hasn't happened to her, she still is angry about the time it happened to a friend, sister, niece, or coworker.

The sexual harassment data in this chapter offer a window into how many women have to fight hard simply to keep working. So does the magnitude of some of these jury awards. Bringing a lawsuit for sexual harassment is a grueling experience: women who do so must be prepared to be grilled ruthlessly about their motives, their clothes, their sexual histories, and of course, the details of their behavior. Women must be prepared to stand up to lawyers who will try to humiliate them, who will imply that they welcomed and encouraged every comment and touch. Accusations must be backed by evidence—witnesses, logbooks, memos, telephone calls. When juries award enormous amounts of money for what a woman endured to keep her paycheck, that's evidence that those jurors' consciences were shocked—that the sexual harassment was *much* worse than they had previously thought possible in the American workplace. And when companies settle sexual harassment charges out of court, it gives you a clue that they thought it would be cheaper to pay a woman off than to risk losing the case or shocking those jurors with how badly she may have been treated. "I was a management lawyer for many years," EEOC Detroit Regional Attorney Adele Rapport said, and when the facts were especially bad, she would tell her client to settle. "I would tell my client, this is indefensible! You certainly don't want the publicity that's going to be engendered by a trial—and then have to pay. Because when a jury hears these facts, you're going to be in hot water." When you see "settlement," keep that advice in mind.

Each of this chapter's short sections will examine a slightly different kind of sexual harassment. Was it just one nasty guy who happened to be in charge? Was it one or two coworkers or supervisors whose offenses (even when women complained) management ignored, in an apparent calculation that the men were more organizationally valuable than the women? Was it an entire workplace—a car dealership, attorney general's office, army base, manufacturing plant—that collectively treated women as fair game for an ongoing group grope? Or was it something even more sinister: Were the *Hustler* centerfolds, lunchtime strippergrams, speakerphone sex acts, and daily demands for oral sex used as weapons in a larger campaign to drive women out of "men's" work such as policing, firefighting, or securities trading?

As you read some of the stories in the following pages, remember that these incidents are not just shocking because they're sexual or illegal. They're shocking because they're *costly*. They account for some of that 23-cent gender wage gap. Having to fight or endure such guerrilla tactics on the job, day in and day out, drains money from many women's pockets. All sexual harassment has this in common: women, not men, pay the emotional—and the financial—price.

One Bad Guy—in Charge

> Gabriella Arango said her boss Masaki Nakashima repeatedly touched her, chased her around the office, hit her with a telephone, and said, "If you obey what I say, you'll get anything you want." . . . She said she was forced at times to lock herself in the office bathroom to get away from her boss.
>
> —Harriet Johnson Brackey, "Jury Hits Mazda Hard in
> Sex-Harassment Case," *The Miami Herald*, February 24, 1999.
> At Mazda North America, based in Miami, Nakashima kept
> his position; Arango was fired. A federal jury awarded her
> $4.4 million, reduced by a judge to $3.4 million in 1999.

Let's start with the kind of sexual harassment that everyone knows is illegal: the boss who leans on women to have sex with him to keep their jobs. Such men behave as if the workplace were their own private fiefdom, that in exchange for their paychecks women must expect to give up their bodily privacy. Their female employees—lawyers, secretaries, finance directors, chief operating officers, dental assistants, chemists, grade school teachers, production line supervisors, egg packers—must try to evade their creepy bosses without losing their self-respect or their wages.

Over and over, the story is the same, with a tiresomely repetitive story line. Here's how it usually happens. Soon after a woman gets a job, her new boss starts telling her how great she looks—a little too often, a little too insistently. He tells a few lugubriously sexual jokes. Since she doesn't want to put her new job in jeopardy or come across as a difficult worker, she grits her teeth and tries to ignore him. Next he starts joking about how great he is in bed, with wince-worthy details about his penis or stamina or technique. He stops by her desk or production station, saying that it's amazing that a beautiful girl like her doesn't have a boyfriend or a husband or suggesting that her boyfriend or husband surely can't please her sexually as much as he could. She repeatedly tries to bring their conversations back to business, backing away when he gets too close. It doesn't help. His "friendly" touches on the hand or shoulder—which soon feel so menacing that she flinches whenever he comes into the room—turn into "playful" gropes of her bottom or breasts or crotch. Maybe he starts rubbing his groin against her bottom when he walks by. Maybe he starts rubbing his genitals while talking to her. Maybe he grabs *her* hand and puts it on his crotch. If she objects, he insists they're just having some harmless fun: For God's sake, lighten up!

By now, she's waking up repeatedly at night with anxiety dreams or even nightmares. Or she has daily headaches from unconsciously grinding her teeth. Dread begins to suffuse her days, but she persistently tries to push it aside, determined not to let that jackass get her down. Maybe she's young and afraid it's her fault. Maybe she's afraid either to speak up or quit, since she has to pay the mortgage or feed her kids. But then he does something that crosses the line. He gives her a picture of himself naked. Or he pins her to the wall so that she can feel his erection. Or he pushes her head toward his unzipped fly. Or he walks into the bathroom while she's there. Suddenly she realizes—correctly, considering many women's experiences—that rape might be next. She quits and, if she has the strength of mind, brings charges.

But here's the point: *She* quits. He doesn't. She has weeks, months, or years of unemployment while searching for another job. He's still the boss, undermining the dignity and income of the next employee.

This sequence of events happens in businesses large and small, to women working for minimum wage and women working for six-figure salaries. But even within this outline, the observer can be repeatedly startled by new and amazing details. For instance, there's the Michigan home for the mentally disabled where, according to the EEOC, a supervisor told a newly hired nurse's aide that a particular chair was the "head" chair—where her predecessor had given him head and where she would do the same. Not long after, the EEOC complaint continued, he grabbed her leg and bit her thigh.[1]

Or there's Dan Wassong, the chief executive of cosmetics company Del Laboratories. When one woman brought sexual harassment charges against him in the mid-1990s, dozens of other women came out of the woodwork to tell the same story. They testified that Wassong had asked for blow jobs in exchange for raises, worked in his underwear, left the restroom door open while he urinated, and walked around the office with his fly down, fingering his genitals. In 1995, with the customary denial of wrongdoing, Del Labs settled with those women for $1.2 million. But apparently Del considered that just the cost of doing business: Wassong stayed on as CEO, still fully in charge.

The story was similar at Simat Helliesen & Eichner (SH&E), an airline consulting firm, where five female employees charged that the company president talked to them while keeping his hand in his crotch, invited them to service him, leered at their breasts, or discussed his sexual prowess. In 2003, the company agreed to a consent decree and a payment of $2.3 million. Then it promoted the offender to chairman and CEO.

Sometimes he does have to pay, especially if he's a public official and the local media keep his misbehavior in front of the public. The speaker of the Virginia House of Delegates, S. Vance Wilkins, Jr., was forced to resign after *The Washington Post* learned that he'd paid out $100,000 in sexual harassment hush money to a clerical worker who accused him of assault. Local outrage forced Milwaukee's mayor, John Norquist, to reimburse the city for the $375,000 it paid an aide who accused him of coercion for sexual favors. But outside politics, when was the last time you read that the top guy on the job was fired for groping?

As you look at the following table, notice the titles: chief executive officer, school principal, mayor, president, owner, founder, chairman, sheriff. Men who harass women—who make it impossible for women to earn a living fairly—are in charge of institutions of every kind, from elementary schools to doctors' offices, from law firms to textile factories, from pizza shops to liquor importers. These bosses are not concentrated in male-dominated industries. They run all sorts of businesses and offices throughout the country.

In chapter 5, we concluded that some chief executives do not acknowledge the discrimination that's happening on their watch because they don't believe it exists. But that's the best-case scenario, in which the top manager genuinely thinks of himself as fair. For the employers who show up in the next table, things are still worse. What CEO (or sheriff or restaurant owner) would possibly acknowledge and fix discrimination—when he himself is its worst perpetrator?

As you scan this chart, note also the wide financial variation among these settlements and jury awards. Most workers, it's easy to see, barely win back the wages they lost by quitting, much less enough money to see a counselor to talk out any anxiety they might still feel. Even the awards that *look* large are split among dozens or even hundreds of employees, who must then pay the law firm that prosecuted the case and pay taxes on what's left. Women who sue for sexual harassment do not get even.

A Few Bad Guys—Ignored by the Company

> Monica Santiago worked at a [Rent-A-Center] store in Arizona, and she too was sexually harassed by her male Store Manager. Santiago's Manager asked her, "Would you consider having sex with me and my other girlfriend?" When the two of them were in the store's delivery truck together, the Manager propositioned her, saying, "pull over, let's get it on right now." On another occasion, the two of them were delivering a bedroom set and the Manager said, "Why don't we park the truck and try these mattresses out." He once said to her, "Why don't you have sex with me for one last fling before you get married? I'll pay you to make it worth your while. I'll even buy the alcohol."
>
> Other times, the Manager rubbed his genitals against her, fondled her breasts, and placed his hand on her buttock. When Santiago reported her Manager's behavior to Market Manager Doug Gray, he responded by telling her, "He's your manager. You have to do what he says or else you'll lose your job."
>
> —From "Plaintiffs' Brief in Support of Their Motion for
> Class Certification," *Wilfong and EEOC v. Rent-a-Center, Inc.*,
> in the United States District Court for the Southern District of
> Illinois, citing sworn deposition testimony

Sometimes the harassment comes not from the top boss but from a manager or coworker whom the woman can't avoid. She has to get along with him or she can't do a good job. Whether he's the guy in the next cubicle, the mechanic sharing the midnight shift, or the prep cook in the restaurant, he can become a real threat.

Take restaurants, where there's an especially high risk of sexual harassment. Restaurant jobs are often taken by women working in isolated situations, who come in very early or leave very late; all too often, that means these become the employment equivalent of a back alley at midnight, dangerous for a woman alone. Often these women desperately need the job; they might be between other jobs, unable to travel to other towns, just coming off welfare, or single moms coming out of a divorce, and feel they have little choice but to put up with the harassment. Or they might be teenagers on their first jobs, as yet unpracticed in recognizing or fending off predatory men; they're still naive enough to feel guilty, ashamed, or implicated when men touch them. Their wages, schedules, or tips might well depend on their ability to get along well with these men. If the prep cook takes a dislike to you, he can make sure your orders regularly come out late; if the assistant manager takes a dislike to you, he can assign you to the slowest shift.

"The worst are the car dealerships and the restaurants," says Adele Rapport, EEOC regional attorney in Detroit. "The restaurant cases just break my heart, because you have these young girls, sixteen, seventeen, eighteen years old, who don't know how to cope with this." Rapport explains that the pattern is predictable. Managers start putting their hands on the girls as they pass by, pulling the girls onto their laps for a second, or "adjusting" the girls' uniforms in the back. "They talk about what their wife will and won't do for them; they talk about what they want to do to the customers; they talk about the features of the women and the girls themselves. Any time a woman gets on her knees to do anything, she must be down there for —. 'While you're down there!' If I counted how many times I've heard that in my litigation: 'While you're down there!' "

One young woman's difficulty came not with her manager but with a coworker.[2] This teenager was still living with her mother and stepfather when she started working at a southern California Pizza Hut. Her coworker "John" was, as the young woman put it, "flirty" from the first meeting. Within a few days of working together, he started asking her out, which she repeatedly declined. She didn't know enough to recognize that insistence as a warning sign. One night, when her mother couldn't pick her up and she faced a long walk home, she accepted

RECENT PAYOUTS FOR WOMEN
WHO CHARGED HARASSMENT BY THE BOSS [3]

Boss's Title	Employer	Employee	Type of Action	Payout Year	Amount[4]
Manager	ABC Pizza, Tampa, Fla.	2 teenage employees	Settlement	2004	$325,000
Manager	Accent Mobile Homes, Inc., Anderson, S.C.	2 sales representatives	Settlement	2004	$50,000
Doctor	Alaska Regional Hospital, Anchorage, Ala.	Nurses, administrative staff over 20 years	Alaska State Medical Board fine	2002	$3,000
Supervisor	Ames Textile, New Hampshire	Machine operator	State commission order	1998	$24,300
CEO and other managers	Astra USA, Westborough, Mass.	Female employees	Settlement and consent decree	1998	$10 million
Manager	A-X Express Mart/ Conoco #155, Socorro, N.Mex.	Employee	Settlement	2004	$180,000
Dentist	Dr. Avery Beall, LaGrange, Ga.	Dental assistant	Jury award	2002	$135,000
Manager	Bennigan's Grill & Tavern, Phoenix, Ariz.	9 waitresses	Settlement	2001	$160,000
Headmaster	Berkshire School, Sheffield, Mass.	Teachers, employees, wives	Massachusetts Commission Against Discrimination finding	2002	Headmaster resigned
Owner	Block's Lighthouse Supper Club, Inc., Texas	4 waitresses	Settlement	2004	$98,000
Owner	Bravo's Pizzeria, Massachusetts	Waitress	Massachusetts Commission Against Discrimination award	2001	$25,000
Manager	Burger King, Peerless Park, Mo.	7 teenage waitresses	Settlement	2004	$400,000
Owner *	Casa del Sol, Las Cruces, N.Mex.	Employee	Settlement	2002	$225,000
Owner	Chesrown Chevrolet, Denver, Colo.	Business development manager	Jury award	2002	$1 million, reduced by judge to $550,000
Sheriff	Clay County, N.Dak.	Deputy sheriff	Settlement	2003	$1.5 million
President	Clifford Electronics, Inc., Chatsworth, Calif.	Marketing executive	Jury award	2000	$682,000

President	Cliff Smith and Associates, Massachusetts	Employee	Jury award, upheld by Massachusetts appellate court	2001	$250,000
Founder and chairman	Colt Services, Phoenix, Ariz.	Several female employees	Settlement	2003	$190,000
Owner and operator	Comfort Inn/Welk Investments, Nevada, Mo.	Motel manager	Jury award	1998	$1,002,500
Inspector general	Cook County, Ill.	Employee	Jury award	2004	$500,000
General manager	Country Kitchen Family Restaurants, Globe, Ariz.	Female employees	Settlement	2002	$75,000
Company founder	Dillard Environmental Services, Byron, Calif.	Office workers	Settlement	2003	$85,000
Manager (owner's brother)	Family Motor Inn, Sullivan, Mo.	3 front desk workers	Settlement	2004	$180,000
City manager	Fayetteville, Ga.	Main Street director	Settlement	2001	$50,000
Supervisor	First Student, Inc., Iowa	Employees: s, r, n.o.	Settlement with consent decree	2003	$145,000
Supervisor	Fort Dodge Animal Health and Fort Dodge Laboratories, Inc., Overland Park, Kans.	6 harassed women employees and 2 dismissed HR employees	Settlement	2002	$487,500
Supervisor	Heartland Disposal, Cadet, Mo.	Secretary/dispatcher	Settlement	2003	$75,000
Partner	Jacobs, Persinger & Parker, New York, N.Y.	Associate	Jury award	2000	$250,000
Manager	Kansas Auto Auction, Elwood, Kans.	2 saleswomen	Settlement	2004	$55,000
Owner, other managers*	L&L Wings, Inc., Myrtle Beach, S.C.	4 female teenage sales associates	Settlement	2002	$115,000
Sheriff	LaSalle County, Illinois	Employees	Settlement	2003	$500,000
Councilman	Los Angeles City Council, Calif.	Aide	Settlement	2000	$175,000
Executive director	Louisiana Levee Board, East Jefferson Levee District, La.	3 employees	Private settlement, disclosed by The Times-Picayune	2003	$143,500
Sheriff and deputy	Marion County, Fla.	Sheriff's deputy detective	Settlement	2003	$155,000

(continued on next page)

Boss's Title	Employer	Employee	Type of Action	Payout Year	Amount[4]
CEO	Medical Center Brace & Limb, Houston, Tex.	COO, administrative staff	Settlement	2002	$200,000
Mayor	Milwaukee, Wis.	Aide	Settlement	2002	$375,000
Magistrate	Mora County, N.Mex.	Employee	Settlement	2003	$107,500
Owner	Munzert's Steak House, Fenton, Mo.	Teenage employee	Jury award	2004	$118,000
Chairman of parent company	New Boston Select Staffing, Mass.	Female employee	Jury award	2002	$2.16 million
President	Paladin Press, Boulder, Colo.	Employee	Jury award	2004	$100,000
Supervisor	Parmalat Bakery Division of North America, Wallington, N.J.	Sales division manager	Settlement	2004	Undisclosed
Manager	Pizza of Florida, Tampa Bay, Fla.	Employee	Settlement	2000	$70,000
Owner	Po Po Family Restaurant, Kendall County, Tex.	2 teenage waitresses	Settlement	2003	$43,000
Manager	Radisson Prince Charles Hotels and Suites, Cumberland County, N.C.	Banquet worker	County court order	2003	$213,433
Manager	Ron-Bar Inc., owner of Burger King, Odessa, Tex.	Employee	Settlement	2003	$35,500
Managing partners	Roquemore, Pringle & Moore, Los Angeles, Calif.	2 paralegals: s, r	Settlement	2002	$135,000
Treasurer–tax collector	San Diego County, Calif.	Chief deputy tax collector	County Board of Supervisors settlement	2002	$100,000
Chief of police	San Francisco Police Department, Calif.	Public relations officer	Settlement	1996	$288,606
Manager	Santa Clara County, California Medical Association, Calif.	3 female employees	Settlement	2002	$73,000
County commissioner	Schuylkill County, Pa.	Secretary	Settlement	2004	$42,000
Principal	Seattle, Wash., public schools	3 elementary school teachers	Lawsuit settlement	2002	$90,000

Doctor	Dr. Sekhon, Yuba City, Calif.	Student	Arbitration	2003	$175,000
President and owner	Sidney Frank Liquor Importing Co. Inc., New York, N.Y.	More than 100 female employees	Settlement	1999	$2.6 million
Company president	Simat, Helliesen & Eichner, Inc., and Reed Elsevier, Inc., New York, N.Y.	Finance director, administrative staff	Settlement with consent decree	2003	$2.3 million
Publisher	*Spin* magazine, New York, N.Y.	Editorial assistant	Jury award	1997	$100,000
Owner's son	Star Concrete, San Jose, Calif.	Employee	Jury award	2002	$250,000
CEO	State Adjustment, Inc., Salem, Oreg.	Clerk	Order, state commissioner, Bureau of Labor and Industries	2002	$10,000
Owner	Dr. George Stewart, Anchorage, Ala.	Employees	Alaska State Medical Board	2002	$3,000
Store manager	Taco Bell, Grants, N.Mex.	4 teenage workers	Settlement	2003	$100,000
Superintendent	Tigard-Tualatin School District, Oreg.	Associate superintendent	Bureau of Labor and Industries–mediated agreement	2001	$155,000
Principal	Tucson Unified School District, Ariz.	Middle school teacher, administrators	Settlement	1996 1996 2000 2001	$500,000 $12,900 $50,000 $15,000
Chief administrative officer	Ventura County, Calif.	Top aide	Settlement	2003	$165,000
Owner	Westlake Manufacturers Representatives, Inc., Minneapolis, Minn.	Office manager/ receptionist	Minnesota Human Rights Commission award	2003	$42,000
Virginia Speaker of the House	Wilkins Construction Company, Amherst County, Va.	Secretary	Private settlement	2002	More than $100,000 (exact amount confidential)

* *The charges included sexual assault.*

Codes: s = sex; r = race; n.o. = national origin.

If you or someone you know is being sexually harassed on the job, you can find more information, resources, and contact numbers at the Web sites of such organizations as the EEOC (www.eeoc.gov), the WAGE Project (www.wageproject.org), the National Women's Law Center (www.nwlc.org), and Equal Rights Advocates (www.equalrights.org).

While all cases mentioned in this chapter involve women charging men with harassment on the job, each year a small number of men file workplace sexual harassment charges. From 1992 to 2002, women accounted for 85 to 90 percent of all sexual harassment charges filed with the EEOC.

John's offer of a ride. Before letting her out of the car, John was all over her, as we used to say in high school. He offered to show her his "manhood," insisting, "Come on, come on, you want to see it, you know you want me." Although she was petrified, she managed to evade his kiss, peel his hands off her thigh, and get out of the car. She told her mom, who advised her daughter to complain to someone if John ever grabbed her at work.

The car ride was an unpleasant and even frightening experience but no more actionable than a bad date. Had John's vulgar behavior stopped there, there would have been no lawsuit. But John started rubbing his groin up against the young woman's bottom as he passed by—when she was cashiering, making pizza, or cleaning the salad bar. She could feel his erection. He kept insisting that they go out together, saying things like he knew she really wanted him, she didn't know how much he could please women, she'd be asking *him* out once they'd had sex. She tried a teenager's basic tactics for discouraging boys: saying no, standing up for herself, ignoring him, glaring at him, walking away. None worked.

One day, while another male coworker looked on, John "teasingly" grabbed her from behind, put the blade of a one-foot-long butcher knife against her throat, and said, "Now tell me no." When she objected, he said, "God, I was only joking." He and the other guy laughed at her.

By now this teenage restaurant worker was asking all her coworkers what to do about John's increasingly frightening attentions. They told her to tell him off or ignore him; she was too embarrassed or ashamed to explain how far beyond that it had gone. She complained to her manager, who asked the young woman whether she wasn't exaggerating; when, offended, she insisted that he wouldn't leave her alone, the manager told John to apologize. Rudely, John apologized, but things got worse. One day as she came out of the freezer, he pinned her against the wall, groping her while insisting that she wanted him, until she managed to shove him off. A few days later, when the two were in the store alone, John tripped her. When she fell backward, he straddled her and pinned her down, groping her and suggesting, "Oh, let's have sex on the floor. That would be so erotic." She escaped because their manager returned to the store unexpectedly, but for the next week John insisted that his victim had enjoyed their flattened encounter.

Many adult women reading this would recognize a potentially dangerous stalker. Why didn't she complain more explicitly to her manager, outlining the details of these attempted assaults? She was young, shy, inexperienced, and embarrassed. She'd been humiliated by her manager's implication that she was a liar, that John probably wasn't so bad, that girls were just oversensitive. And she *was* telling her coworkers; to her it seemed that everyone knew what was going on. Meanwhile, John's behavior was taking its toll on her sleep, her health, and her peace of mind. "Not knowing what was going to happen when I went to work—like the stress gave me headaches," she said in a deposition. "It was going to work every day and not knowing what was going to happen." And so she again complained to her unsympathetic manager, asking to be put on another shift. The manager concluded that the teenage girl was the difficult one and cut her hours. The teenager quit.

Fortunately, she was quickly able to get another low-wage job, this time at Blockbuster. But she was still "waking up in cold sweats, just thinking about the situation that happened, and having nightmares about it." She mentioned the experience to a male coworker at Blockbuster, who called Pizza Hut regional management to complain. She confided the details to a former Pizza Hut coworker. This second woman had had her run-ins with John as well. Emboldened by hearing about the teenager's experiences, the older woman complained all the way up the Pizza Hut hierarchy. No response. So she filed charges with the EEOC. In the end, Pizza Hut paid a $360,000 settlement to four women for its manager's refusal to take John's menacing behavior seriously.

Seen from one angle, this is a minor incident, the kind millions of women have faced and managed to put behind them. Who *hasn't* had a guy refuse to take no for an answer, a guy who grabs her repeatedly until she somehow manages to escape his view? But it's not minor at all—precisely *because* millions of women have faced it. In order to protect themselves from the daily threat of assault, too many women must quit and start over again at the bottom of the ladder. Even if they respond like the older Pizza Hut worker, staying on out of need and stubbornness, for those months that they were fending off their harasser, they weren't advancing on the job. At worst, the experience of working while under attack can damage women's stability and their ability to work effectively and move up in the future.

What management too often doesn't realize is that many such men are serial harassers. The problem isn't her; it's him. If one woman quits, her replacement becomes his next sacrificial offering. For instance, Rena Weeks was hardly the first woman who complained about senior partner Martin Greenstein at the law firm Baker & McKenzie, then the largest law firm in the United States. In fact, she was the seventh. But as sexual harassment expert Dr. Freada Klein told *The Washington Post*, often companies decide to pay off women without making any other changes because they believe that "this is the cost of doing business . . . this guy brings in millions of dollars in business a year."[5]

That's not the attitude of every employer, of course. Many—most, one hopes—intervene quickly when any employee feels threatened, preventing things from escalating, as you'll see at the end of this chapter. But as can be seen in the table below, far too many do not. And in this table, once again, you can see that employers in *every* industry and economic sector have thought they could look the other way when their female employees were harassed. But in this list you can see something quite troubling: women in the most vulnerable positions are the most often targeted. For instance, the egg-processing workers at DeCoster, who charged sexual harassment and, in some cases, assault, were immigrants who didn't always speak English. Many others are young women starting out as waitresses or women working in very-low-paying jobs, such as cashier, clerk, secretary, and production line workers—women who are working because they desperately need that paycheck. "I often have this vision of a lion watching a gazelle pack run by," EEOC's Adele Rapport said, who "sees one limping in the back and goes after that one. I mean, the woman may be vulnerable because she's a single mother and she can't afford to lose her job, she may be vulnerable because she's going through a difficult divorce, because she may have

PAYOUTS FOR WOMEN WHOSE EMPLOYERS
DISMISSED HARASSMENT COMPLAINTS

Title	Employer	Employee	Type of Action	Payout Year	Amount
Supervisor	Airguide Corporation Hialeah, Fla.	3 plant employees	Settlement	2004	$1 million
Manager	Applied Technologies, Inc., Lexington, Ky.	Employee	Jury award	1997	$125,000
Police officer	Aurora, Colo.	Police officer	Jury award	2000	$964,326
Coworker/Supervisor	Benchmark Residential Services, Inc., Pinconning, Mich.	Nurse's aide	Settlement and consent decree	2004	$62,000 and reinstate-ment
Supervisor	Beaumont Housing Authority, insurance companies, Texas	Employee	Settlement	1998	$44,500
Cook	Bravo's Pizzeria, Massachusetts	Waitress	Massachusetts Commission Against Discrimination award	2001	$25,000
Assistant manager	Brinker International Inc., Chili's of Maryland, Chili's of Bel Air, Md.	4 servers	Settlement with consent decree	2004	$283,000
Supervisor and shift sergeant	Central Missouri State University, Missouri	Campus police dispatcher	Federal jury award, reduced by trial judge, reinstated by Eighth Circuit Appellate Court	2004	$242,272
Supervisor	Chartwell's Dining Services, New York	Assistant marketing coordinator	Jury award	2004	$15.145 million
Coworker	Chelsea Clock Co., Massachusetts	Customer service representative	Massachusetts Commission Against Discrimination award	2001	$32,620
Store manager*	Church's Chicken, Wichita, Kans.	14-year-old employee	Settlement	2002	$150,000
Supervisor	Columbia University, New York, N.Y.	Female employee	Jury award	1996	$450,000
Supervisor	Control Building Services, Inc., New Jersey and New York	2 female cleaners and maintenance man	Consent decree	2003	$575,000

(continued on next page)

Title	Employer	Employee	Type of Action	Payout Year	Amount
Coworker	Cook County Forest Preserve District, Illinois	Police officer	Jury award	2001	$3 million, reduced to $300,000 under federal damages cap
Supervisors	Decoster Farms, Wright County, Iowa	Egg-processing workers	Settlement	2002	$1.525 million
Employee	Delta Faucet, Chickasha, Okla.	Employees	Settlement	2002	$50,000
Manager	Denny's, Carbondale, Ill.	Employee	Settlement	2002	$135,000
District manager	Disc Jockey, United States	Sales manager	Jury award, upheld in appellate court	2000	$446,159
Manager	EZ Buy & EZ Sell Recycler Corporation, of Southern California	3 employees	Settlement	2003	$380,000
Store manager **	Fashion Cents, Miami, Fla.	Sales clerks	Settlement	2002	$250,000
Supervisor	First Transit, Alabama	Special-needs bus driver	Settlement	2003	$85,000
Supervisor	Florida County, Fla.	Air-conditioning mechanic	Jury award	2003	$330,000
Coworkers	Ford Motor Company, Dearborn, Mich.	Plant employees	Settlement	2002	Undisclosed
Line foreman	Forest River Corporation, Goshen, Ind.	Plant worker	Jury award	2001	$320,000
Deputy sheriff	Forsyth County Sheriff's Office, N.C.	Employee	Settlement	2001	$150,000
Plant superintendent	General Motors, Willow Run, Mich.	20-year factory employee	Settlement	1998	$1 million
Assistant superintendent	Georgia Department of Corrections	Probation officer, prison counselor	Jury award	2000	$1.75 million
Supervisor	Golden Valley Produce and William Bolthouse Farms, Bakersfield, Calif.	2 female processing/ distribution plant employees	Settlement	2001	$150,000
General sales manager	Golf Galaxy, Inc., Goshen, Ind.	Customer service manager	Settlement	2002	$80,000
Terminal manager	Groendyke Transport, Inc., Enid, Okla.	Chemical dispatcher	Settlement	2003	$150,000

Coworker	Haffner's Service Stations, Massachusetts	Cashier	Massachusetts Commission Against Discrimination order	2001	$30,000
Managers	Hooters, Newport, Ky.	Waitress	Jury award	2000	$275,000
Coworkers	Huntwood Industries, Spokane, Wash.	Female cabinetmaker	Settlement with consent decree	2004	$100,000
Coworker	Hy-Vee Inc., Gladstone, Mo.	2 teenage employees	Settlement	2001	$850,000
Supervisor	International House of Pancakes, Alabama	Female employees	Settlement	2003	$180,000
Shift leader	Jack in the Box, Arizona	Female employees	Settlement	2002	$92,500
Manager, coworkers	JB's Restaurants, Utah	Female employees	Settlement	2004	$300,000
Supervisor	Jerry Chambers Chevrolet, Inc., Bellingham, Wash.	Female salesperson	Settlement	2004	$70,000
Supervisor and coworkers	Jiffy Lube franchise, Lynwood, Calif.	Female employees, including 2 teenagers	Settlement and consent decree	2004	$299,000 and training to employees
Coworker	Kimbrell's Furniture, Statesville, N.C.	Female employee	Settlement	2003	$25,000
Supervisor	Krispy Kreme, Issaquah, Wash.	Employees	Settlement	2004	Undisclosed
Supervisor	Kroger, Marion, Ill.	Female employees	Settlement	2001	$750,000
Supervisor	Little America Hotel, Salt Lake City, Utah	Laundry worker	Jury award	2002	$88,000
Coworkers	Loca Luna Restaurant, Atlanta, Ga.	Female employee	Mediation agreement	2004	$50,000
Assistant manager	LongHorn Steakhouse, Tampa, Fla.	3 teenage employees	Settlement	2003	$200,000
Coworker	Lumberton Municipal Utility District, Texas	4 female employees	Settlement	2000	$90,000
Doctor †	Lutheran Medical Center, New York, N.Y.	More than 1,200 employees	Settlement	2003	$5.425 million
Coworkers	Matador Mexican Food Restaurant, Phoenix, Ariz.	Bartenders	Settlement	2003	$71,614

(continued on next page)

Title	Employer	Employee	Type of Action	Payout Year	Amount
Supervisor	Mazda North America, Miami, Fla.	Marketing associate	Jury award	1999	$4.4 million, reduced to $3.5 million
Coworker/supervisor	Meade Lexus, Southfield, Mich.	7 female employees	Settlement and consent decree	2004	$85,000
Coworker	Mortgage.com, Sunrise, Fla.	4 female employees	Settlement	2001	$100,000
Supervisor	New England Serum Company, Topsfield, Mass.	Employees	Settlement	2003	$150,000
Trainer	New Prime Inc., Kans.	Truck driver trainee	Jury award	2003	$95,000
Police supervisor	New York City Police Department, N.Y.	Police officer	Jury award	2002	$470,159
6 police officers	New York City Police Department, N.Y.	Police officer	Jury award	2002	$1.85 million
Supervisor	North Little Rock School Department, Arkansas	Secretary	Settlement and consent decree	2001	$70,000
Youth counselor *	Oakland, Calif.	Teenage employee	County court settlement	2001	$80,000 plus four years in prison
Youth counselor (same as above)	Oakland, Calif.	Teenage employee	County court settlement	1999	$825,000
Coworker	Pizza Hut, Diamond Bar, Calif.	4 employees	Settlement	2003	$360,000
Manager	Porcelanosa, Farmingdale, N.Y.	Female employees	Jury award	2004	$1.6 million
Police sergeant	Portsmouth, Va.	Police officers	Settlement	2002	$300,000
Coworkers	Pro-Tem Inc., and Personnel Research Inc., Albuquerque, N.Mex.	Account manager	Jury award	2001	$456,300
Supervisor	Regional Transportation District, Denver, Colo.	Clerical worker	Jury award	2000	$375,000
Coworker‡	Reynolds Metals Company and Local 400, United Steelworkers of America, United States, Richmond, Va.	Machine worker	Settlement	2003	$75,000

Supervisor	Richmond, Calif., Police Department	City jail worker	Settlement	2004	$100,000
Assistant manager	Rio Bravo International, Inc., and Innovative Restaurant Concepts, Inc., Florida	Female servers	Jury award	2003	$1.55 million
Assistant manager	Rogers & Hollands Jewelers, Milwaukee, Wis.	3 employees	Settlement	2003	$155,000
Supervisor	Roy's Poipu Bar & Grill, Kauai, Hawaii	3 employees	Settlement	2003	$245,000
Vice president	Sacramento Kings, Sacramento, Calif.	Assistant	Settlement	2002	Undisclosed
Coworker	Salsbury Dodge City, Baton Rouge, La.	Car mechanic	Jury award	2004	$904,923
Coworkers	Salt Lake County, Utah	Paramedics	Jury award	1996	$2 million
Coworkers	San Francisco Municipal Railway, California	Custodian	Settlement	2002	$450,000
Coworker	Sears, Greensboro, N.C.	Female employees	Settlement	2002	$20,000
Sergeant	Shelby County Sheriff's Office, Tennessee	Deputy	Jury award	2003	$952,000
Shift supervisor	Taco Bell, Glenolden, Pa.	16-year-old food service worker	Settlement	2003	$151,500
Manager	Tigard-Tualatin, Oreg., School District	Counselor	Settlement	2000	$5,000
Restaurant employees	Tri-Spur Investment Co, Inc., Utah	6 female employees	Settlement	2004	$80,000
Coworkers	U.S. Department of the Navy	Employee	EEOC administrative judge	2002	$5,000
Colonel	U.S. Department of the Navy, Fort Bliss, Tex.	Civilian employee	EEOC administrative judge	1997	$300,000
Manager	U.S. Postal Service, United States	Employee	Administrative law judge order	2003	$50,000

(continued on next page)

Title	Employer	Employee	Type of Action	Payout Year	Amount
Coworker	Village of Bloomingdale, Ill., Engineering Department	Secretary	Jury award	2003	$1.1 million
Supervisor	Wal-Mart, Atoka, Okla.	Cashier	Jury award	2000	$63,750
Pharmacist	Wal-Mart, Boone, Iowa	Pharmacy clerk	Jury award, upheld by appeals court	1998	$28,000
Supervisor	Wal-Mart, Glen Carbon, Ill.	Stock clerk	Jury award	2000	$107,000
Supervisor, assistant manager	Wal-Mart, Warsaw, Mo.	Associate	Jury award, reduced by appeals court	1996, 1997	$50 million jury award, reduced to $383,000
Bakery manager	Wal-Mart, Texas	Female bakery employee	Settlement with consent decree	2003	$150,000
Supervisor	Wellesley College, Wellesley, Mass.	Kitchen worker	Jury award	1996	$150,000
Coworker, union president	Western State Hospital, Tacoma, Wash.	Medical administrator and 12 others	Settlement	2003	$896,000

* The charges included sexual assault, for which the offender went to prison.

** This female store manager was fired when she complained that her male fellow store manager was harassing the female salesclerks.

† During a mandatory medical employment screening for more than 1,200 women, this doctor asked offensive sexual questions and fondled the women's genitals and breasts during "gynecological" exams. The women involved ranged from nurses to file clerks.

‡ This woman was fired after her coworker and stalker—who'd been convicted of criminally assaulting her and was under court order to stay away from her—attacked her on company property. The union backed him.

EEOC: Equal Employment Opportunity Commission.

If you or someone you know is being sexually harassed on the job, you can find more information, resources, and contact numbers at the Web sites of such organizations as the EEOC (www.eeoc.gov), the WAGE Project (www.wageproject.org), the National Women's Law Center (www.nwlc.org), and Equal Rights Advocates (www.equalrights.org).

been abused earlier in her life. She may have serious self-esteem issues. These women become the victims. Because they look inviting to these predators."

As you look at the list, you'll also see a great many cases of sexual harassment in traditionally male jobs. When women try to work in a formerly male preserve—as a bus driver, car salesperson, police officer, firefighter, probation officer—they're seen as a real threat. Sexual harassment is a tool to drive them out. Often they're the only woman, or one of a very few, in an area where men have felt traditionally free to disparage women or boast about their sex lives. Such trailblazing women can often expect to be treated unfairly—less likely to be promoted or equally paid—*and* to be sexually harassed.

Group Grope: Abandon All Hope, Ye Who Enter Here

Alison Kornegay worked at a [Rent-A-Center] store in Florida. . . . Kornegay's male Store Manager and other male employees constantly subjected her to inappropriate sexual comments. For example, they talked about her breasts, asked her if she "did oral sex," viewed pornography on the computer, and even talked about having sex with Kornegay's 15-year-old daughter. On one occasion, the Manager knowingly walked into the restroom when Kornegay was using one of the stalls. She told him to leave, but he refused. As he followed her out of the restroom, he grabbed her buttock.

> —From "Plaintiffs' Brief in Support of Their Motion for Class
> Certification," *Wilfong et al. and EEOC v. Rent-a-Center, Inc.,*
> in the United States District Court for the Southern District
> of Illinois, citing sworn deposition testimony

When plaintiff Althea Rapier went to work for Ford [at the Chicago assembly plant], the head of the Labor Relations office told the women who, like Ms. Rapier, were just beginning their first day of orientation at the Company: "When you go downstairs [on the plant floor], you're on your own. It's a different world down there." Moreover, supervisors told women when they complained about sexual harassment, "That's why I don't let my wife work here."

> —From *First Amended Class Action Complaint, Althea Rapier,*
> *et al., v. Ford Motor Company,* Case no. 98C 5287, January 22,
> 1999. (Ford subsequently settled for $9 million.)

[Foreman] leered at Ms. Evans as she worked, brushed up against her so that he touched her breasts and buttocks, and on two occasions in 1992, grabbed her and pulled her close to him. After the first incident, Ms. Evans told [foreman] that if he grabbed her again, she would call her union committeeman. When he grabbed her the second time, she complained to her committeeman . . . who told her, "Rhonda, you know he likes you, you're so pretty, I'm over here looking at you myself. . . . You can't write a grievance for that." . . .

In December of 1997, another co-worker put his hands between her legs and lifted Ms. Evans up off the ground. She complained about this incident, but was told only, "Oh, you know he's crazy."

—From *First Amended Class Action Complaint, Althea Rapier, et al., v. Ford Motor Company,* Case no. 98C 5287, January 22, 1999

There's a third category of sexual harassment that can strike an observer as nearly surreal: situations in which the entire workplace gives the nod to men who insult, proposition, grab, fondle, and even assault women. Such workplaces have been found in situations as different as an attorney general's office and a liquor-importing firm. They've been found ludicrously often in the financial industry, police and firefighting stations, car dealerships, and manufacturing plants.

Whether the worksite is white- or blue-collar, the harassment pattern is fairly standard. The walls are plastered with *Hustler* centerfolds, which sometimes show up labeled with female employees' names; the guys openly watch porn in the break room or in their cubicles; celebrations and staff meetings take place at strip joints. Women are repeatedly asked for oral sex. Their bodies are lewdly assessed, aloud, when they walk by. At the annual holiday party, a few women are pressed to the wall and groped, find themselves sandwiched between two men pressing their groins against them, or are fondled through their clothes. Slowly, women realize that they're risking assault or rape if they walk into an empty conference room, a dark part of the plant, or a distant section of the parking lot. Complaints are useless, since the top bosses—owner, manager, sheriff, vice president, union leader—are serial harassers themselves or see harassment as harmless.

When sexual harassment metastasizes throughout a workplace in this way, are men consciously using it to drive women out of their industry? Are they simply having fun, as some insist, and genuinely believe it's a game to the women as well? Are they testing women for toughness? Moving in on the most vulnerable prey? The answers may differ from one man to the next, from one workplace to the next. What doesn't differ is the fact that the women, not the men, suffer the financial costs.

A good white-collar example comes from the many brokerage firms and financial institutions Susan Antilla wrote about in *Tales from the Boom-Boom Room: Women vs. Wall Street.*[6] Throughout the 1990s, securities firms and banks routinely refused women jobs, raises, and promotions; forced women to take and retake tests that men didn't have to pass; demoted or fired women when they got pregnant; and stripped women of any accounts (or bank branches) they'd made profitable. All this was documented in large and highly publicized lawsuits. According to Antilla, in 1995, women occupied 2.67 percent of all Smith Barney jobs paying between $450,000 and $549,000—and none of the many jobs paying more than that. Even proportionate to their numbers, women were way behind, making up 36 percent of the 1995 investment banking workforce but bringing home *11 percent* of the payroll.

That blatant discrimination was buttressed by a ceaseless background of sexual hazing. Women regularly—sometimes daily—faced demands for sex, lurid comments about their bodies, detailed descriptions of coworkers' sexual exploits or fantasies, and requirements to attend office strip shows, and received "gifts" of chocolate or pastry shaped like a penis. They were regularly called sluts, whores, bitches, tramps, pussies, or cunts. Men grabbed their breasts, pulled down their pants, and rubbed their groins against the women's bottoms.

For instance, here's how Antilla summarized the charges against Shearson Lehman made in a sexual harassment lawsuit that was filed in 1996, a lawsuit that was settled in 1997 with up to possibly 20,000 affected female employees, each forced to settle her claim through mediation and arbitration. By 2004, Shearson had paid an estimated $100 million dollars for behavior like this:

> In 1982, two men—a trader and an officer in the municipal bond
> department—sent [Lydia Klein] a calzone shaped like a penis,

with ricotta cheese seeping from a hole in the pastry. The harassment Klein says she experienced was constant and public. The same trader would stare at her breasts and ask "How they hanging?" He approached her at a business dinner making lewd remarks as he hung a banana outside his pants zipper. Another man—a supervisor—would stare at her breasts and say, "Oooh, I love them, booby booby boo." A male coworker once bit her ankles at work, tearing out patches of her nylons . . .

[A broker in New Jersey] took his penis out of his pants in front of female colleagues, put it in his drink at a party, and told them "It's thirsty." Another male broker at an office in California cornered a wire operator against the wall, placed his right hand against the wall, his left hand up her skirt and on her buttocks, and told her "This is going to be so good, I've wanted to do this for such a long time." He then rubbed his erect penis, through his pants, up and down her buttocks. When the branch manager learned of the conduct, he said the broker should be left alone because he was "going through a mid-life crisis."[7]

Which is not to say that Shearson Lehman was unusual. Similar behavior permeated many companies in the financial industry, from small to large, in New Jersey, New York, and Chicago. If women left their firms after filing charges, as often happened, management used a special parting weapon: discharging them with a bad comment on their U-5 termination form, an explanation for their discharge required by the SEC. A bad U-5 could destroy a career, making it impossible for a woman to get hired in the industry again. Sexual harassment on its own had financial consequences: it could stop women from advancing, effectively holding their incomes to half or less what comparably qualified or comparably successful men were earning. But *complaining* about sexual harassment could end a woman's financial industry career entirely—sending her into a career where her earnings were halved again, or worse.

By the late 1990s, enough women had gotten fed up to bring charges against such firms as Shearson Lehman/Smith Barney, Merrill Lynch,

Rodman & Renshaw, Josephthal, Olde Discount Corporation, and other financial institutions, dragging them through the courts before settling for millions of dollars.

In one sense, the financial industry was unusual: Most women haven't lived through anything quite that bad on the job. But it was hardly unique. Many readers would like to believe, for instance, that since women have made up close to 50 percent of most law school classes for the past decade, female attorneys must have integrated their profession enough to wipe out crude comments, turning it into a world as sternly focused on duty as the *Law & Order* offices.

But it's not so. Take New Jersey's Division of Criminal Justice. During the 1990s, that office was just as bad as the worst office at Shearson Lehman. At trial, witnesses testified that the office was blatantly hostile to women, or as Iver Peterson of *The New York Times* wrote, "rife with sexual banter and touching, where male superiors openly conducted sexual affairs with subordinate women and where a woman's physical attributes were fair game for public comment even after death, in gruesome crime scene photographs." One man kept a penis statue on his desk; many of the guys made crude sexual jokes about female murder victims; women working there were aggressively propositioned. Barbara Davis testified that her boss, Richard Carley, stuffed money in her bra, and that he groped her breasts and bottom. In the *New York Times* interview, she explained, "He would come up behind me and grab me. He would ask for oral sex. He would ask me if I was wearing any underwear that day. It was just devastating." *The New York Times* reported that Alan Hyde, a professor at Rutgers Law School in Newark, N.J., commented that "You can't hang a sign on the door that says 'Men Only' in words, but this case seems to say they hung the sign not with words but with deeds." The jury awarded Davis $350,000.[8] If that's what was going on during the 1990s in the office charged with upholding the law, what was happening elsewhere?

Group grope isn't limited to testosterone-heavy white-collar jobs with large amounts of money or prestige at stake. And confusingly, it's not always as openly and obviously hostile as it was in the financial industry or the New Jersey attorney general's office during the 1990s.

That's what becomes clear on hearing the story of one production line supervisor[9] who, midway through a fast-rising career, found herself at one such work site—although it took her a while to recognize it as such.

At first, this supervisor thought that the Dial manufacturing plant in Aurora, Illinois, an economically depressed town outside Chicago, would be a relaxed and even enjoyable place to work. (We'll call her "June Smith," because she asked for anonymity in this book, as she wanted to put this experience behind her.) June had joined Dial because it seemed like a smart career move. With an undergraduate degree in chemistry, she'd spent a few years working for Mobil, where she'd been fast-tracked into the management training program. Mobil promoted her regularly from one of its heavy product plants to another, where she oversaw the production on the plant floor. But the promotional tour involved moving every eighteen months, which June found lonely. Ambitious, capable, and practical, June had set her career sights on being a plant manager—and decided that she could get there outside Mobil just as well as within it. When she landed in Chicago, where her family lived, she quit.

She took a job overseeing high-speed packaging in retail products at the Dial Corporation, at the $36,000-per-year salary she'd had at Mobil. The structure was amazingly informal, so relaxed that she was able to pick her shift and her position. She thought, "Well, this is nice, this is really gonna work out nicely."

The Dial plant was large—so large that, sitting at one end, you couldn't see the other. Distributed across the floor were sixteen production lines, run almost entirely by women in the lowest-wage positions. The higher-paying positions, the line supervisors and mechanics whose job it was to fix anything that broke, were held almost entirely by men. June was one of only two female supervisors (and no female mechanics) on her midnight shift.

June was surprised by the degree of what she called "friendliness" in that office, to which at first she didn't give much serious attention. When she commented that a particular man and woman must be very good friends since they were seen together so regularly, she was assured that everyone knew that those two were longtime lovers, even though he had a wife and family on the outside. She was surprised to learn how many married men were having a series of affairs within the plant. "They told me, though, that Dial has gotten *so* much—oh, this place is *so* much better now . . . There wasn't a dark corner in this place where you couldn't . . . find some people screwing. I'd say, you're kidding! Oh my God—all the comments, all the conversations—it was an interesting place."

At first she didn't put this together with the nasty way the guys talked about some of the women on the production floor. "The two maintenance supervisors used to make fun of how ugly [Mary] was . . . but how she had this great body. I thought, that doesn't seem to be the right thing to do, she really can't help how she looks," June said. On the other hand, she could see that "Mary" had a very nasty attitude toward the mechanics and thought to herself, "She's probably irritated these people to death, and so that's how they vent and make fun of her." It took a number of months before she revised that assessment, realizing that they were making fun of every woman. One young intern was a "three-bagger": you'd need to put three bags over her head to have sex with her. "I'd listen to, over the summer, all the supervisors in that office make fun of the women out there, how big their asses were, how ugly their faces were." These guys were commenting sexually on every woman on the floor.

June had the same slow awakening about what at first she had called "friendliness." Every day, work discussions involved a hand on the shoulder, a hand on the arm. Over time, it occurred to her that one of her fellow supervisors "would always be rubbing my back and putting his hands on my hands and all this friendliness, and it was really—sickening. But this was *okay* there," she said with some incredulity.

One day, June asked one of her fellow supervisors for help. He was another of those who had a wife at home and a longtime mistress at the plant, an open arrangement about which June was somewhat startled. But her attitude was, live and let live. Then one day he was helping her examine a stalled production line. "So I'm looking over this glass guard . . . when all of a sudden I feel this body like pressed up against me behind me, and—and—he has an erection! And I can feel it! I go, 'Oh my God! Aren't you getting a little close? Get back!' And I push back. And it turns out, he goes, 'We could get a lot closer.' And I look at him, and go, 'What are you talking about?! Are you insane? I don't need to get any closer. This is all the closeness I need.' And I just walked away."

June's voice was quite disgusted when she spoke about it. "I tried not to show too much shock, but I was just really surprised. I guess the body part was kind of offensive to me. That somebody would be so close to you that you could feel *stuff*. That wigged me out." At that point, June Smith realized that what she had at first taken for "friendliness" was sexual harassment: an insidious and even sinister sense that women were there for the touching.

There was no question of reporting it. All the women said that this was the Dial way, had been since the plant opened in the 1960s, and happened at the very top. More important, if you made a stink, the guys—the mechanics and production supervisors—could get you demoted and fired by sabotaging your production. For instance, a woman might complain about one of the worst serial harassers, especially one in particular, who had on-the-record complaints against him filed by forty or more separate women. As a result, the other mechanics would decide that the latest to complain was a bitch. Then her lines would stop working. Explained June, "You'd have a problem with your line, and you'd ask your mechanic to come out, and your mechanic wouldn't be around: 'Oh, he's working on something else that's more pressing, he'll be there when he can.' Your line would stay down. Then when he'd come out, he might tinker around for another half hour or forty-five minutes. So you might lose a night or half a night's worth of production. And this could go on for several days. After a while your production would start to go down." And you would pay the cost.

That's what had happened with "Mary," whom June Smith had first noticed the men complaining about. Mary got a bad review. That took money out of her pocket: her regular raise was delayed, through no fault of her own. June found her barricaded in the women's restroom, sobbing over the accumulated strain of holding off the men, on the one hand, and trying to earn a living, on the other. But what were her options? Dial was the only game in their rural Illinois town.

June had managed, through her time at Dial, to avoid one of her more relentless admirers: the all-shift supervisor who'd originally hired her, whom I will call "Big Dan." In fact, she regularly passed up opportunities for promotions, since all of them involved working on day shift under Big Dan. Another $10,000 (plus additional benefits) a year did *not* seem like enough compensation for the loss of peace of mind.

But one year, at the annual Christmas celebration, June found herself seated with her now husband to one side and Big Dan on the other. "So we sit down, and [Dan] immediately goes, 'God, you look *great!*' I go, 'Thanks, [Dan].' He goes, '*God,* you look *wonderful!* I don't think I've ever seen you look so good!' And he starts with that, and I thought, Thanks, thanks very much. And he does not stop." For the next forty-five minutes, Big Dan kept hitting on June. He was praising her looks. He was rubbing her back. He did not take his eyes off her long enough to glance down at his *own* girlfriend at the table's other end. June's husband was somewhat deaf, so he didn't notice and June couldn't get his attention. Her own shift supervisor, seated across the table, tried to drag Big Dan onto another topic of conversation, to no avail. Big Dan kept on coming on.

Of course June couldn't openly reject him: This was her boss's boss. "I mean, I didn't plan on living at Dial. I was going to do some time there to get some experience on a résumé, and get out of there. There was no way in hell I was going to cause trouble and wreck my life for this. I was not going to get into a giant war with [Big Dan], lose recommendations, possibly get fired: No. I wasn't going to do that." Eventually she fled to the women's room, where she stayed for fifteen minutes, until it was time to leave.

But the pervasive sense of threat was affecting her more than she realized. Before Dial, she'd worked in situations where she'd endured nasty comments about her race. She'd worked in a plant where the union/management hostility was so strong that, June said, one of her colleagues had carried a loaded gun during negotiations. Neither situation had especially upset her. "But at Dial, people would *touch you!* Oh God. Oh my God, it was incredible. Every other day, every day! Somebody'd come up and rub your hand, put their hand on your back—I *hated,* I *hated* that. When I look back on it, I think maybe that might've been the number one thing that drove me out of there. It just drove me *insane.* I couldn't take the chance of going back into another world like that. I was like, I've gotta get out of here. Not only will these people touch you, but—I always got the feeling that if you were at the Dial plant in the wrong place in the warehouse—I always got the feeling that something bad could happen to you."

So June decided that under no circumstances was she ever, ever willing to work in manufacturing again. She tore up her ambitious career plan. She went back to school in tax accounting—starting from scratch in a career where she could work hundreds of miles from her supervisors, far from the risk of being touched.

June Smith, the production line supervisor, wasn't assaulted, as the teenage Pizza Hut worker had been. But she testified that she was regularly propositioned; she was touched too often and too intimately; she lived under the perpetual threat of retaliation (either financial or physical) should she ever complain about her coworkers' "friendly" treatment; she slowly came to feel (accurately, as it turns out) that assault was a daily possibility. All of this is disgusting—and that disgust is what most women who've endured sexual harassment tend to focus on. The emotional toll, the cost in personal integrity: that's what they add up. They forget to add up what it cost them in dollars and cents.

So let's roughly calculate how much the production line supervisor actually lost financially—mind you, through no fault of her own but because of Dial's "hostile environment."

Start with the two years when June earned $10,000 less each year than she'd have gotten on the day shift, for a loss of $20,000. During the next five years, while June was in school, she took an even bigger cut from what she'd have made had she continued in her promising manufacturing career. To support herself during those years, she took a $24,000-per-year job because its hours and location made it easy to get to campus. Had she stayed in manufacturing, let's assume she'd have continued to get regular promotions and raises, as she had in the past, and would have moved incrementally up from the $50,000 per year she would have made on day shift to $60,000 per year. That's a five-year loss of $155,000, without even counting the benefits she wasn't getting or the funds she wasn't accruing toward a pension. So, over seven years, June already had more than $175,000 in losses. Now add in the cost of school loans, for another $52,000 (plus interest). Just to make a career change after being harassed out of her chosen career cost her at least $227,000 in lost income and expenses.

In 2003, the former production line supervisor finally started her new career, making $48,000 per year. Had she stayed in manufacturing without interruption, she would in 2003 have been making $60,000 per year. In her new career, she can never make up that jump: any increases she makes now will build incrementally from that $48,000 base. That $12,000-per-year difference widens as it travels, causing more damage each year. But again, to be conservative, she will lose at least $36,000 over three years—on top of the $227,000 permanently lost.

Then let's subtract what June won in the class action settlement. Out of a sense of responsibility, June had agreed to be one of the named plaintiffs in the EEOC's case against Dial. "I wasn't too thrilled with going through those—those questions," as she put it. "The deposition wasn't thrilling. I wasn't looking forward to trial." But she was willing to do what she had to do to bring the perpetrators to justice. Fortunately, testifying at trial wasn't necessary: at the last minute, Dial settled for $10 million and a consent decree that included two and a half years of court oversight. In 2003, June received $200,000 as her share of the class settlement. That sounds like a big award, doesn't it? Except that $200,000—even before she paid taxes on that lump sum, bringing her actual award to something closer to $140,000—does not cover even the most *conservative* estimate of her financial losses. It doesn't approach repaying her for her emotional distress. And what's most significant is this: she will remain financially disadvantaged for the rest of her working life.

June Smith got off easily. Noelle Brennan, the EEOC supervisory trial attorney who oversaw the charges against Dial, confirms that June was absolutely correct in her sense that "something bad could happen" in some dark corner at Dial.[10] Something bad *did* happen to many of her female coworkers. More than sixty women—out of four hundred who'd worked at Dial's Aurora plant during the eleven years covered by the lawsuit—were willing to testify that they'd been sexually harassed, threatened, or assaulted by male coworkers or supervisors. More than *one hundred* were willing to go on record as named plaintiffs in the lawsuit, testifying to years of sundry taunts, grabs, and sexual hostility.

Some women simply couldn't bring themselves to talk about their experiences publicly.

Nevertheless, *one-fourth* of the plant's female workforce were willing to testify publicly about some of the worst moments of their lives; to release their medical records; to have hostile strangers grill about them about their psychological and sexual histories; and to go to court and be named in the newspapers as suing their company—with no guarantee of reward. Here's what their testimony revealed: At Dial, men regularly called women cunts, sluts, whores, bitches, and so on; ripped off their shirts; grabbed their breasts or buttocks; pinned them against the wall and groped them, sometimes while other men watched; unzipped their own pants and "offered" women their penises; pointed to the pornography posted on their desks, above their lockers, or on their toolboxes and suggested that the women would enjoy those acts; and repeatedly rubbed their penises against women's buttocks. It didn't happen constantly. It didn't happen to everyone every day. But over time, "something bad," as June put it, happened to almost every woman there.

For instance, Plaintiff 90, a janitor, walked into an unlit office one night. When she tried to turn on the lights, a man grabbed her from behind and started groping her. His mouth was on her; his penis was out and erect. She started screaming. A coworker came into the room and flipped on the lights. Her assailant was her supervisor. He kept his job.

Plaintiff 100 actually got one of her harassers temporarily dismissed. The guys were furious and ostracized her, Brennan says. One day, one of the mechanics came up behind her, grabbed her by the crotch, and lifted her, jerking her up and down, saying, "You fucking bitch, you think that was harassment? This is harassment!" She begged him to put her down. When he did, laughing, he insisted that she had liked it. Says Brennan, "She just—she never really recovered from that." The harasser she'd gotten fired was later hired back as an independent contractor. The man who had jerked her up and down wasn't reprimanded and kept his job.

At first Dial responded that this couldn't have been harassment; it had, rather, been mutual flirtation. Had the women felt harassed, they wouldn't have stayed on for ten, twenty, thirty years. But most had come to Dial—the town's only major employer—right out of high school. By early 2000, they had worked their way up to a wage of $15 or $20 an hour, a good wage for a high school graduate. June Smith, the production line supervisor, had had the skills, education, experience, and motivation to leave. Most of the other women, having never worked elsewhere, didn't know whether things would be different. Their choice seemed to be: suffer at work and pay the rent—or suffer at home by living on nearly nothing. The women stayed because they had no economic choice. An EEOC brief explained it this way: "As Victim 96 . . . who described sexual harassment at Dial as 'a way of life,' put it, "[I] just continued to work because I had—I had to work to make a living." [11]

At Dial, sexual harassment served as an ongoing warning to women who might have otherwise sought to move up from the lowest-paying jobs in the plant. If a qualified woman applied for a higher-paying job as a mechanic, she was harassed that much more ferociously—often with a group of men looking on. Sexual harassment functioned effectively to keep these women from trying to make more money or be treated as men's equals.

None of the plaintiffs got rich off the settlement. If the difference between a woman's production line job and a man's mechanic's job averaged $10 an hour, many of these women had been deprived of $20,800 per year for roughly twenty years apiece. That's a loss of $416,000 each, without counting overtime, benefits, or pension accruals. And that's just the straight loss of being underpaid, without adding combat pay for spending a lifetime working in a war zone, for the cost of psychological breakdowns or ongoing posttraumatic stress reactions.

Even a $10 million lawsuit settlement did not get these women even.

Sexual harassment, like more straightforward forms of discrimination in hiring, pay, and promotions, is an equal opportunity offender. It happens at the highest- and lowest-earning ends of the wage spectrum. And it can be terrible for immigrants who speak little or no English. Demands for sex in exchange for jobs, assaults in the fields or on the plant floor, being fired or locked in the plant freezer after refusing to have sex with a supervisor: Latin American immigrants charged that one or more of these things happened at such employers as Grace Culinary Systems in Townsend, Md.; at New England Serum Co., Inc., in

GROUP GROPE: SOME OF THE PAYOUTS FOR LARGE-SCALE "HOSTILE ENVIRONMENT" SEXUAL HARASSMENT CLAIMS BETWEEN 1998 AND 2004

Employer	Facility	Based In	Type of Action	Payout Year	Amount
Arapahoe County	Government office	Colorado	Settlement	2004	$170,000
Bob Watson Chevrolet, Inc.	Car dealership	Harvey, Ill.	Settlement	2002	$300,000
Charoen Pokphand USA, Inc.	Chicken-processing plant	Eufaula, Ala.	Settlement	2001	$485,000
Cheap Tickets, Inc.	Discount leisure travel products	California	Settlement	2003	$1.1 million
Clippinger's Chevrolet and West Covina Dodge	Car dealership	West Covina, Calif.	Settlement	2003	$75,000
Coachmen Automotive	RV manufacturing and sales	Elkhart, Ind.	Settlement	2001	$57,500
Colonial Ice Cream, Inc.	Family restaurants	Crystal Lake, Ill.	Settlement	2003	$368,000
Continental Airlines	Airline	Houston, Tex.	Jury award	1997	$875,000
Cook County, Ill.	Police force	Cook County, Ill.	Jury award	2002	$3 million, later reduced to $300,000
Dial, Inc.	Consumer goods packaging plant	Montgomery, Ill.	Settlement and consent decree	2003	$10 million
Double T Diner	Restaurant	White Marsh, Md.	Settlement	2002	$300,000
Eagle Tannery	Tannery	Waterloo, Ohio	Settlement	2002	Undisclosed amount
Electric Boat Division of General Dynamics Corporation	Submarine builder	Groton, Conn.	Jury award, reduced by judge to cap	2000	$750,000, reduced to $300,000
Equicredit Corporation of America	Mortgage financier	Pennsylvania	Settlement	2003	$190,000
Eveleth Mines	Mining	Eveleth, Minn.	Jury award	1999	Undisclosed amount: *The Washington Post* reported it to be more than $1 million

FedEx	Delivery service	Middleton, Pa.	Jury award	2004	$3.24 million
Fifth Third Bank	Financial services	Illinois	Settlement with consent decree	2004	$225,000
Ford Motor Company	Car manufacturing	Chicago, Ill.	Settlement	1999	$9 million
Ford Motor Company	Truck assembly plant	Norfolk, Va.	Settlement	2002	Undisclosed amount
Foster Wheeler Constructors, Inc.	Construction site	Robbins, Ill.	Settlement: s, r	2000	$1.325 million
Garban LLC	Financial services	New York, N.Y.	Settlement	2000	$200,000
General Motors	Car manufacturing plant	Linden, N.J.	Settlement	2001	$1.25 million
Glendale, California	Police department	California	Jury award	2003	$3.5 million
Good Samaritan Community Health Care	Surgery center	Puyallup, Wash.	Settlement	2002	$170,000
Grace Culinary Systems (W. R. Grace) and Townsend Culinary, Inc.	Food processing plant	Laurel, Md.	Settlement	2000	$1 million
Great American Foods Corporation's Catfish King	Restaurant	Idabel, Okla.	Settlement	2003	$81,000
Gruntal & Co.	Financial services	New York, N.Y.	Settlement	1997	$750,000
Gurtz Electric Company and Pickus Construction and Equipment Company	Construction	Illinois	Settlement	2003	$79,750
Hall-Copeland Ford Lincoln Mercury	Car dealership	Lewiston, Idaho	Settlement	2000	$42,500
Hanson Motors, Inc.	Car dealership	Olympia, Wash.	Settlement	2002	$670,000
Interstate Brands Corporation	Bakery	Philadelphia, Pa.	Settlement	2004	$222,000
Interstate Hotels & Resorts (Radisson)	Hotel	Henrietta, N.Y.	Settlement	2003	$625,000
I Sector Corporation and All Star Systems, Inc.	Computer parts company	Houston, Tex.	Settlement	2003	$175,000

(continued on next page)

Employer	Facility	Based In	Type of Action	Payout Year	Amount
John Elway AutoNation	Car dealership	Boulder, Colo.	Jury award	2002	$1 million
Josephthal	Financial services	Washington, D.C.	Settlement	2000	$330,000
King Soopers	Grocery	Denver, Colo.	Jury award	2002	$500,000
London International Group	Condom manufacturer	Eufaula, Ala.	Settlement: s, r	2000	$625,000
Marin Municipal Water District	Government agency	San Francisco, Calif.	Jury award	1997	$635,000
Meristar Management Co., LLC, Radisson Inn Rochester, et al.	Hotels	Rochester, N.Y.	Settlement	2003	$625,000
Merrill Lynch	Financial services	New York, N.Y.	Mediated settlements	1998	$100 million
Merrill Lynch	Financial services	New York, N.Y.	Arbitration panel	2003	$500,000
Merrill Lynch	Financial services	San Antonio, Tex.	Arbitration panel	2004	$2.2 million
Minnesota Beef Industries	Beef processor	Buffalo Lake, Minn.	Settlement	2004	$140,000
Mitsubishi Manufacturing	Manufacturing plant	Normal, Ill.	Settlement	1998	$34 million
New Jersey Division of Criminal Justice	Attorney general's office	New Jersey	Jury award	1998	$350,000
New Mexico Department of Public Safety	Public safety	New Mexico	Settlement	2001	Award under separate agreement
Nielsen & Bainbridge, LLC	Manufacturing and distribution	Bedford Park, Ill.	Settlement	2002	$155,000
Northwest New Mexico Regional Solid Waste Authority	Waste disposal operation	New Mexico	Settlement	2003	$148,000
PJAX	Interstate trucking	Pennsylvania	Settlement	2003	$500,000
Quality Art, LLC	Manufacturing	Gilbert, Ariz.	Settlement	2001	$3.5 million
River Oaks Diagnostic Center	Medical facility	Houston, Tex.	Settlement	2001	$275,000
RPM Auto Sales, Inc.	Car dealership	Flint and Saginaw, Mich.	Jury award	2003	$137,000
Salomon Smith Barney	Financial services	Garden City, N.Y.	Settlement	1997	$15 million plus individual settlements

Salomon Smith Barney	Financial services	Los Angeles, Calif.	Arbitration panel	2002	$3.2 million
San Joachin County, Calif., Office of Substance Abuse	Government agency	San Joachin County, Calif.	Jury award	2002	$562,000
Select Pre-Owned Homes	Mobile home dealer	San Antonio, Tex.	Settlement	2004	$16,500
South Beach Beverage Company (division of PepsiCo)	Beverage manufacturing	Norwalk, Conn.	Settlement	2002	$1.79 million
Southwest Supermarkets, Inc.	Grocery	Arizona	Settlement	1999	$1 million
Tanimura & Antle	Agriculture	Salinas, Calif., and Yuma, Ariz.	Settlement	1999	$1.855 million
Teaneck, N.J., Police Department	Police	Teaneck, N.J.	Jury award, upheld by New Jersey Supreme Court	2002	$1.1 million
Technicolor Videocassette**	DVD/video manufacturing	Camarillo, Calif.	Settlement	2002	$875,000
Thistledown Race Track	Horse racing	Cuyahoga County, Ohio	Jury award	2003	$500,000
Titanium Metals Corp. d/b/a TIMET	Manufacturer	Henderson, Nev.	Settlement	2003	$217,500
Trans World Airlines	Airline	New York, N.Y.	Settlement	2001	$2.6 million
Tualatin Valley Builders Supply	Retail supply	Oregon	Settlement	2001	$35,000
24 Hour Fitness	Health club	Florida	Arbitration award	2003	$3.5 million
Tyson Foods*	Poultry-processing plants	Alabama, Miss.	Settlement	1999	$3.2 million
UNICCO Service Company**	Janitorial services	Newton, Mass.	Settlement	2002	$1.54 million
UPS	Shipping	Des Moines, Iowa	Jury award	1998	$80.7 million, reduced to $800,000 under federal damages cap
Urban Retail Properties	Property management	Chicago, Ill.	Settlement	2003	$250,000
U.S. Postal Service	Government agency	Portland, Me.	Jury award	2001	$1 million

(continued on next page)

Employer	Facility	Based In	Type of Action	Payout Year	Amount
U.S. Postal Service†	Government agency	United States	Jury award	1998	$5.5 million
Ventura County, Calif., Fire Department	Fire department	Ventura County, Calif.	Jury award	2002	$28,000
Washington, D.C., Department of Corrections	Prisons	Washington, D.C.	Settlement	2002	$9.6 million

The charges include sex harassment and racial harassment.

**The victims were recent immigrants who were not always fluent in English.*

† *Awarded to survivors after a USPS employee committed suicide, blaming coworkers' harassment in her note.*

Codes: s = sex; r = race.

If you or someone you know is being sexually harassed on the job, you can find more information, resources, and contact numbers on the Web sites of such organizations as the EEOC (www.eeoc.gov), the WAGE Project (www.wageproject.org), the National Women's Law Center (www.nwlc.org), and Equal Rights Advocates (www.equalrights.org).

Topsfield, Mass.; at Technicolor Videocassette in Camarillo, Calif.; at DeCoster Farms in Iowa; at Quality Art in Gilbert, Ariz.

Or take the nation's largest employer of women, the Department of Defense. Some of the military's group-grope sites have been painstakingly documented over the past decade. Congressional hearings, military investigators, and in-depth newspaper, magazine, radio, and television coverage have all revealed petri dishes of sexual harassment, assault, and rape at such outposts as the Army's training bases in Aberdeen, Maryland; Fort Jackson, South Carolina; and Fort Wood, Missouri; and at the Tailhook convention of Navy and Marine aviators. The top Army boss, Major General Larry Smith, was found guilty of groping and harassment. In fact, a study showed that women in the military are four times more likely to suffer from posttraumatic stress disorder (PTSD) from sexual harassment than from combat.[12]

Why does large-scale sexual harassment happen? Sometimes a workplace culture turns into a group grope because a few unbalanced men sense an opportunity; because men who might otherwise behave decently are resocialized by the workplace culture to feel it's okay to behave badly; and because men who might object are afraid of being retaliated against as well. Sometimes it happens because a group of men are angry that their paychecks are disappearing and lash out at the women who, the men believe, are trying to steal their jobs. Some observers theorize that sexual harassment is about power: that men are using it to derail female competition for jobs, raises, and promotions. Sometimes, lesser sexual harassment can be fended off by determined women who are strong enough to play just as hard as their male tormenters. But that's not always possible. Whatever the men's reasons might be, the outcome is the same: *women's* psyches and paychecks are the ones that suffer.

The final table in this chapter is a list of employers throughout the United States that were charged with allowing disturbing cultures of sexual harassment to persist—and that had to pay. Once again, you'll see that hostile environments that threaten women's wages are a problem in every corner of the economy and of the country. You'll see a racetrack, a chemical-processing plant, a tannery, a chicken-processing plant, and manufacturers of cars, soap products, and DVDs. Sometimes sexual harassment drains women's wallets at enormous employers'; sometimes it sets back women's wages in small offices. Many of the employers on this list, such as prison systems and car manufacturers, have long been strongholds of male work cultures, but you'll also see that hostile environment discrimination has been proven in a health club, grocery stores, and government offices.

For decades, surveys have documented that *most* working women say they have encountered sexual harassment at work. As you'll see in the table, it's not going away: every year, new employers are nailed for this outrageous, criminal, discriminatory behavior. Why does it continue?

Because too many CEOs let it go on, without consequences to the harassers—or the harassers' managers. Let's be clear: no matter how bad a workplace gets, the CEO can always put a stop to sexual harassment. The person who issues the paychecks and stamps the promotions is the person who has the final say in what's acceptable and what's not on the job. If he (or, less often, she) is outraged by any hint of sexual harassment; if he insists that every worker must be trained to recognize the difference between flirtation and exploitation; if he insists that every sexual harassment allegation be investigated fairly; and if he holds every manager fully accountable if any illegal behavior is allowed to continue—you can bet that workplace will clear up. In the worst cases, as we'll see in the last part of this book, change may require the intervention of outside observers' studies and recommendations, in order to alter the workplace culture. But no outsider (or midlevel manager) can eliminate sexual harassment unless the top boss wants it accomplished.

Can you name one top executive in the country who, without first being hit by a media storm of scrutiny and outrage, has said, "We have a problem with sexual harassment, and I'm going to fix it"?

Neither can I.

Once Again, Nobody Loves a Lawsuit

> The supervisor asked us if it was OK to bring him [the alleged harasser] back because of the workload. I said no. The word spread . . . I broke out in hives and constantly couldn't sleep and got threatening phone calls through the night.[13]
> —Linda McFarland, who sued Coachmen Industries for sexual harassment and retaliation and won a $57,500 settlement in 2001

> [Anne Berry] said in a recent interview that the lawsuit was as much an ordeal as her brief tenure as assistant to [Sacramento Kings Vice President Alton] Byrd, 44. "I was warned that they would do everything they could to make me out a slut," Berry said. "That turned out to be an understatement. It was hell."
> The Sacramento Bee, October 3, 2002[14]

> This has taken four years of my life and I lost a job that I loved. I gave GM the best years of my life and they refused to protect me.
> —Julie DeRossett, The Detroit News, August 28, 1998

The vast majority of these women were reluctant to sue. Most of them came forward with their stories only after some other woman, someone with a strong sense of self-respect or moral outrage, stuck her neck out first. All of them knew what they were risking: retaliation on the job, career suicide, marital discord, hostile grilling, media attacks, and repeated exposure of the worst moments of their lives.

Even when they won, the women lost financially. Sexual harassment makes it impossible for women to concentrate on their jobs, to hope to move up, and sometimes to continue earning at all. By suing, women forgo not just jobs but careers and reputations: Who will hire such a trou-blemaker again? And that's if they're in any condition to hold a job. Many of these women were too paralyzed with flashbacks to work again or, like Barbara Carter and Vera Brummell, who'd once been with the Washing-ton, D.C., Department of Corrections, remained on workers' compen-sation or medication to cope with crippling depression and anxiety.[15]

While the women lost their jobs, the men almost always kept theirs. Most of the women who reported such treatment left their jobs and careers—while the men who harassed them were scarcely punished, if at all. The men saw, at most, a temporary dip in their paychecks—or were sometimes even promoted. By contrast, women lost promotions, jobs, and sometimes the very ability to work. Shelly Mehringer, for instance, a secretary in Bloomingdale, Illinois's, Engineering Depart-ment for eleven years, complained that her coworker James Monk-meyer was harassing her. As a result, she was given a bad review for causing tension in the workplace. Monkmeyer was promoted to assis-tant director of village services.

No organization, of course, can entirely stop all its employees from behaving badly. "The question is, what do they do when they find out about it?" asks Adele Rapport, Detroit EEOC regional attorney. Here's what an employer *should* do: swiftly and visibly punish those who step out of line. Some employers do exactly that when they hear about sex-ual harassment. Rapport, who as EEOC regional attorney has prose-cuted or overseen the prosecution of dozens of sexual harassment cases, knows personally what it's like to work under a corporate zero-tolerance policy. In fact, she was surprised, when she first went to work for the EEOC, to find out how many corporations and organizations ignore sexual harassment charges for far too long. Her own corporate experi-ence was quite different.

"I represented Sears for many years, and they didn't wait until some-thing rose to the level of a hostile work environment," Rapport ex-plained. Courts have made it clear that merely vulgar behavior may be immature and uncomfortable, but it's not legally actionable. Neverthe-less, Sears punished such misbehavior immediately. "If there was one dirty joke by a manager, one offensive touching, they were fired!" One could speculate that Sears' diligence was influenced by the fact that it had faced an EEOC class action sex discrimination lawsuit, filed in 1973 and finally decided in Sears' favor in 1988; if so, women won that lawsuit in spirit, even if not in court.

June Smith had had a similar experience, in her pre-Dial jobs, of knowing she was backed by management. At Mobil, "I was the only woman in a two-hundred-man plant one night," she said. "But those guys all knew if anything happened to me, it was my word against theirs. The company would come down *against* them, *for* me, immediately, and they would lose their jobs. There was never a question."

Even group-grope worksites can be reformed—sometimes by legal action. In May 2002, the Washington state Department of Labor and Industries fired four employees and disciplined a handful of others for e-mailing sexually explicit messages on the government's system, as part of its response to an earlier sexual harassment claim. And as we'll see in chapter 11, Mitsubishi went from condoning one of the most sexually harassing cultures in the industry to aiming to be the best environment for women workers, according to Nancy Kreiter, one of three court-appointed monitors who oversaw the company's reform while it was operating under a consent decree. (For guidelines on good sexual harassment policies, go to www.eeoc.gov, various women's law centers, or professional human resources organizations.)

Legal action that affects any company in an industry can make its competitors take notice. For instance, in 2003, J.P. Morgan Chase fired two investment bankers, Managing Director Palden Gyuimed Namgyal and Vice President Norman Gretzinger, after other employees reported that, after a holiday party, Namgyal and Gretzinger had "sandwiched" a junior female investment banker between them, rubbing up against her from both sides and propositioning her. The firings were widely interpreted as meaning that, after a decade of multimillion-dollar sexual harassment lawsuits, at least this Wall Street firm had gotten the zero-tolerance message.[16]

Despite the amount of illegal misbehavior she prosecutes, EEOC Attorney Adele Rapport believes that most corporations do the right thing. Far too many don't. And women's paychecks (with all that means, including a poorer quality of life and a damaged ability to retire comfortably) suffer.

CHAPTER 7

Women's Work

In the [aircraft] dispatch area, it was almost all men. The men were pretty demeaning toward women. It was pretty hostile. It wasn't unusual to walk down in the hangars and see nude pin-ups on men's toolboxes. This was the mechanic environment, and it was very difficult to be looked at as an equal.
> —Former airline executive [1]

It was an incredibly masculine office. The model was older married men and younger single women; there were no women in between. It was clear where all the power and glamour was. I wasn't prepared for the mighty WHO [World Health Organization] to feel like 1955.
> —Former public health administrator,
> U.S.-based international organization [2]

In the world of fund-raising, men tend to work for bigger institutions that pay bigger salaries. And the men tend to be the ones to do planned giving, which also pays them bigger money.
> —Lawyer and former nonprofit development director, Missouri [3]

Men's work and women's work sound like ideas from a distant past. Economists once theorized that women's work was poorly paid because women were allowed to work only in certain kinds of jobs: as teachers, nurses, editorial assistants, shop clerks, typists, and so on. Artificial social barriers crowded too many women into few job categories. If, no matter what their qualifications, women only could be teachers and nurses, there would be a tremendous oversupply of labor for those limited jobs, driving wages down.

With the combination of second-wave feminism and Title VII of the 1964 Civil Rights Act, many women thought that the bad old days of workplace sex segregation were numbered. The doors to all professions and occupations were supposed to have been flung open wide: women should now be free to be doctors, lawyers, pilots, plumbers, professors, welders, and anything else to which they might aspire. Many believed that as women fanned out into jobs traditionally held by men, women would soon be paid as well as men. If the economists' theories were true, that should have happened.

But the pink and blue paychecks remain. In 2000, two thirds of all U.S. working women were still crowded into 21 of the five hundred occupational categories. The women's top ten list wouldn't surprise Austin Powers, that time traveler from the 1960s: receptionist, secretary, cashier, sales worker, registered nurse, elementary school teacher, nursing aide, bookkeeper/accountant/auditor, and waitress. Women still make up 80 to 98 percent of all the workers in those categories—and only 2 to 20 percent of all engineers, police officers, firefighters, mechanics, and construction equipment operators.

And that's without counting the way women are segregated *inside* professions, occupations, or industries. Even inside an individual employer or occupation, it's still possible to see a ravine between male and female jobs, such as (male) orthopedic surgeons on the one side and (female) pediatricians on the other. Does this happen because women don't have the skills for or interest in men's work, such as the hand-eye coordination required to stitch up surgical incisions? Or is it that men don't want to have to compete with twice as many people (not just qualified men, but also qualified women) for those higher-paying jobs? Perhaps the reason wouldn't matter—except that men's jobs still pay much more than women's.

As you read on, you'll notice that this chapter—unlike the previous two—includes few cases where women won lawsuits or got settlement payments. That doesn't mean that wages for women's work in occupationally sex-segregated jobs are fair; social scientists say this discrimination is so damaging to women's earnings that it's a major reason for the wage gap.[4] The dearth of lawsuit settlements in this chapter is for two reasons. The first is straightforward; in chapter 5, we already covered the most egregious kind of sex segregation: refusing to hire women for "men's" jobs.

The second reason is that women in "pink" jobs who make "pink" paychecks (paychecks that are cramped compared to a male's blue dollar) aren't able to take their claims of discrimination to court. After the passage of Title VII of the 1964 Civil Rights Act, women did sue over "comparable worth," the idea that jobs with comparable skills should be paid similar wages—even if one job is dominated by women and another by men. Why—except for sex—should social workers make less than probation officers or kitchen workers less than janitors? But over time, federal courts narrowed what could be litigated. By 1990, the courts had all but closed the door to women's complaints of discrimination by sex segregation.

Yet even though the courts would not hold employers liable for paying higher wages for "men's" jobs than for "women's" jobs, more than 1,700 state, county, and local governments voluntarily called a halt to that unfair practice. They passed "comparable worth" legislation that covered their own employees. As employers, those governments then systematically and objectively evaluated such job categories as secretary and maintenance worker, adjusting wages to be fair and equitable. The state of Minnesota actually managed to close the wage gap almost entirely: that government's female workers now make 97 cents to a male worker's dollar. It's a success story that *Getting Even* will examine in more detail in chapter 11.

But here's the important point to remember. When an employer— whether a hospital, government, engineering firm, grocery store, or brokerage firm—drives women into "pink" jobs and pays them less than men in corresponding "blue" jobs, that can be just as illegal as plain old discrimination or sexual harassment. Sex-segregated jobs add one more notch to the wage gap.

Girls Keep Out!

> The men on the [mattress factory] line worked wonderfully with me, but as soon as the manager came in to personally supervise the line . . . he just attributed every error that came through that line to me. And then he took me off after two or three mattresses to go and do tidy-up work.
>
> —Full-time temporary worker, Olympia, Washington[5]

> I got off a hoist elevator on a construction site and had my breast grabbed. There was an effigy of me with my work clothes hung outside the building they were working on, which I had to see upon my approach to work. I am a short person, as well as female, and I would be standing in an elevator hoist with about eight or nine guys telling rape jokes. I couldn't even see their faces. Those are pretty common experiences.
>
> —Lauren Sugerman, former electrician,
> now president, Chicago Women in Trades

We all smile at those old movies and books in which boys, battling desperately to stay away from girls' "cooties," barricade their clubhouse with a "Girls keep out!" sign. Unfortunately, many boys keep up that clubhouse mentality well into adulthood—and bring it into the workplace.

Some observers believe that the clubhouse doors are wide open—and that women simply *like* certain kinds of work better. According to this theory, girls overwhelmingly prefer words to numbers, indoor desks to outdoor dirt, human relationships to hard facts, filing to forklifting, making a difference to making money. They don't want to break their nails or mess up their hair paving highways or repairing cars. They don't want to stay late to battle for power in corporate halls; they're sensible enough to prefer to leave early so they can do homework with their kids.

This sounds very much like the idea, popular in the early 1970s, that only boys wanted to play sports. Not until the enforcement of Title IX did girls show that, if given the chance, they would throw themselves enthusiastically into such sweaty and unladylike pursuits as soccer, basketball, and track. Today an entire generation of young women believes it's their birthright to be strong, agile, and physically competent: running marathons, passing basketballs, lifting weights, staying healthy — and winning.

Still, perhaps it's true that some, or even most, women freely choose to pursue stereotypically female interests. But not all of them do. Sociologists have shown definitively that women are far from dedicated to doing women's work. In fact, they've found that at just about any age, women will jump into "men's" work if it pays more. "The occupational choices of women of all ages are quite responsive to new opportunities in male-dominated fields," writes the sociologist Barbara Reskin, widely considered to be one of the top academic researchers of occupational segregation. In fact, women with children are *more* likely than non-moms to shift into "male" jobs — because "men's" work pays enough to support a family. "Hence, factors such as early sex-role socialization and occupation-specific investments in human capital are far less consequential than the supply-siders would have us believe."[6]

Why, then, are there so few women in "men's" jobs? Because they're not always allowed in. Too often, men have actively hazed and harassed women who wanted to do "men's" work. That's what happened to the women at Rent-A-Center and to Sharon Pollard, the supervisor at a DuPont chemical plant. It's what happened to Barbara Davis when she tried working as a New Jersey assistant attorney general, where hands-on sexual harassment (such as her boss's stuffing money into her bra) was just the tip of the iceberg. It's what happened to the women at Dial, where sexual harassment increased to the point of violence when women tried to move up from (low-paid) line worker to (higher-paid) mechanic. For all these women, the message was clear: "Girls keep out!"

Some employers flatly insist that they want only men for certain jobs—say, electrical repair—and only women for others—say, receptionist or filing clerk. We saw that in the Advantage Staffing lawsuit.[7] That's what happened to one woman, who, after losing a computer programming job in 2000 during the national downturn, spent three years trying to get well-paying day work in Olympia, Washington. Since she was five feet nine, athletic, and physically strong, she decided to apply for unskilled "light industrial" work, which paid $10 or $12 per hour, rather than clerical work, which paid $7 per hour. "Temporary clerical work starts at minimum wage and stays at minimum wage," the woman explained. "The blue-collar stuff started at one, two, or three dollars an hour more and then quickly moved up. Those are living wages in this area. But $7.01 per hour, which is minimum wage in Washington—you can't make it on that."

That seemed like a sensible enough decision. But employers balked. At one staffing agency, "the person behind the desk blandly said, 'We have women's jobs, we have telemarketing.' And I said, 'You don't mean you have women's jobs and men's jobs? That's illegal.' This was in the year 2000!" But no matter how often this woman explained the law— occasionally in terms that made clear the possibility of an EEOC charge—she simply wasn't called to the desk for manual labor jobs. One manager, whom she described as short and slight, told her, " 'You have to be able to lift fifty pounds; I can because I'm a man.' I was standing over him! Most women can lift that with very little training. I can do it because I've been athletic all my life. Most women can get there in almost a heartbeat. They lift children all day!"

When she called to apply for another temporary light industrial job, she was told, " 'Oh, we tried some women, and they didn't work out.' And I said, 'Well, I'd still like to apply.' She said, 'No, they just didn't work out.' " When she did get onto a few manual labor job sites, "I got along with the crew, many of whom were ex-cons and recent immigrants, but the invariably male managers did not want women, and said so. At one construction site, where I moved furniture up three flights of stairs right along with the men, the male manager finally noticed me, after I had worked most of the day. He called me over and asked, 'Why'd they send a damn woman?' " At another light industrial job, the foreman refused to give her lifting work and assigned her instead to take inventory—"because women write so neatly," she said incredulously.

At still another manufacturing job, this woman explained that she wanted to apply for light industrial, which by definition involves lifting fifty pounds or less. The woman who answered the phone, however, told her, "Oh, you have to be able to lift 140 pounds." She was shocked at what she knew to be an outright lie. "I said, 'I don't think there are many men that can lift that.' She said, 'Oh yes, all of our people can do it.' But 140 pounds is over the OSHA safety limits in the state of Washington for lifting unassisted."

And so, during her period of professional unemployment, this woman ended up losing her house and car. "I could not support myself on a woman's wage," she said. "Women cannot. That's why they depend on men." She knew she was unusual in understanding, as many other women wouldn't, that her rejections had been outright violations of federal law. "The key figures here are the ones who applied for these jobs, and then did what any normal human being, less motivated than myself, would have done: they applied, and they were discouraged, and they went and did something else. And they don't talk about it. Failure is embarrassing." You could say that, unlike this determined woman, those women decided they'd rather do women's work. But was it a free choice? Or did those women "choose" to stop beating their heads against an illegal brick wall?

Men at Work: Women and the Trades

As bad as things are in entry-level manual labor, it's just as bad or worse in the skilled trades. In chapter 5, we saw that Home Depot's founders tried to explain away the fact that women were overwhelmingly hired to be (lower-paid) cashiers while men were overwhelmingly hired to be (higher-paid) sales associates this way: "We recruit in the construction trades; it is no secret that the construction trades are predominantly male. In fact, a scant 2.6 percent of the people working in these trades are female."[8] The implication was clear: it wasn't Home Depot's fault that women weren't in the trades. So whose fault *was* it?

Many men in the trades would say it's women's fault. Women don't want to do this kind of work. Or, women didn't grow up with hammers in their hands, helping their dads in the workshop, like we did. Or, women just don't have what it takes to lift and carry heavy loads, visualize floor plans in three dimensions, or understand electricity flow. But is that true about *that* many women? Or are those very *ideas* about women being used to rationalize unfair treatment, which either drives women out or makes it impossible for them to succeed?

Let's consider the second possibility, which is the one most social scientists would endorse. The first people who try to desegregate a workplace or an occupation, according to the past few decades of social science research, are seen through the distorted lens of stereotyping. Stereotyping isn't by definition evil; it's a necessary and often useful skill, growing from human beings' capacity to sort things into abstract groups. Sorting is a skill we need throughout our lives: to understand that red means stop and green means go; to declare that a ball is inside or outside the strike zone; to determine whether a client can bring charges for a particular wrong and, if so, under which statute or legal theory.

But if stereotypes are not confronted, that habit of matching things to their pattern can become dangerous overgeneralizing. If *some* women want to be home at 3 P.M. when their kids get home from school, men may assume that *all* women are unreliable because of their kids. Or if, on average, men are stronger than women, *all* men may be seen as stronger than *all* women—regardless of the individual evidence if, say, Serena Williams and Woody Allen were to apply for the same job. One woman on a construction site will stand out like one yellow square on a page of blue circles—which means, sociologists say, that the guys will more quickly remember anything she does that matches the way "women" behave. If the guys' stereotyped idea is that "women" complain too much, a request for a private toilet (when all the guys are satisfied with an open bucket in the corner) will confirm their suspicions. If they think of "women" as being too emotional, a woman who gets upset when the guys spend lunch hour showing hard-core porn movies will prove she's one of those oversensitive females. If they believe that "women" screw everything up, a woman who makes a mistake proves her uselessness—even if her mistake happened because, say, nobody told her which wire is neutral or which tools should be used for which task.

Social scientists explain that the resulting discrimination can be broken down if active and conscious efforts are made to counter those stereotypes or if there's a critical mass of the new group, enough that it's obvious that each woman (or African American or Muslim) is different and individual.[9]

But in 2003, women still made up fewer than 2 percent of those working in each skilled trade: carpenters, plumbers, pipefitters, ironworkers, machinists, sheet metal workers, boilermakers, bricklayers, masons, operating engineers, painters, mechanics, and so on. As a result, a woman in construction is almost always the only one on her job site. Everything she does is going to be seen as cripplingly female, from how she holds a hammer to how long it takes her to engage a clutch.

The more recalcitrant trades have shown a clear pattern in how they keep women out. For some reason—a lawsuit, a presidential order, community pressure—the organization is forced to agree to hire women. But agreeing in theory doesn't mean the guys have changed their minds in practice. So when women do apply, their applications mysteriously go missing. Or the letter telling them when and where to show up for the interview somehow gets lost in the mail. Or their entrance exam is invalidated for some obscure technical reason and they have to retake the test. Or they're allowed to take the training and pay their union dues, but somehow no job openings turn up over the next two or three years. That's what happened in the northern California carpenters' union in the 1990s, after a labor-employer organization called the Joint Apprenticeship and Training Committee was ordered (in *Eldredge v. Carpenters*, a lawsuit that dragged on for more than twenty years and twice reached the ninth circuit U.S. Court of Appeals) to refer female apprentices onto construction jobs at least one out of five times. JATC would put a minimum number of women to work one day a quarter—just enough to be able to list them on its quarterly report to the court monitor—and then never send those women out to work another day, according to Debra Smith, director of the Equal Rights Advocates tradeswomen's legal advocacy project. Of course those women got the message. They pursued some other line of work where they had a hope of actually being paid more than four days a year. You could say that those women "chose" other jobs. But was it a free choice—or were they forced out?

Dying to Work in Construction?

Things aren't necessarily much better if some woman does actually manage to get hired in blue-collar work: too often, the guys make it nearly impossible for her to succeed. For one thing, no one will show her how to do the job. Instead, they stand by while she does it wrong and then tell her that women are stupid and useless. For another, she's pounced upon for any slight deviation from the rules—even if it's a rule that none of the guys follows. If she ever asks for time off for a personal or family responsibility, such as a doctor's appointment or a parent-teacher meeting, she's told no and that she has to choose between having a career and having a family. And yet, somehow, the guys themselves get time off for exactly the same reasons, since they're just being "good family men." That's what happened to one of Debra Smith's clients, a journeywoman in pile driving. While working on the San Francisco Bay Bridge in 2003, this female journeyman asked for a day off to sign her child up for school, since the school required parents to do so in person. She got the date wrong and had to ask for a second day off. "The boss said, 'This is why we don't want women in construction,' " Smith told us. "And the guy with him said, 'That's why my wife stays home with my kids.' " Suddenly she was getting written reprimands for such "infractions" as taking her required life jacket off, as they all did, when she had to squeeze into the portapotty.

All the tactics seen in earlier chapters are used to push a woman out of skilled blue-collar work. She's given the ugliest, hardest, least appreciated assignments in the hope that she'll get discouraged and leave—flagging around the construction site, for instance, which is simultaneously boring and dangerous. Or porn is pasted in her locker or toolbox, as happened to women who insisted on becoming mechanics at Dial. Or she's groped in unguarded moments, as happened to women who tried to work at Ford's Chicago assembly plant. Or she's handed broken or dangerous equipment that no one else will use. Or all of the above. And when, despite all this, she sticks around, they put her into the deep freeze, refusing to eat with her or speak to her, as happened to Sharon Pollard at DuPont. According to Debra Smith, the lack of welcome extends to such basics as failing to have equipment that would fit women, from safety harnesses to work gloves to bathrooms that are something more than buckets in a corner of a muddy field.

Hostility toward women naturally varies from one job site to another and from one union local to another. Some are welcoming and fair. Too many aren't. Sometimes men refuse to teach women, instead waiting to see whether they can prove their fitness. "If a woman is asked to move a hundred two-by-fours, all the men will watch," explained Debra Smith, "instead of stepping forward and saying, 'Look, this is how you do this,' or, 'This is an easier way to do it.' Women get injured on the job because men don't pass on their knowledge of how to do things the way that's safest and least hard on your body."

In the previous chapter, a female production line supervisor realized that men were sabotaging women's work at Dial. In the trades, such sabotage can be deadly. "All the man two floors above has to do is drop a hammer," Smith explains. That hammer might or might not hit the woman below him. "He just says, 'Oh, I had an accident, I dropped it.' You can't prove it wasn't. Women fear for their lives." That fear for their lives is often what drives even the most determined women out, according to Lauren Sugerman of Chicago Women in the Trades. Early in the 1980s, she managed to get a position as an apprentice elevator technician under the auspices of the local union.[10] She liked her co-workers and thought they got along well. One day she was working on the tenth floor of an eleven-story building site, amid 480 volts of electricity, dangerous moving equipment, and live cables. Suddenly she realized that everyone else had signed out early and gone home, leaving her alone on a potentially deadly job site, with no help should something go wrong. "That did it for me," she said. "I'll put up with everything else, but I'm not going to put my life in danger for higher wages." Sugerman instead started advocating for women in the trades, the kind of nonprofit office job—a female job—she'd hoped to avoid. You could say that she chose women's work of her own free will. And it's true. She did choose to abandon her career in the trades in order to advocate for others. But was her choice really a free choice—or was she forced out?

None of this is inevitable. Consider the experiences of Mary Ruggiero, who'd been a "Rosie the Riveter" right out of high school, during World War II. "Management treated us like VIPs," she said. "People were so patriotic! Nobody wondered whether you could do the job, because the need was there. . . . We got paid the same as men and got the same work and training."[11] All that ended with the war. According to Ruggiero, "I was a damn good welder. But after the war nobody would hire us. Employers would look at me and say, 'What are you, some kind of freak? A woman can't weld.'" Ruggiero got the message. She did what women in the 1950s were supposed to do: gave up and stayed home to raise her family.

But thirty years later, Ruggiero went back to welding—and was startled by how much *worse* she was treated in the 1980s. "The guys at work had a real different attitude than during the war years. Most men didn't want a woman around. They made fun of me, they'd sabotage my workbench and my tools. One guy said, 'I got a woman at home, who needs one on the job?' Management is responsible for a lot of the harassment. They support the fellows' hostility rather than stick up for us."[12]

My Father Is My Idol: The End of a Dream

Like the trades, police and fire departments—especially the smaller ones, far from the urban centers that were roiled by race riots in the 1960s and 1970s and were therefore forced toward diversity by court and community pressure—have often been determined to keep women out. It's not always that way. According to Women in the Fire Service,[13] the first American woman to be paid for fighting fires was Sandra Forcier, hired as a public safety officer (a combination police officer and firefighter) by the city of Winston-Salem, North Carolina, on July 1, 1973. By 2003, Forcier was Battalion Chief Sandra Waldron, still on the job with Winston-Salem after thirty years.

But Forcier-Waldron is an anomaly. In 2002, only about 6,000 women (of a total of 225,000 nationwide) were employed as firefighters, making up a grand total of 2.7 percent of the occupation.[14] Is that because women don't want to risk their lives for their community—or is it because men don't want them there? The story of one young female firefighter and her father offers some insight into the question.[15]

In 2001, when his daughter applied to become a firefighter, Tom McKinney was the president of the firefighters' union in Muskogee, Oklahoma (population 38,310), where he'd been a firefighter since 1979. Tom is a plainspoken midwesterner. When asked whether he had wanted his daughter to become the first female firefighter in the department's 103-year history, he said bluntly, "No. Not originally I didn't." As his daughter explained, "He was a little biased about women being in the workplace."

But his daughter Amy was determined. "My father has been a firefighter since a month before I was born," she said. "And I've always been interested in following in my father's footsteps. My father is my idol. I look up to my dad."

So Amy McKinney went all out to prepare for the firefighting test. She studied everything she could get her hands on about firefighting and fire safety. While a secretary for a local business, she put herself through a year of rigorous physical training, taking up weight lifting and running. Seeing her stubborn effort, her father changed his mind. "When she proved to me that that was the job she wanted, I said, 'Okay, I'll help you out any way I can. I'll back you all the way.'"

The father, however, knew better than the daughter what she was going up against. "As soon as it was determined that we were going to have a female taking the test for becoming a member of the fire department," he explained, "the crap started. Immediately. 'We don't need any women on here, and we're going to make sure, *damn* sure, that they won't get on here.' They simply did not want to break up the good-ol'-boys' club." According to him, the guys wanted their clubhouse to be female-free for a very simple reason: "So they can say and do whatever they wanted to. They can be away from their wives and girlfriends, speak any way they wanted to, watch any programs, TV, movies." Asked whether he meant pornography, Tom McKinney quickly agreed.

Amy McKinney first aced the written exam. Then she aced the physical agility test, in which she ran a mile and a half in less than thirteen minutes; dragged a 200-pound dummy while outfitted in fire gear; dragged a fully loaded water hose 100 feet; lifted and maneuvered 150 pounds of equipment; climbed a fully extended ladder from a ladder truck; and stayed inside a smoke-filled room, wearing fire mask and air tank, for twenty minutes. Out of eighteen applicants, the firefighter's daughter was one of only three who passed. "Captain Doe" applied to the state board to invalidate the test as not meeting regulations. The board mandated a new test. Amy McKinney passed that one as well. She was confident that, through hard work, she would win the other firefighters to her side, just as she had won over her father.

But Doe and his cronies didn't care whether she was qualified, said Tom McKinney. "When she passed it the second time, the statement was made point-blank to me as president of the union, 'Well, she won't make it. We'll make damn sure that she won't make it.' "

His daughter was ready for a little opposition and discomfort. "Before I came along there was sexual material on the walls, I'd hear a lot of vulgar stuff. It didn't bother me." She didn't expect the guys to change anything just for her. Nor, at first, did she mind the petty annoyances, she said, such as the fact that other firefighters refused to partner with her in practice runs. Or that out of twenty-four captains, only four (including her father) would train her as they were supposed to; others simply told her to clean the station and wouldn't even show her what was on the truck. Or that a couple of captains refused to have her work on their shifts at all. Or that many of the drivers, who were next in seniority to the captains, refused to speak to her. As a result, despite her stellar initial showing, she got poor monthly scores on her ongoing training, "because no one would show me the proper way of doing things." But she was willing to continue: she was certain that she could change their attitudes.

Amy McKinney was willing to endure the fact that, when she came in for meals, everyone else would leave the room; if they had to be in the same room with her, they gave her the collective cold shoulder. The younger men encouraged her privately but went along with the silent treatment in front of the veterans, lest the veterans drive them out too. The veterans' attitude shocked her. "I grew up around most of the veterans on the department," she explained. "I went to Christmas parties, Easter egg hunts, drives for muscular dystrophy—you name it, my dad was the main person that they ran to for any type of function. I mean, I've known these guys forever, since I was in diapers. It really surprised me."

One day, the young female firefighter was assigned to work under Captain Doe, who spent three hours putting her through impossible training exercises. He insisted that she work while wearing firefighting gloves and suit that were vastly too big, before those specially ordered for her small size had arrived. He berated and barked at her every step of the way, saying essentially, according to the young woman, "People are watching you! People are saying, this is a firefighter who can't do her job! She's nothing but a wimp!" He had her move a ladder while goading her for being too short to do the job. He assigned her to pull a hose from the truck. This particular "jump line" had been incorrectly loaded: it was wet, which added unwieldy weight; 150 feet of hose had been jammed into a compartment designed for just 100 feet; and it had been shoved in rather than correctly loaded. As a result, it was nearly impossible to drag out. While she tried, Doe yelled and sneered at her for being so slow. "I had to jump on top of the bumper and keep jerking and pulling and jerking and pulling. I could not pull it out of there. I fussed and I fought and I started to cry. I'm crying, but I'm still out there trying to pull the hose out. And then he scores me for crying. 'Look at this firefighter! She's crying on the job! I can't take this!' "

Her father explained the attitude toward her sarcastically, saying, "She and two other people were hired on the exact same day. They were all supposed to be going through the exact same training. The men got preferential treatment; if they did something wrong, they got showed how to correct it. With her, it's just a dumb-ass woman, that's about the way it is." Written reprimands began to pile up.

Amy McKinney refused to report her treatment to her superiors; she was determined to tough it out and get ahead on her merits. She contacted some of the field's female pioneers and got advice about winning over her department from a New York City firefighter who had eventually become a chief. But before she had a chance to use those tactics, Captain Doe accused the young woman of cleaning the toilet inadequately and called in the assistant chief as a witness. The assistant chief watched as she was forced to reclean toilets and showers and was then punished further by being ordered to clean long-neglected storage rooms, light fixtures, and so on, in an ever-lengthening list of humiliating chores. Word of the incident got back to the chief. The personnel director started an investigation. And all heck broke loose in Muskogee.

The press picked up the story. Soon Amy McKinney and the Muskogee Fire Department were front-page news—not just in Muskogee but across the state, debated in the capital's paper and in the state's land-grant college classrooms, reported on by the AP. She was instructed to keep notebooks documenting everything that happened to her; other firefighters watched her constant scribbling with suspicion and antagonism. Firefighters who were called into the hearings were furious, assuming she had accused them of nefarious deeds. The cold-shoulder treatment got even more frigid.

Meanwhile, the union confronted her father. In one meeting, Doe and his cronies demanded that their longtime colleague back the union's version of events and not his daughter's. "They came right out in the union meeting and told me that I couldn't help her because she's not a union member," Tom McKinney said indignantly. "And I said, 'No. Absolutely no way.' I was not going to stand for it. I was going to stick with my daughter, because I knew what had happened." Union members retaliated. Tom McKinney was voted out of his presidency of the firefighting union. He and the three other captains who had backed the young woman were given the silent treatment, spoken about but never to. No longer would fellow firefighters ask her father and these other three to work overtime to cover their shifts, the McKinneys said. As they lost overtime, the former union president's (and the other three captains') incomes were cut, in some cases in half.

As the investigation dragged on for more than two months, things got worse. A union member wrote a letter to the Muskogee paper, accusing the now ex–union president of having sexually harassed him when the union member was a private; he then filed a lawsuit that he later dropped. This lifelong firefighter had been a proud leading community member for two decades. Suddenly, crushingly, Tom McKinney saw his name dragged through the mud. "My heart was so broke," said his daughter Amy. "I didn't know what to do. He cried. He got depressed."

The city personnel director's investigation upheld the discrimination charges against Doe and demoted him. But after the demotion, Doe appealed to the city's civil service commission, contending that he'd merely treated Amy as he would have treated any male private and was just doing his job. After three days of public hearings, the commission voted 2-1 to reverse the demotion. One commissioner commented that "some other steps should have been taken by the City, suspension or something, other than demoting a 25 year employee." [16]

Doe's reinstatement took place on an abominably hot and humid August day, a day that left Amy McKinney discouraged and her father, Tom McKinney, depressed—a day on which much of the department was called into what Tom described as "one of the darkest, hottest fires I can remember," reaching 110 degrees and emitting thick black smoke. While pausing for a drink of water, Amy saw her father double over and grab his chest, a moment that he later described as feeling "just like somebody had stepped on my chest with an elephant." None of his fellow firefighters moved to touch him. She ran and gave him oxygen. Still no one else came over. She ran down the block and flagged the assistant chief to call an ambulance. Tom McKinney was hospitalized with what, fortunately, was not a heart attack but merely a dangerous level of smoke inhalation and dehydration.

"So that made my decision," Amy McKinney said grimly. In her mind, the stress was literally killing her father, who had been worrying that the company might leave her to die in a fire. "If they're going to let my father—that they've been friends with, or so-called friends with, for twenty-some odd years—lay there and suffer, what are they going to do to me when my dad's gone? It just wasn't worth my health. And it wasn't worth my father's health. That was my quitting point. It's one of the hardest things I've ever had to do. But it had to be."

The young woman's attempt to integrate Muskogee's firefighting service was exhausting and costly—emotionally, physically, and financially. When she quit, her income dropped dramatically. As a firefighter, she had made $16,250 a year, accompanied by generous health insurance, disability insurance, life insurance, funeral benefits, and full pension benefits that kicked in after twenty-five years of service. Further, firefighting lent itself to having a second job. Muskogee firefighters were on duty for twenty-four hours and then off for forty-eight. On her two off days, she worked part-time, earning another $12,000 a year. As a result, she said, her income was "pretty high for [this state], especially for a woman. I brought home more money than my husband did, and that felt good! It did, it really did!"

That financial security fell apart when McKinney left the fire department. She won a lawsuit settlement from the city—accompanied by the familiar denial of wrongdoing—that she said was just enough to tide her family over for several months, until she got a full-time office manager job. When we spoke in late 2003, more than a year after she'd quit, the young woman was again earning $16,250. But she no longer had either the generous benefits or a schedule that enabled her to hold a second job. Her earnings had, in effect, been cut by nearly $15,000 a year.

"I lost what I'd worked for," Amy McKinney said. "They took my closeness with my father away from me, that I felt I needed. They took my money that would bring my—I was hoping to have another child within the next couple of years, but times are tough right now, and I can't do that." She'd lost both money and her dream.

This woman is a fighter. When we spoke, McKinney had already started training for a new career—as an ob/gyn nurse. "I never, never want to work with a male-dominant facility again," she said with concentrated fury. "Because they have given me a very biased outlook toward men." You could say that she has chosen to take up "women's work." And that's true. She has. But was it really a voluntary choice—or was she forced to?

Pink-Collar Ghetto: Keeping Wages Down

> I was an in-home family counselor, and I loved that too. Mostly women worked there. One or two men were doing counseling, mostly as a part-time job. Again, most of the men were in management. In the mental health field, they are so thrilled to have a man that I think they give them a lot of extra. I think they've always been paid more than we have.
>
> —Substance abuse counselor, Iowa

One rationale for paying men more has been that men's work is physical work. But so is women's. Is a housekeeper doing less physical labor than a maintenance man? Is reading an electric meter more physically demanding than reading a parking meter? Consider four new 1990s job categories: child care workers and elder care workers, on the one hand, and messengers and private security guards, on the other. Which do you think paid more? Was that because carrying a gun is heavier than carrying a toddler or because carrying documents is more physically exhausting than lifting an elderly man into and out of a tub?

Anthropologists have suggested a different interpretation: a task categorized as "men's work" is prized more highly than the same task when classed as "women's work"—whether weaving baskets or grilling meat, editing books or approving mortgages. After all, brawn no longer contributes that much more to the GDP than does brain. Today most American jobs, even those that used to be physical, rely on mental and social skills: calculating and communicating, managing and persuading, manipulating and maneuvering, asking and answering. From machinist to funeral home director, from air traffic controller to astronomer, "men's" jobs lean primarily on mental and social skills—just as "women's" jobs do.

In fact, "women's" jobs can be more skilled than "men's"—and still pay less, for no clear reason. We've already seen, in chapters 5 and 6, how much less women are paid within a single organization when there's an unofficial but nearly complete divide between women's and men's job titles—"housecleaners" versus "janitors" or "production workers" versus "mechanics"—even if the skill level, or the work itself, is the same.

Consider the experience of a secretary who worked in housing code enforcement in what she described as an "upper-crust" municipality. The department's clerical staff was all female, while the inspectors were all male. The inspectors would travel around the city, making notes when they saw lawns that weren't properly mowed and houses that weren't properly painted or checking on tenants' complaints about such things as leaky roofs. Meanwhile, the clerical staff maintained all the records, managed and tracked the issuance of and response to citations, and answered questions about the codes and requirements.

Called "clerks" and "secretaries," they were administrative staff with computer and secretarial skills and had to be familiar with the housing and zoning codes, just as inspectors did. Guess which job paid more? Now imagine the situation reversed. Picture men working in the office, called "code managers" or "enforcement overseers." Picture women working in the field, observing and taking notes on home maintenance standards and called "code maids." Which jobs do you think would pay more?

"The inspectors get a lot more money than clerical does," the secretary said, but that wasn't all. "The guys who clean our toilet were getting paid more than the clerical staff. I had come to that job with skills. The guys who were out picking up sofas—you know, if you were moving out of your house and you left your old ratty sofa behind—they didn't have to come to that job with any skills. They were getting paid more than me. I found that unfair."[17]

Or consider the fact that, even within "women's" jobs, there's a wage gap: men in those jobs are paid *more* than women in those same jobs. For instance, can you think of a job that's more female than nursing? According to the U.S. Department of Labor, in the year 2000, women held 97.8 percent of all RN jobs. And yet female nurses made, on average, only 87.9 cents to a male nurse's dollar. Cashier is, as we've seen, another female-dominated job. Yet female cashiers make only 88 cents to a male cashier's dollar. The same is true in all women's jobs: schoolteachers, file clerks, librarians, bookkeepers, waitresses. If sex segregation exists because women are *naturally* better at some kinds of work, shouldn't women in those job categories make *more than* men in the same job?

The wage gap is slightly smaller in "women's jobs" than it is overall. In professional jobs that were once "men's"—doctor, lawyer, banker, manager—women talk about a glass ceiling. But in women's jobs, the problem has been called the "sticky floor" or the "glass escalator." Women get stuck there. Men with equal or fewer qualifications are promoted up and out twice as fast, as social scientists have shown, into management or some other more promising career track.[18] We've seen that in chapters 5 and 6, as Home Depot, Publix Super Markets, Dial, and many other large employers regularly left women in the bottom-rung jobs.

Occupation	Percentage of women in the job	Gender wage gap in this job
Miscellaneous administrative support	84.2 percent	$.16
Registered nurses	97 percent	$.13
Cashiers	77.5 percent	$.12
Grade school teachers	83.3 percent	$.19
Bookkeepers, accounting, auditing clerks	92.1 percent	$.12
General office clerks	83.6 percent	$.09

Women often see that happening around them in ways that aren't upsetting enough or blatant enough to set off a lawsuit. The secretary who got angry at the pay disparity in her city code enforcement department left civil service to become a secretary in a large corporation. There, she reported, "Men get hired along with women into the clerical categories. But I have seen them lifted up out of clerical and brought into management at a higher rate than women." Asked why, the secretary speculated that male managers just "felt more comfortable" with other men. When the corporation's managers saw a good female secretary—someone talented at organizing, coordinating, anticipating problems, and creatively suggesting solutions—they saw a good secretary. But when the same managers saw a good male secretary— someone talented at organizing, coordinating, anticipating problems, and creatively suggesting solutions—they saw management potential. Organized male = manager; organized female = secretary. That's stereotyping in action: the mind matches characteristics to a pattern.[19] When it's acted on, that's discrimination—and it keeps women from getting even.

White-Collar Jobs—
but with Pink Tracks and Blue Tracks

There were certainly equal numbers of men and women in faculty positions. . . . Men predominated in the sciences and they were paid considerably more than those of us who were weren't, who tended to be female.

—Former writing program director,
community college, Massachusetts[20]

All the other groups had male heads. This one had me as its head. It really became perceived as a woman's group and women's work. Scientists were always on a lower [pay] scale than the engineers. . . . I know women engineers that were so turned off by the [masculine engineering] culture after awhile that they just couldn't stand being there anymore. I know one that went out and was making sandwiches in a sandwich shop off in Colorado, and another one that ended up designing dresses on her own. [Women were] taking enormous pay cuts just to get out of the culture.

—Environmental planner, engineering firm, East Coast[21]

There is a mind-set that women working in the not-for-profit sector should probably just be doing this as volunteers. Women are supposed to volunteer their time to make the world a better place. Whereas men in not-for-profit—there is a concept that these are men working and doing jobs and need to be compensated.

—Karel Amaranth, executive director,
victim services agency, New York

It's easy to see the stark divide between low-wage pink-collar work and well-waged blue-collar work. Call to get your water heater fixed, and you quickly notice which sex answers the telephone and which sex pulls up at the door with a toolbox. In these long-standing occupations we've become so accustomed to sex segregation that we take it for granted, scarcely noticing that the "Men Working" highway sign has a subtext: "No Women Need Apply."

Less visible is the new *white*-collar sex segregation—but it's there nevertheless. Take, for instance, those promising "new economy" jobs, where women and men should have found a level playing field, an arena free from hundreds of years of sex-segregated history. In the booming information technology industry, the high-paying jobs, such as senior software engineer, computer software architect, and computer hardware engineer, are held almost entirely by men. How did that happen so quickly? And when women *do* enter IT's high-paying "men's" jobs, the wage gap is just as persistent as in those "men's" jobs that are centuries old. Female computer systems analysts and scientists make only 82 cents for every dollar men make; female computer programmers earn 86 cents; and female computer operators make 82 cents.

Of course, even if the technology jobs themselves are new, engineering and math have a long history as a male domain. So are things any better in the new and growing service-sector jobs such as advertising, public relations, and communications? These industries draw employees from liberal arts majors such as English, art history, and design, which have long been dominated by women and use the "soft" skills in which women are said to excel (at least in high school and college), such as persuasion, creativity, and teamwork.

The answer is no. Even in these industries, men outpace women— sometimes dramatically so. Female public relations specialists earn, on average, only 84 cents to a male's PR dollar. In small advertising agencies, a female creative director makes only 70 cents to her male counterpart's dollar—a wage gap that's even wider than the average overall. If she works for a large advertising agency, where a female creative director is paid on average $113,000 per year, she's still getting only 74 cents to a male creative director's dollar. And that wage gap exists all the way down the line, in almost every job, top to bottom. There is an exception, however. When working as copywriters (in small agencies) and art directors (in large agencies)—which are the very bottom, entry-level rungs of the advertising industry—women make either as much as or slightly more than men. So long as they're not promoted, that is. That's the "sticky floor" at work: talented women get stuck in the bottom jobs, at decent entry-level salaries. Talented men move up.

The new brain-driven economy, in other words, has its pink and blue paychecks, just like the old brawn-driven economy. Meet the new boss, same as the old boss.

And that's true throughout the white-collar world, despite the enormous progress women have made breaking into professional jobs. Doctor, lawyer, engineer, journalist, scientist, MBA: these days, it's hard to find a graduate school program without a sizable and high-achieving group of female students, women who usually believe that nothing but their own drive and skill can limit their careers. In 2002, women made up 64.1 percent of journalism and communications undergrads and two thirds of those in journalism graduate schools.[22] In biology, according to MIT biology professor Nancy Hopkins, women make up 50 percent of the undergraduate students, 45 percent of those in graduate programs, and 35 percent of those with postdoctoral fellowships. And in one of the fields most often pointed to as a female success story, women make up nearly half of all law students and 34 percent of all lawyers.[23]

But instead of being segregated *out of* white-collar professions, women are now segregated *within* them—into the lower-paying jobs. For instance, in 2003, more women than men applied to medical schools and nearly one third of all doctors were female. But those full-time female doctors make only 58 *cents* to a full-time male doctor's dollar. These numbers count full-time doctors only, without including women working part-time. So why the gap?

If you compare doctors within a specialty—male GPs to female GPs, say—the wage gap doesn't look quite as bad, as you can see in the table below.

But the numbers look much worse once you notice the sex segregation *within the profession*. Women and men may look equal going into medical school, with equally high MCAT scores and GPAs. But by the time they come out of their residencies and fellowships eight or ten years later, many have been slotted into pink- and blue-stethoscope specialties, with enormous consequences for their future earnings. The medical pink-stethoscope ghetto is financially more comfortable than

GENDER WAGE GAP BY MEDICAL SPECIALTY[24]

	Females	Males	Wage Gap
Family practitioners	$140,000	$150,000	7 cents
Internists	$120,000	$155,000	23 cents
Pediatricians	$120,000	$150,000	20 cents
All physicians	$125,000	$180,000	31 cents

the clerical pink-collar ghetto; gynecologists can at least pay for mortgages and child care. But a female doctor will still be living on that much less than a male doctor at every stage of her life: while working, while putting her kids through school, and throughout her longer retirement.

Underneath the "men's work" and "women's work" labels lies the stereotypical idea that men's work is serious, important, and hard, while women's work is intuitive, inessential, and easy. Men fix; women tend. Men blaze new trails and get things done; women keep things going. That's reflected in the pay: When a job "tips" into being seen as a woman's job, it's paid less than when it's seen as a man's. And the further it tips, the worse the pay. Sociologist Cheri Ostroff, a professor at Columbia University, has shown that that's true even on the microlevel: the more women you work with (making your job "women's work"), whether as colleagues, peers, or subordinates, the lower your pay. The effect starts as soon as your group is 51 percent female and increases rapidly as the percentage of women in your group increases. That's true for managers as well, as Ostroff found in a study of thousands of managers in several organizations. Whether you're a man or a woman, if you manage a group made up of only female employees, you'll be paid roughly 15 percent less than if you manage a comparable group of only male employees.[25]

Your pay takes another hit if you're female yourself. Controlling for such things as experience, education, age, and occupation, Ostroff said, female managers make 9 percent less than male managers. Pay goes down still more if all three are true: if you're a woman, managing mostly women, with managerial peers who are mostly women. Guess what that means for your salary if you're a nursing supervisor, if you manage a group of female secretaries, or if you run a domestic violence project?

Here's what it means: when you're a woman doing women's work, you're earning an extrapink paycheck. Many women suspect this. "There aren't too many GS-14s [here]," said one lawyer[26] who ran a government office that focused on a "woman's issue." "Of the forty-two people on staff, forty are women. And honestly, there's really some incredible feeling against [our] office. I've been told, 'Oh, maybe you'd get a little more work done there if you had a few more men.' That's an actual comment by a person in power!"

Doing Good for Less: The Nonprofit Wage Gap

Just as there are pink and blue tracks within what were once "men's" white-collar professions, so there are pink and blue tracks within the "women's" white-collar jobs — such as nonprofit and fund-raising jobs.

If professional women have a traditional field, it is helping others. And if women have traditional skills, surely those are the skills needed in nonprofit organizations and development: talking, writing, persuading, arranging, managing, organizing. Nonprofit leaders must work together with many constituencies, keeping many different community members happy, harmonizing everyone's interests so that they stay involved in fulfilling the main mission. They must speak and write about the importance of the organization's shared goals or services and ensure that those services are delivered. Fund-raisers must persuade others that they have a personal interest in giving toward something that's bigger than the self. This is the kind of work that middle-class women were allowed to do (albeit without salary) back in the 1950s or that upper-class women did in the Victorian era. If ever there were an occupation where women should be making more than men, you'd think this would be it: running charitable organizations and raising money.

But it's not so. Nonprofits — from human services organizations to philanthropic foundations — have the same "sticky floor" as do most

MEDIAN PAY FOR FUND-RAISERS[27]

	Men	Women	Wage Gap
Chief executive officers	$68,333	$49,167	28 cents
Chief development officers	$73,000	$50,000	32 cents
Deputy development officers	$65,250	$48,000	26 cents

MEDIAN PAY FOR EXECUTIVE DIRECTORS[28]

Size of Budget	Men	Women	Wage Gap
More than $50 million	$271,032	$186,088	31 cents
$25 million to $50 million	$175,913	$143,188	19 cents
$10 million to $25 million	$135,885	$111,545	18 cents
$5 million to $10 million	$105,699	$91,179	14 cents

Note: *Of groups with annual budgets of $5 million or more, 25 percent are headed by women.*

businesses. Women dominate at the bottom and middle rungs and then thin out amazingly in the higher ranks—where the pay is higher. In the foundation world, for instance, 75.6 percent of the staff is female, as you might expect. But check out the distribution across the salary range. Women hold 92 percent of the administrative assistant jobs, 67.8 percent of the professional jobs—and only 54 percent of the CEO positions. Things are even worse in nonprofits as a whole, where women hold 70 percent of all the jobs—but only *25 percent* of the top jobs if the budget is $5 million or more. And the higher the nonprofit executive's salary, the less likely it will be going to a woman.

Even when women do head nonprofits, they make much less than the men who do.[29] Among nonprofit leaders of groups whose budgets are between $25 million and $50 million, women earn 81 cents for every dollar men are paid. And the wage gap is wider in the larger and wealthier nonprofits. Among groups with budgets of $50 million or more, female leaders make only *69 cents* to a male leader's dollar.

So why are women in nonprofits underpaid compared to men? Many hold the theory held by one woman who had worked in nonprofit jobs for more than twenty years. In 2001, Karel Amaranth was a non-profit veteran and director of an East Coast victims' services agency, overseeing a staff of twenty-three and making $70,000 a year. Noting that women were hired to head badly funded agencies while men were hired to run nonprofits with healthy endowments, she believed that the reason was simple: "Women are supposed to volunteer their time to make the world a better place. There is an attitude: 'Whatever you get paid, you're lucky.' Or 'You're doing good work, so you should be satis-fied.' Or 'You've chosen this, so you shouldn't make money anyway.' It's pretty amazing." In fact, she told me, some people she met were taken aback that she actually accepted money for her work.

Some suggest that men in nonprofits are paid more than women be-cause they come from the corporate world and have a higher salary his-tory from which to negotiate. But that theory doesn't work for women who do the same. In 2003, I spoke with a woman[30] who had had a high-earning career, with impeccable credentials. Her undergraduate de-gree was from one of the top ten universities in the country; her M.B.A. came from one of the top five. When this manager left corporate life, she had been a vice president of marketing making $120,000, with an-nual bonuses of $20,000 to $30,000, a $5,000-a-year car allowance, stock options, and generous benefits and pension plan.

And yet when this accomplished manager accepted a position in a nonprofit energy consulting firm in the fall of 2003, her entering salary was $58,000 — roughly the same salary being earned by her two female peers but only *half* the $120,000 salary of the male executive director, to whom the three women reported. Within months, this manager had al-ready negotiated the largest contract her nonprofit had ever held, more than enough to support a raise. But how do you negotiate a raise that will close a salary gap that vast?

There's a long list of possible reasons for the nonprofit wage gap—

and none of them seems much different than the reasons for the wage gap at large. Maybe women are simply paid less . . . because they're women, and too many bosses think women don't deserve as much money as men.

Pink Paychecks and Blue Paychecks

Here at the beginning of the twenty-first century, most of us take for granted that some kinds of jobs are "women's work" and others are "men's work." But few of us have realized just how widespread and pervasive that pink and blue slotting system is—affecting men and women at every earning level, from struggling clerks to highly paid professionals. The lowest-paid workers are segregated openly: women can be file clerks and telemarketers for minimum wage, while men can do "light industrial" and unskilled construction work for up to one third more an hour. Midwage workers are segregated more subtly into specific jobs and job titles within companies: women work on the production line while men are machinists; women are data analysts while men are programmers; women are researchers while men are policy analysts. And in the upper managerial and professional ranks, women are segregated into the lower-earning tracks of the same professions: women are executive directors of smaller nonprofits while men are CEOs of large ones; women are pediatricians and men are orthopedic surgeons.

Walk into any employer—a bank, a car rental company, an ad agency, an airport—and ask yourself, "Where are the women?" If the women's jobs are earning more, please let me know—because you'll be inside a very unusual organization indeed, one whose existence I would like to document.

CHAPTER 8

Everyday Discrimination:
Working While Female

[The vice president] only talked to the males. When you came to him with an idea, you got a brush-off. He had no time for you. There were very few women in the shop, other than in the office. And even the ones in the office ran into the same thing. Mostly they didn't even bother trying to talk to him because they got nowhere.

—Woodworker,[1] small private company, New Hampshire

The guys all went home, and we worked late. You could walk around the halls of [the corporation] and you would see the women there. You just had to do it. You sit there and go, "Well, I've got two kids, do I want to fight it or is this something that you just live with?"

—Middle manager, Fortune 100 corporation, eastern United States[2]

Until this chapter, *Getting Even* has considered measured and measurable forms of discrimination. But all those lawsuits and numbers don't quite capture something I heard from nearly

everyone. Many women—whether they're earning $10 an hour or
$100,000 a year—encounter an undercurrent of bias that holds them
back, even when that bias isn't blatant enough to take to a court of law.
How can you measure a financial setback from offhand jokes or minor
incidents? It's harder to articulate, harder to quantify, and nearly impossible to document or prove. Call it everyday discrimination. It's what
happens when a woman's ideas are dismissed—only to be discussed
seriously when made by a man. Or when employers turn to old-boy networks rather than public postings to recruit new talent. Or when interviews or applications evaluate masculine characteristics more highly,
even when women's strengths and communication styles could accom-
plish the job just as well, and perhaps better.

Underlying the blatant sex discrimination, the sexual harassment,
and the occupational and job title segregation, there's a pernicious form
of discrimination at work. In a thousand insidious ways, everyday discrimination eats away at women's pay. It may or may not become offensive or obvious enough to launch a lawsuit. But women know that,
repeatedly and subtly, they're being diminished and devalued—and
that this eats directly into their paychecks.

It doesn't happen everywhere, or all the time. But when you ask, almost every woman has a story of the time she lost out—on recognition,
or praise, or promotions, or pay—simply because she was Working
While Female.

Few women dwell on these insulting moments. Some are reluctant
to think poorly of their colleagues and quick to blame themselves.
Some wonder, Was I really unfairly overlooked while the guys around
me were being promoted, or was it my fault because I didn't know how
to play the game? Some decide that, since they can't reeducate their
coworkers, they're better off outperforming the guys so spectacularly
that they can't be left back. Some just set aside those snubs and keep
their noses to the grindstone, since they can't afford to get angry and
lose that much-needed paycheck.

But at some point—maybe at age 35 or 40 or 50—many women
abruptly hit their limit. One last insult (and it's often a small one, far
from the worst of their lives) topples the entire shaky pile of slights, re-
fusals, delayed promotions, overlooked achievements, was-it-me-or-

was-it-unfair moments that have for so long been shoved to the back of the mind. Women are suddenly overwhelmed with outrage. "I could hear the scales falling from my eyes," one 60-year-old corporate manager said about the moment she realized that she'd been held back and underpaid throughout her career.

For younger women especially, this moment of awakening can be a nasty surprise. In 1985 or 1990 or 1995, when this generation entered the labor force, it was taken for granted that things were already fair. Teachers, coaches, and professors had always treated these girls and boys as equals. Some went to schools where girls held the top positions, such as valedictorian, class president, school newspaper editor, basketball star, or debate team leader. Their mothers had worked; they had seen highly visible women—Marian Wright Edelman, Mia Hamm, Connie Chung, Carly Fiorina, Madeleine Albright, Ruth Bader Ginsburg—at (or near) the top of just about every profession. Media coverage had concluded that sex discrimination was a thing of the past. So these young women were astonished when, once they entered the workforce, men with equal or lesser talents and accomplishments sped past them to higher positions and higher salaries, for no good reason.

This chapter and the next will look into the below-the-threshold experiences that remind women on the job that others' biased expectations and behavior are holding them back—and are pinching their paychecks. These fleeting impressions of unfair treatment may be just as illegal as some of what you've read about in earlier chapters, even if they have not been so outrageous as to push women into visiting a lawyer. And to those of us who want to understand the wage gap, these experiences are just as important as major lawsuit settlements. Why? Because *most women have them.* Many women tend to doubt themselves, asking: Was it him, or was it me? Seeing how many other women have them should prompt you to take them seriously as an indication of others' attitudes—and therefore of subtle discrimination against you at the office. Each time you encounter such hints that you're being treated as less than equal, think not just of your offended dignity *but of your wallet.* When your boss neglects to give you credit for what you've done, or when your colleagues or coworkers swap office gossip in an all-male huddle, or when you're the only female manager in the conference room, see it as a sign that money is being subtracted from your next bonus, raise, or promotion. Take these moments seriously; they're pointers to your own personal wage gap.

This chapter won't discuss what you should *do* about such incidents. I'll lay out action plans in a later chapter. For now, this chapter's message is simply: Pay attention. As you read, regularly ask yourself: Has anything like this ever happened to me? Every time you answer "yes," it's another notch in the wage gap.

Twice as Good to Get Half as Far

> I was getting called in to do presentations for projects my name wasn't legitimately on—because there would be a woman on the [client's] review team. Excuse me?!
>
> —Environmental planner, engineering firm, Boston

> Women were the lowest on the totem pole, they were treated like crap, and they didn't make much money. No one took anything they said seriously. They would say, "Oh, [she] can't do such and such, she's not very smart, she doesn't know how to work conceptually." Or, "She's so antagonistic, she can't really work with the clients."
>
> —Art director, advertising agency, southwestern United States

Most women want to believe that they're going to advance based on their own talents, proving themselves on the job. What they don't recognize (often until it's too late) is that others' expectations can stringently limit what they do. Nothing needs to be said out loud; it all happens in the mind of the observer. Unbeknown to the woman herself, her motivations are questioned, her actions are suspected, and her performance attributed to luck rather than talent—while men around her are given the benefit of the doubt. The problem is that, if it's the boss who mindlessly organizes the world into men versus women, competent versus incompetent, rational versus nurturing, and so on, he can make his beliefs self-fulfilling: giving women less training, fewer chances to work on challenging or significant projects, lower perfor-

mance ratings, and lower pay than men with equivalent resumes and results.[3] And when women are treated this way, their *own* automatic fears
of being stereotyped can cause them to choke, questioning or double-
checking everything they do and hurting their performance.[4] Meanwhile, even men who truly aren't biased can easily miss the fact that
women around them are being treated unfairly; it's happening too far
below perception, inside their colleagues' minds. That means that
good, fair-minded guys truly may not see that they're living in a different, more welcoming job climate than their female peers—nor can
they see that some of their success is due to the fact that they have the
wind at their backs, while women are facing into the driving wind.

How so? As we saw in chapter 7, stereotyping can click in automatically, erasing a real individual and substituting a prefab idea of how
everyone in that person's category is supposed to behave. Few people
stereotype viciously. It happens without much thought.

According to two decades of research,[5] stereotyping is amazingly
persistent and self-perpetuating, "abating only when the evidence to the
contrary is indisputable."[6] Consider the following chart, adapted from
an article by American University law professor Joan Williams, which
illustrates research into such social science concepts as "prescriptive
stereotyping," "descriptive stereotyping," "attribution bias," "leniency
bias," and "role incongruity."[7]

When a woman does anything that cracks her category—say, by
being outstandingly productive or hardworking or quick with figures or
talented with machines—that fact is shed as irrelevant. Her success is
attributed to accident, not talent or effort; she's thought to have gotten
lucky or to be doing work that's easy anyway. In other words, according
to social scientists, it's true: women really *do* have to be twice as good to
get half as far.

And that costs her money. Stereotyping quickly becomes everyday
paycheck discrimination. Too often, women are treated as if they will accept any job they can find. They're paid less for the same work. They're
not told about possible job openings, promotions, or raises—because
(without asking) the men in power assume women won't travel
overnight or stay late. When women ask point-blank to move up, they're
told that they wouldn't be able to combine work and family. They're

HE'S LATE/SHE'S LATE, 1:
WORKING MEN, WORKING WOMEN

He's late; there must be a traffic jam.	She's late; she's probably shopping.
He's still on the phone; he must be closing a deal.	She's still on the phone; she's such a gossip.
He's very thoughtful and deliberate.	She has trouble making up her mind.
His last project turned out well; promote him fast, before someone else gets him.	Her last project turned out well; she's lucky that she had such an easy customer.
He's assertive and a natural leader; he motivates people to get things done.	She's too aggressive and abrasive; her coworkers think she's a bitch.
He went to lunch with the boss; he must be up for promotion.	She went to lunch with the boss; they must be sleeping together.

told that men have families to support (as if women don't). They're told that women don't need more money because, after all, they have husbands—even if they don't. Such comments are anything but neutral. They reveal not merely personal beliefs but beliefs that can translate into illegal and discriminatory actions—actions that unfairly cut into women's pay. They show that the speaker is blind to the reality of the actual, individual worker in front of him and is instead seeing a chimerical idea about how she will behave—an idea that will prevent him from treating her fairly.

And yet such attitudes remain pervasive. No wonder a study of one M.B.A. graduating class showed that women with equivalent résumés and experiences were offered starting salaries that were 9 percent less than their male peers'.[8] Since raises are usually awarded as percentages of salaries, that starting wage gap will *widen* in the years to come.

Invisible . . . or Too Visible?

For many women, everyday discrimination comes in the form of feeling invisible on the job. Their views, recommendations, or ideas are ignored at meetings. Or their successes are attributed to someone else. Or they're refused such minor amenities as office space, administrative support, or pension benefits equal to those of their peers. Consider, for instance, the experiences of one property manager[9] who worked for a midsized California firm in the 1990s. By any objective measure, she was one of her company's most efficient and effective performers: she always met her deadline and budget and had the lowest staff turnover of any manager.

Nevertheless, like so many women, the property manager didn't get credit for her work. "I would take a project up to the point of glory," she said with some resignation, "and they would take it away from me and give it to a man, who would walk out with the flag. That was consistent. One time we took over a new property and I read the bond documents. I kept saying, 'There's something not right here.' " Repeatedly, she was told that she was wrong: The lawyer and the contracts department had gone carefully over the documents, and everything was correct. But she had spotted a bit of information that no one else had noticed. This information released the building from rent control limits and would thus enable her company to charge much higher rents, increasing the property's value.

No one believed her. The property manager pursued the issue through one city department after another. Sure enough, she was right. Her company could indeed charge higher rents. Because of her persistence, the building was worth about a million dollars more. Proud to be vindicated, the property manager delivered the supporting documents to her company, documents that were then stamped by the (male) company attorney.

But at the company Christmas party, her boss publicly thanked the male *attorney*—not the female property manager—for finding the mistake. "It was 'We want to thank him for his diligence for following through on this,' " the property manager said, still angry at the memory. "Not only did I find it, but I had had to convince them that I was right!"

Many male corporate managers, of course, have had the jaw-dropping experience of seeing someone steal credit for their project; they either learn to tout their accomplishments or accept (bitterly or otherwise) that their career has been sidelined. But this was something more. This was because the property manager was working while female. Stereotypically, male corporate attorneys were smart; working women were drudges. The boss quickly (and incorrectly) assigned the million-dollar credit to the person in the "right" category. No matter what she did, the property manager couldn't crack through that super-imposed stereotype. "It was just consistent," she explained. "I really struggled. My compensation was always a tad below everybody else." When put together with a variety of other, similar dismissals, she knew, as many women do, that it was because she was working while female.

For other women, everyday discrimination is the feeling of being *too* visible, too closely watched because no one believes she can succeed. It happens when she's told that she "thinks like a man" and is expected to hear that as a compliment. "I remember going to my first project meeting," said the environmental planner introduced in the previous chapter, who had launched an environmental impact department in a major engineering firm. As she walked into the conference room, she noticed that she was the only woman there. When each of the guys gave his report, lively discussion followed. But "when they came to me there was dead silence," she said. "And it was all eyes on me, kind of staring at me. 'Well, what is she going to say? What can she contribute to this?' It was a real eye-opening experience. I had never expected that at all."

These individual anecdotes would prove nothing—except for the fact that so many women could tell similar stories. Have you felt either invisible, or too visible, on the job, just because you were female? Add that into your wage gap.

Pushed Out . . . or Left Out

Sometimes everyday discrimination reminds women that they're outsiders, excluded from the male power club that governs the workplace. They miss out on chances to advance not because of one man's biases but because the male group thoughtlessly excludes her. That can occur in fairly obvious forms. It's what one female vice president encountered in the early 1990s while running a midsized department at a major East Coast financial services firm. Suddenly her female boss left, and her group was assigned a new executive vice president. "I was the only woman on his management team," the female VP said. She soon found the group untenable. For instance, she explained, "we would be in a staff meeting and he would look for his watch and it wouldn't be on his wrist. And he would say, 'Ah, f——, I left my watch — boy I'm not even gonna tell ya on whose bedtable this watch is, but man, this was a blonde that—' I had no way to respond. It was extremely clear to me that I wouldn't survive under this guy." This woman was facing the same kind of hostile, coarse environment that, elsewhere, has led to more obvious and severe incidents of sexual harassment. She ultimately did leave — at the cost, however, of her six-figure job and her valuable stock options.

By getting out instead of simply trying to endure that hostile environment, she saved herself a lot of heartache, as she learned later from friends who had not left. This particular executive spent a costly year outside the job market, building her family's house and reevaluating her career options. Eventually she landed another six-figure job as the second in command at a major medical nonprofit. But why should she have had to choose between her sanity and her paycheck in the first place — a forced choice that cost her more than $100,000?

Sometimes the message that women aren't welcome is delivered in a manner that's far less obvious — even to the guys themselves. That's what happens when an in-group of male employees socializes with other men but not the women: whether or not they intend to do so, they're excluding their female coworkers from the informal alliances through which things really get done. Exactly that happened to one female doctor. Soon after this woman took a job at a major teaching hospital in 1997, her boss and her boss's boss, she said, "were going to a ball game. They had an extra ticket, and they asked me to ask my husband if he wanted to go, and he did. In retrospect, I now think: I like watching baseball, I could've gone! But I just didn't even think to ask, 'Can I go instead?' " And if she had, she said, they'd probably have felt uncomfortable: they thought they were socializing not with their colleagues but with other guys. The insidiousness of this encounter didn't strike her till much later—when she found out she'd been left behind while men were promoted, as you'll see in a story in the next chapter.

Going to a ball game or a weekly lunch with colleagues is how professional networks are built. Casual socializing, especially over something as neutral as food or sports, builds the camaraderie and trust through which colleagues swap gossip (men call it "information") about projects, opportunities, ideas, promotions, pay, and openings elsewhere. Socializing is how inside information travels, how younger colleagues are taken up and mentored, how alliances are formed. Over time, being left out means being left behind—in real dollars and cents.

Nowhere is that more obvious than in sales, where every minute of face time is another chance to close a deal, learn about a potential client's worries, or build the bond that will lead to the next sale. For most of the 1980s and 1990s, one salesperson said, she had been treated fairly at a small consulting company run by a husband-and-wife team. "They paid me what the market bore, what I was worth, regardless of sex," she explained. "I flourished in the job." And so she expected nothing less. But in 1997, she took a job in Florida selling high-tech consulting services. Every year, her firm hosted "a huge golfing event where you would take your potential clients. I automatically assumed that I was going. [The manager] turned around and said, 'Oh no, it's just the guys.' I couldn't believe it. He said, 'Oh no, it's nothing personal, it's just for guys.' "

That manager knew perfectly well that every time he threw his sales force and their potential clients together, he boosted profits. So this was an astonishing statement, showing that his stereotypes could actually blind him to the bottom line. The saleswoman and her female peers argued with him that no business event could be boys only. "He could not see it. No one had ever challenged him before. And I was furious. I hadn't encountered that kind of blatant bias since the old days." What manager would ignore a chance to help his sales force sell? A manager so mindlessly awash in his stereotypes that he couldn't imagine they were blurring his vision.

Once again, reading stories like this is important because they illustrate what so many women feel on the job but try to ignore, hoping that their colleagues really mean well, despite some occasional slipups. Maybe they do. But when you face a slight like this, it's far from minor. If your boss or colleagues are willing to say things to your face that reveal that you're not seen as a full and equal member of the team, you can be sure that they're overlooking or undervaluing you when you're not around.

Double Standards for Performance, Promotion, and Pay

> I started there [in 1994] at $50,000 and two years later, I left at $55,000. I was the first development officer hired in that college and I was the only woman in that office except for the secretaries. I was the only professional woman. The men— they were making much, much more, double the salary I was making.
>
> —Development director, West Coast

> It's funny, because [my husband and I] started off at the same range of pay and he just completely left me behind. He just went off—his salary just kept going up and up every year and mine just went up incrementally. And I would never ever have reached his.
>
> —Academic program coordinator, mid-Atlantic seaboard

Women often see that they're held to different standards—in their performance reviews, promotions, and paychecks. The double standard is what's happening when a man who drives his team hard is said to get things done, while a woman who drives her team hard is said to be a bitch. It's what happens when men are promoted on potential while women are promoted after they prove themselves. It's what happens when men are given bigger raises because they have families to support—even when the women do, too. Social science research finds it grows from the subterranean presumption that, until proven otherwise, men are competent and women incompetent. In other words, it's everyday discrimination.

It's what happened to Diane Levin, who eventually became a high-performing manager several times in her career. For instance, while a student at one of the top five business degree programs in the country, Levin took a summer job working for a major telecommunications firm. At the summer's end, her manager told her, "You have been the best performer I have ever seen. You are really exceptional in every-thing. But if I put that in there, they would have thought I'm sleeping with you, so I've thought it through and I only put you down as excep-tional in half of these categories." Levin was actually told she was twice as good and yet would be evaluated as doing half as well, since no one would believe that a female could do so well on her own merits. A man with her skills would have been heavily recruited for a higher position; she was, psychologically, pushed out the door. "I was stunned," she said. "I didn't do anything because it was a summer job, and I knew I was not going back there, but—that was awful."

Why was it awful? Because it implied that no woman could perform outstandingly—except in bed. Being cut down to a sexual stereo-type was appalling. By revealing his own biased assumptions, this man-ager had made it clear that, within this company, Levin would most certainly be held back on the job. His company had lost out on a strong performer. Sure, she didn't want the job anyway. But this is how women's expectations are cut down to size: one insult at a time.

Such men may not believe they are doing anything wrong. They simply haven't corrected for the fact that their minds swiftly fill in the culturally implicit assumption that men will be competent, and women will not. That's why managers will promote a man for showing promise, but will wait for evidence before promoting a woman. "It took us longer to become vice presidents," said one financial executive at a major New England bank about her tenure during the late 1990s. "It was pretty clear the bar was higher for us. We needed to be better longer." One middle manager in a large service corporation told a story about a young man who had been promoted too quickly to run a forty-person office. "To go from being a project manager to an office manager of such a large office was a *huge* leap," she explained. His leapfrog promotion came not because of any real indications that he had the skills but because, in his bosses' minds, he fit the stereotype of the young man who makes good. "It was because he was a tall, good-looking guy; it's like, let's bet on the rising star. He failed, miserably. He was just a *total failure*."

The "rising star" stereotype had turned out to be wrong—just as wrong as the stereotype that only a woman who was sleeping with her manager would get outstanding performance reviews. The corollary was that women were scrutinized more closely than men. Said the middle manager, "Women had to prove our way first. I think that's true in every organization. [The attitude toward promoting men is] 'Let's just do it, he's really great, he's one of us.' But women always have to show their competence before they'll get compensated." Not only male managers but also female managers can be guilty of this. Men are put on the fast track. Women are put on the pink track.

What's at work here is the same biased "tap on the shoulder" promotion method, that "gut instinct" about a candidate's promise, that in chapter 5 we saw turned out to be so costly at Home Depot, at Publix Super Markets, and so on. Gut instinct isn't evil. But it has to be carefully scrutinized, or it's run by bias. And whether it reveals itself in offhand comments about promoting women "if they're qualified," or whether it reveals itself in statistics showing that men are promoted faster and far more often than women, it results in women being routinely held back and underpaid.

Over time, all these small delays and gaps in a woman's career add up. Maybe she gets a lower performance rating because her supervisor is trying to avoid the appearance of favoritism, or his boss's disbelief. Or she's hired at a slightly lower rank and salary because it's assumed that she has less background (in holding a hammer, carrying out garbage, or understanding insurance) than all men are thought to have. Or she's left out of the socializing by which men learn the ropes and make the connections that help them get ahead. Or she gets promoted more slowly because she doesn't quite have the rising star "look" (tall, white, male, confident) that can trigger managers' stereotypical trust.

Nowhere along this pink track, this career-long chain of small delays, are these slights egregious enough to trigger a lawsuit. Yet their costly effects are even acknowledged by the federal government and some business leaders.[10] Over time, each delay compounds, with interest. If she's a few cents behind at the beginning, she's many dollars—even a million dollars—behind by the end.

One accounting clerk, based at a small manufacturing firm in Tucson, said that when she looked at her firm's salaries in the course of her job, "I can see the differences just because it's a woman." At every rank within the company, women were paid significantly less. "Even in the yearly raises, for some reason. The yearly raises for the men are always higher than what they are for the women. In our sales department there is one woman salesperson versus five males. Many of these men have been with the company less time. When the raises come out, hers is invariably less than the men's. They are earning more than she is. I am sure she is happy because she is making a good salary. But if she were aware of the difference!"

Women's careers are affected by discrimination every day. These effects accumulate. The paycheck losses accumulate, too. Two short stories can illustrate how this below-the-lawsuit discrimination plays out over years for women—subtracting thousands upon thousands of dollars over a lifetime. (For more such stories, please go to www .wageproject.org.) Every woman's story will be a little different than every other story. No two workplaces hold women back in quite the same way. But as you read these stories, consider: Has your work life ever included roadblocks or incidents at all like these? Did they hurt your pay—and if so, by how much? If you look back, can you see that, since then, your advancement has fallen behind that of men you thought were your peers?

Tale of a Pink Paycheck, 1: If I Were a Carpenter

Back in 1972, a young woman named B. J. Wilkinson decided that, more than anything, she wanted to become a carpenter. With women breaking into every profession, and barriers falling left and right, anything seemed possible. B.J. worked on a Florida construction site for awhile and then took a break to get married and have children. Her marriage fell apart. After she'd moved up to New Hampshire, she went back to woodworking; she had fallen in love with the work. She got some wonderful experience in custom woodworking shops, building elegant craft furniture and boxes under the eyes of a master craftsman. Although she was earning only $11.50 per hour, she became so skilled that she was drawing up detailed, highly accurate plans and overseeing the other apprentice woodworkers. But her employer had more talent than business savvy. He ran out of orders, and had to lay off the entire staff.

As the sole support of three boys, Wilkinson needed a steady job immediately. A local wooden box manufacturer hired her at $7 per hour, drawing up plans that had to be accurate to within 1/64 of an inch. Soon after, the manufacturer hired a young man who had less than half her experience for $12 per hour. Imagine what that meant to her. Since she was caring for herself and three sons on $14,500 a year, his additional $10,000 was way off the charts. "I didn't waltz in there and scream and yell," Wilkinson said. "I got very upset. I did. But at the time I still had three children, single mother. I felt there was not a whole lot I could do about it other than put up with it. I had to feed my kids."

For the next two years, Wilkinson steadily worked her way up at this new company. "I was in charge of doing all the samples, the prototypes, working out all the processes, how it was going to be run through the shop, adjusting the blueprints for it, adjusting the process to make sure it would go through efficiently and actually work," she explained. Out of sixty employees, she was one of only five in charge of precision work. She earned small raises along the way, until she finally reached $11.50 an hour again. She had not, however, caught up with her peers. The male managers were always making "a couple of dollars an hour" more than she was. They were on salary, which meant they got the health benefits that she desperately needed for her family and the pension contributions that she knew she needed but couldn't imagine how to get. Hers was a wage gap of roughly 20 to 30 percent.

Wilkinson never confronted management about the inequity. One of her female colleagues did. "The woman that ran the spray department, where they put all the finish on everything, would go round and round and round with the plant manager about it," she said. "His story for why this was okay was: The guys were supporting families." Of course, so was the woodworker, which was why she wasn't prepared to argue about her pay—until she was given an assistant.

"This is what I was told, that this guy was my assistant," Wilkinson said. But he certainly didn't act like one. "First day there, I went in to have him do some work for me, to help me out on a project. His comment was 'I don't think a salaried employee is going to be working for an hourly employee.' " B.J. was livid. She walked into the manager's office and confronted him. Why was she still hourly when her "assistant" was salaried—and making more than she was, to boot? "That was it. I was leaving. I had enough." Her manager tried to talk her out of it. Too late: Wilkinson moved across the state and married the man she'd been seeing on weekends. When she told this part of the story, her husband yelled from another room, "I was just an excuse to quit!" She laughed.

There, in 2000, Wilkinson found a job at a small firm that made high-end children's furniture. "I took in my résumé with photographs," she explained, "and two letters of recommendation from [both previous employers] that recommended me highly. They had some good stuff to say, which was nice. And still, with that, I started out at $7 an hour." It was an insulting wage, considering her advanced experience. But she was told, "That's what they start everyone at, because even with good résumés and yada yada yada, they can't always trust that the information is accurate, so they want to have a trial period." Six months later, a 23-year-old man was hired at $10 per hour. When Wilkinson objected, she was brought up to his hourly wage, or roughly $20,800 per year, no benefits.

"Basically, I knew more than my boss did," B.J. said cheerfully. "He would pick my brain and have me teach him. He was the shop supervisor, and he was on salary, making $40,000 a year." Wilkinson laughed when asked if she was making the same as her peers. By 2002, she was making $12 per hour with no benefits, or $24,960 per year—far below where she should have started, for a wage gap of nearly (if you add in benefits) 50 percent. By then she was one of the top three shop managers, responsible for training and overseeing most of production.

Why did Wilkinson stay? "I'm stubborn," she explained. "I stayed in there and pushed." By 2003, her three sons were out on their own, so she didn't have to worry about supporting them. Her husband had a good government job, so she didn't worry about health insurance. She loved the work, and there wasn't anything else like it in town. So she just kept doing the best she could—including figuring out a low-cost way to buy a computer-controlled router for the company, which brought down production costs and increased speed and accuracy.

That computer-controlled router was a boon. For ratcheting up the company's profits, Wilkinson was rewarded with an official promotion, her own office, and a raise—to $30,000 a year—in 2003. She managed ten out of the company's thirty-five employees, the computer-controlled router, and certain areas of production. Often, when her two fellow supervisors were gone, she ran the entire plant. By then her former supervisor, now peer—the boss she had trained in her advanced techniques when she had first joined the company—was making $45,000. It had taken Wilkinson four years at the company to make two thirds of what was made by the man she had once tutored.

B.J. had a cheerful attitude and a complete lack of resentment. "I'm so used to settling for what I could get," Wilkinson explained. "Whether it's what rightfully I should have or not—I guess I haven't really thought that way." But while her upbeat attitude was surely good for her emotional health, her pink paycheck had been bad for her wallet. The woodworker was asked to sit down and figure out what, had she been a man, she would have made over those thirty years. She was shocked when she added it up—and decided that she would have made another $500,000. That estimate seemed conservative. But whether she lost $500,000 or $750,000 over her lifetime, it was money she could ill afford to miss. That half-million-plus would have been immensely useful in those scrimping years when she was raising her kids. And it will be keenly missed when she retires.

But there's good news to this story. After facing up to her losses, B.J. decided to take control of her work life. Keep her story in mind. In chapter 12, Women Working from the Inside Up, you'll learn how she stood up for herself—with the goal of getting even.

Tale of a Pink Paycheck, 2:
You Can't Get There from Here

In 1983, one hardworking woman was in her early thirties—and thought she had it made. Although she had only an associate's degree, she had worked her way up from a childhood of poverty into a state job.

Sure, it was just part-time bus driving, and sure, she was treated badly, but everyone knows the good part of working for the government: it takes a lot to be fired. Hunger was in the past. Her future was secure.

Our bus driver was ambitious, so she worked a split shift (morning and evening routes), went to school in between, earned her bachelor's degree, and moved inside. By 1986, she was making $18,000 a year as the lowest-grade clerk-typist. "They were unionized employees, but the bottom of the barrel," she said, adding proudly, "Let's see how fast I moved. Thirteen months later I was an executive." Quickly she had seen that the department ran on connections, so she made plenty. "I really should have run for office. They used to call me the mayor of [headquarters]. 'Hi, Mark, how are you!' I played *their* game. And I was very good at playing it." She networked until she became the deputy general manager's right-hand executive assistant, which was a management position. By 1989, she was making $28,000, with good benefits.

But the transportation manager wanted a promotion that recognized her skills and real responsibilities. Told that there wasn't much further she could go in her position, she applied for and landed a job in human resources at $31,000 per year. Then she got a slap in the face. The man who replaced her at her previous job was called a "manager" and paid $56,000 — a much higher rank and double her salary for doing the same work. She was furious.

But don't get mad, get even, right? The transportation manager swallowed her rage and buckled down. By 1998, she was an operations manager, running a small department and making $53,000. She was still not quite even with the $56,000 she *should* have been making in 1989. Nor was she even with the men who worked in similar positions, all of whom were making between $6,000 and $8,000 more than she was. When she asked for a promotion, her boss recommended that she get more education. One month later, she was in night school pursuing her M.P.A., master's of public administration.

As she closed in on her degree, she kept asking for the promotion and raise — but was told that she still didn't meet the requirements, which kept changing. When she finished school in the fall of 2002, she graduated first in her class. So she asked again for the raise. "I went in and said, 'I've done what you want,' " she said. " 'I want to see what the organization is going to pay me back now for this effort I've made on Saturdays, and nights, and weekends, spending thirty-five grand to get an education."

Her boss's answer: Budget crisis. No money. Sorry.

The transportation manager was insulted but practical. With only five more years before she could take her retirement, she needed a higher salary to ensure a higher pension. "I didn't want to leave that position, I love operations," she said. But with retirement nearing, "I had to go where the money is." She found a job that sported a lower title but paid $63,000 per year.

But remember what had happened to her in 1989? She had left a post—and the man who replaced her was given a much higher title and salary. In 2002, she had déjà vu all over again. Her $56,000 managerial job—in a department where she'd been told there was no money available for a raise—was renamed deputy chief of administration. As she related who had gotten the job, she was so angry that she sputtered, unable even to complete her sentences. "White male, fifty some-odd, $74,800. Okay!?! I speak to the new director: 'This is bullshit. You and I both know that's my effin' job.' I was wild."

By that time, she had long been happily remarried to a man with a higher-level job in the same transportation department. "You know, men have said to me over the years, 'What are you worried about? You're going to have [your husband's] pension,'" she said. "To which I say, 'If [he] drops dead, what do you think I'm going to do, eat cat food?' I have to find a way to survive and a way to take care of myself. This isn't about him. This is about me and my career."

In 2002, the transportation manager was agonizing about whether to bring a lawsuit. On the one hand, employment lawyers told her that the facts and records were clearly on her side. On the other hand, as she explained, "Do I take the chance with forty-four months left to go [before retirement], to sue the organization? Because we all know what's going to happen if I do! I'm not a coward. But I'm not crazy either. I'm not sure whether I have the strength, the inclination to take this on. Some days I have all the strength in the world, and say, I'm going to go after those bastards. And other days I say, do your time, and go after them some other way."

There should have been a third choice. She should have been paid and promoted fairly. The transportation manager is a lesson in what happens when women aren't paid fairly early on. If we start clocking her losses only at her second confrontation with unfair treatment—when her replacement was paid $19,000 more than she had been, for the same job—she lost $250,000 over the rest of her career. (That figure assumes that, at age 52, she would continue to work until age 65, earning that additional $19,000 for another thirteen years. Even if she did retire from her government job and went to work elsewhere, any new salary negotiations would take place from that base.)

Sure, a quarter-million dollars is a lot of money. But in 1990, the 40-year-old transportation manager had left her then job—only to have her replacement get paid $56,000 for what she had done for half that amount. If, in *that* job, she had been paid as much her replacement— and then earned that additional $28,000 a year for the next twenty-five years of her working life—she would have made an additional $700,000 throughout her career. And that's without counting any additional benefits or retirement pay. Nor does it count the probability that all her incremental raises over the next twenty-five years would have been larger, based as they were on a larger base salary.

But $700,000 in lifetime losses is a whopping amount for an energetic woman who has worked her way up from childhood poverty—a loss she endured just because she was working while female.

CHAPTER 9

Working While Mother:
The Mommy Penalty

A little over four years ago, my wife, Cheryl, and I announced to the world, through our family and friends, that we were expecting our first child. It was truly one of the proudest moments of our lives. Included in that list of friends was my wife's employer. However, within a week of the "good news," she was terminated from her employment because her boss feared that she might not return from maternity leave.

—Samuel E. Joyner, *Tulsa Law Journal*, Spring 2001 [1]

One Virginia employer fired a woman after she gave birth, reasoning that "she was no longer dependable since she had delivered a child; that [her] place was at home with her child; that babies get sick sometimes and [she] would have to miss work to care for her child; and that [the employer] needed someone more dependable."

—*Bailey v. Scott-Gallaher, Inc.*, 253 Va. 121 (Sup. Ct. 1997) [2]

For the past ten years, public discussion about working women's careers has been shorthanded into a single phrase: the "mommy track." Women—especially those in high-end careers—are said to "choose" to drop out rather than run themselves to death on the gerbil wheel of corporate advancement. They'd rather oversee homework than head count. They'd rather take their children to piano lessons than take a meeting. This simplistic, outdated explanation is a media favorite, making it into the influential *New York Times Magazine* twice in recent years: once in 1998 and again (this time on its cover) in 2003.[3] But is this how women themselves see the "mommy track"?

Perhaps some do—especially those with husbands so wealthy that, even if the marriage is one of the 49 percent that ends in divorce, the woman and her child are guaranteed a good cushion for years to come. But most of the women I've spoken to discovered that they had been "mommy-tracked" without being asked. When they got pregnant or had a child, these women found they were no longer considered for promotion—because, without asking, their managers automatically assumed that the new moms would soon be working part-time, would refuse to travel overnight, or would no longer show up reliably at important meetings. Or when these women returned from maternity leave, they discovered that they were kept off important (read: promotion-track) projects, since managers assumed their "work-family conflict" would slow them down. And if they did ask to work part-time for a while, their salaries and career possibilities were penalized far out of proportion to the time they put into their kids. When they returned to full-time work, their salaries were lower than when they'd left.

Getting Even has noted before how mothers get held back unfairly. In addition to looking at winning lawsuits about other basic forms of sex discrimination—such as refusal to hire or unequal pay—chapter 5, ("Plain Old Discrimination") included examples of women who had sued and won court awards or settlements after charging that they had been shunted aside, demoted, or fired when employers realized they were pregnant, a complaint that EEOC and plaintiff bias lawyers say has been increasing rapidly in the early years of the twenty-first century. Chapter 7, "Women's Work," mentioned a San Francisco piledriver who was late two days in a row because her child's school required her to show up in person for registration—and whose brief absence was followed by harsh scrutiny and eventually the loss of her job. Two mornings of showing up late had triggered her coworkers' twin stereotypes about mothers: on the one hand, that mothers should be home with the kids; and on the other, that mothers were useless and unreliable on the job.

By examining the experiences of women who were *not* willing to go to court, this chapter looks more squarely at how the "mommy track" results from employers' mother stereotypes—stereotypes that result in unfair, punitive, and, yes, costly discrimination against working moms. Do women "choose" the mommy track? Maybe some would, if offered the choice. But too often, women's employers make the choice about their work and career options *for* them—without consulting the women themselves, and certainly without getting their consent. As you'll see in the stories below, and as you saw in the lawsuits in chapter 5, women's only choices lie in how they react.

As you read these stories, keep in mind—as you did while reading the previous chapter—that each woman's story will be a little bit different than yours. But while your experience may not have been the same, it may have been *similar*. That's the purpose of this chapter: to prompt you to ask yourself whether anything similar has happened to you or women you know. Have you ever suspected that you were being dismissed, overlooked, or treated less seriously just because you were a mother—and because your boss and colleagues assumed (despite the evidence of your successful, productive efforts) that mothers always work with half their brain preoccupied with worries about their children? Be honest. Don't make excuses for your bosses, or worry that you may have brought it on yourself. If you've been treated unfairly, you won't ever be able to fix it unless you face it. Ask yourself: Has anything like this ever happened to me?

Consider, for instance, what happened to the fast-rising doctor you met in chapter 8, whose boss and colleagues had invited not her but her *husband* to come with them to a baseball game—an incident whose implications she didn't see until later. Like so many young professionals, this doctor had met her husband while they were in training together. After the pair finished their residencies at a top teaching hospital, the young doctor was hired to create and launch a new service there, while her husband took up a postdoctoral research fellowship. That made her the family's breadwinner.

This young doctor's specialty is highly advanced, desperately needed, and very expensive; there are few qualified others in her field. After six years in her job, she realized, as she put it, "that to be recognized and accepted and valued I needed to be promoted." She asked her division chief about it. She paraphrased his response this way: "He said, 'Oh well, yeah, it looks like you could be promoted. I just never came and talked to you because we thought that you wouldn't be staying around, you might want to be part-time because you're married and you have children.' " This particular doctor is a reserved, quiet woman; I had to lean in to hear her. Her voice was trembling with anger. "I just was—stunned."

This doctor's division chief had apparently drawn his conclusions based on his *ideas* about mothers, not on anything that she, as an individual worker, had either said or done. As it happened, she was more productive than her fellow doctors. Since she had been recruited to launch her service, the group's patients (and its income) had tripled. She was bringing in one fifth of the six-person department's revenues, seeing more patients than anyone else there, and overseeing all the medical students who were rotating through her life-or-death specialty. Between teaching, research, and patient care, her responsibilities had grown so grueling that at one point she asked her boss to lighten her clinical obligations and bring in some help. He responded, she said, by saying "that I should cut back to half-time and get a pay cut."

Thinking back on it in late 2003, she was furious. Her boss hadn't recognized either her productivity or her well-founded concern for her patients' well-being, given her increasing work crush. Instead of looking at her and seeing a productive employee or a breadwinner, he had seen a mommy who just couldn't juggle work and family. Without asking, he had assumed that she would do what married moms are supposed to do: follow her husband to the ends of the earth, working part-time so she could stay home with the kids. "If I had been male, with a wife who was a postdoc, and a two-year-old at home," she said with that quiet resentment, "I don't think anyone would have assumed that, because I wanted fewer clinical obligations, I wanted to be part-time and that I didn't really care about being promoted." Had she been a man, her boss would have assumed that (s)he was the family breadwinner and therefore that (s)he was ambitious and needed more money—and would have suggested the promotion three or four years earlier. She had been financially mommy-tracked—that is, financially penalized—without her consent.

Being financially mommy-tracked meant that the specialist had been cheated out of three or more years' increased salary. Men in her position, she later found, were usually promoted (with a raise) after two or three years on the job. She had waited six—and would now have to wait another six months to a year for her official review to be completed before she got her raise. "What I make now is about $110,000 a year," she said. After checking to see what doctors in comparable positions made, she concluded that "to be fair, it should be at least $130,000." In just a few years, the specialist had lost $60,000 (plus pension accruals) because she was working while mother. And with that bite into her salary early in her career, her raises and promotions for her next thirty years would be forever be handicapped, based on that early lag and therefore significantly behind her male peers'.

The specialist's experience had shocked her because she had genuinely believed that women were recognized and rewarded fairly. She took it for granted that sex discrimination had been beaten decades ago.

And, probably, so did her division chief. If the specialist had suggested that her boss had discriminated against her based on sex, he'd almost surely be appalled and indignant. Like many male managers, he probably believed himself to be open-minded and even-handed, fairly evaluating every doctor without considering sex. It would never have occurred to him that paying a female parent less than he would have paid a male parent, based on nothing but his own unconfirmed beliefs, would be breaking the law.

But, as law professor Joan Williams has noted, cluelessness is not a legal defense. Someone who doesn't realize he's driving a hundred miles an hour will get a ticket, because—intentionally or not—he's still endangering others. He was wrong. She was penalized. Has anything like that ever happened to you?

Just Say the Words: The Mommy Penalty and the Daddy Bonus

> Two years ago, Marylyn Pickler became part of an Arizona employment trend: She got fired for being pregnant, according to federal court records. . . . Complaints for discrimination against child-carrying women statewide have increased 182 percent in the past decade, dramatically outpacing a 27 percent rise nationally.
>
> —*The Arizona Republic*, January 24, 2003[4]

> I was going to put you in charge of the office, but look at you now.
>
> —Employer to pregnant worker,
> cited in *Moore v. Alabama State University*, 1997

> When I returned from maternity leave, I was given the work of a paralegal and I wanted to say, "Look, I had a baby, not a lobotomy."
>
> —Lawyer, large corporate firm, United States[5]

It doesn't take much to push a woman into the highly charged and less respected category of "mother." Court cases show that discrimination against a pregnant woman can start even before she shows any physical signs of pregnancy. All a woman has to do is tell her boss that she's *going* to have a baby and suddenly her work can change dramatically, as we saw in chapter 5. For instance, when Bean Lumber Company—whose company policy was to send home anyone more than four months into her pregnancy—found out that Ginger Rowland was pregnant, it not only denied her a promised promotion; it fired her.[6] Actually, women who mention they're pregnant can lose a job before they even get a boss. That's what happened to a former clothing clerk who interviewed to be rehired at a Wal-Mart store in Arizona. "Come back after you've had your baby," Jamey Stearn said she was told.

According to law professor Joan Williams, the mother stereotype gets triggered at three points in a woman's parental life. The first is when she tells her boss or others at work that she's pregnant. Her body soon becomes a constant reminder, triggering coworkers to stereotype her every move. What's more visibly and exaggeratedly female than that swollen belly (or, in a later phase, the expressed milk stored in the office fridge)? Pregnancy and nursing can both dramatically amplify otherwise latent stereotypes of women as overly emotional and irrational, arbitrary and whimsical, ruled by their (sexual) bodies rather than their minds. No wonder one study of female managers found that their performance ratings "plummeted" after their pregnancies started to show.[7] And when a manager's performance ratings drop, so do her bonuses, raises, and promotions—which means that simply being visibly pregnant is costing her in real dollars and cents. "[M]ost women, like my wife, have enough stress in their lives just with being pregnant, so after being fired, they do not challenge an employer by filing a complaint with the EEOC," wrote law professor Samuel Joyner after his wife lost her job after letting it be known that she was pregnant.[8]

The second trigger moment for the mother stereotype comes when a woman returns from maternity leave. In chapters 5 and 8, there are stories in which women returned from maternity leave—only to find that, while they were out, they were laid off or their jobs were reorganized out of existence. That's illegal. Some women are so outraged that they sue. Remember, for instance, the state cop who took her employer to court because pregnant officers had been sidelined for no good reason. She and her fellow officers won that lawsuit. But most new mothers don't have the time, energy, or willingness to go into court, get a reputation as a troublemaker, and perhaps jeopardize their jobs.

The third moment comes when a mother asks for any accommodation, however temporary or slight, for her family responsibilities. That accommodation can be flextime, telecommuting, a temporary part-time schedule, or just two days of coming to work an hour late because, as happened to the journeywoman piledriver, the school required a parent's presence. Even if women aren't fired, they're sidelined and financially penalized far out of proportion to their time out.

Why? Because the American stereotype of mothering is left over from the 1950s: unlike a father, a mother is someone who is available to respond to her child at any moment of the day or night. If being a mom is a twenty-four-hour-a-day job and being a *worker* involves a full-time commitment to a job, too, the two roles are mutually exclusive. The insurance firm The Hartford, Inc., based in Connecticut, was sued when one manager said he wouldn't consider an employee for a promotion because, as he put it, "women are not good planners, especially women with kids," adding that women cannot be both good mothers and good workers, since "I don't see how you can do either job well."[9] A comment like that is not just discriminatory; it reveals attitudes and behaviors that may be illegal and actionable. The Hartford settled the lawsuit.

But that manager's crude statement is useful, because it perfectly captures the double bind conveyed by the phrase "working mother." This label implies that if a worker so much as *thinks* about anything but the production line or the bottom line, he (yes, he) will be forever rendered useless on the job. A lawyer might be able to juggle the demands of many complex cases in various stages of research and negotiation, or a grocery manager might be able to juggle dozens of delivery deadlines and worker schedules—but should she have so much as a fleeting thought about a pediatrician's appointment, her on-the-job reliability will evaporate. In this way, the phrase "working mother" is heard as something similar to "deadbeat dad": both phrases suggest people who are not fulfilling their "God-given responsibilities." Such stereotypes click into place invisibly, the way carbon monoxide can poison a room without anyone noticing. And they hold back women's paychecks.

An entirely different stereotype kicks in for working fathers. A father at his desk is a serious, hardworking provider, a go-getter, a responsible breadwinner, a family man, a reliable guy. If he also tries to "help out" at home, he's exceptional and ought to be rewarded. Take the case of Illinois governor Rod Blagojevich, who, during a budget crisis in the fall of 2003, flew home every night (from Springfield, the state capital, to Chicago) to kiss his kids good night—on the taxpayers' tab. He took a little flak, but he didn't face anything like the vituperation spewed at Massachusetts Lieutenant Governor Jane Swift two years earlier, when she flew home across the state to see a sick child. Swift was eviscerated; Blagojevich was a good guy. "I wanted to go home and see my seven-year-old and kiss my baby," Blagojevich was quoted as saying. "If you're

HE'S LATE/SHE'S LATE, 2:
WORKING DADS AND WORKING MOMS

He just had a baby; give him that big project, since he'll be working harder now that he has to support a family.	She just had a baby; don't give her that big project, she won't be able to travel or even get here on time anymore.
He's late; he must have had a breakfast meeting.	She's late; she must have child care problems.
He stays late every night; he's really dedicated.	She stays late every night; what a heartless mother.
His performance is down; he must be helping his wife out with that colicky baby. He'll be back to normal in a few months.	Her performance is down; women are useless once they have kids, always putting their families before work.
He just had a baby; give him that raise, he's really going to need it.	She just had a baby; wait on that promotion offer, since she'll want to go part-time soon.

asking me if I'm guilty of that, I plead guilty. And I did it and that's what I'll continue to do." Can you imagine a woman saying such a thing and getting away with it? Chicago columnist Cindy Richards tried:

> [W]hen a man announced with chin-jutting bravado that he wants to spend time with his kids, it's considered endearing. "See, honey, isn't it great that he wants to kiss his kids? I wish more men understood that kids need to see more of their dads."
>
> When a woman does it, she is considered to be less than committed to her job. "See, I told you we shouldn't have hired a woman in her child-bearing years. She might not have had kids when she started, but she does now, and we're lucky to keep her in the office 40 hours a week." . . .

I can only wonder whether the treatment would have been rougher if you were, say, Gov. Rhonda Blagojevich. Had you been a female governor choosing to cuddle up to her children rather than some legislator, I suspect we would have heard more outrage. . . . "Gov. Mom not on the job." To be followed quickly by "Gov. Mom must make choices." And the final blow: "Gov. Mom heads home, should stay there."[10]

Whether women can see it happening or not, those clashing stereotypes (working mother = undependable, working father = go-getter) show up in the paycheck. Among full-time workers, a GAO study found that, for working fathers, each child *increases* earnings about 2.1 percent, while for working mothers, each child *subtracts* 2.5 percent from earnings.[11] That's stereotyping where it hurts.

Working While Mother: Performance, Pay, and Promotion

In the last chapter, we saw that, simply because they are working while female, women are held to different (read: double) standards to get raises and recognition for top performance. When the mother stereotype *also* clicks into the boss's mind, women suddenly have that much more to overcome—and that much less likelihood of getting paid fairly.

Consider, for instance, the property manager whose story appeared in the last chapter. She was ignored when she announced that she had found an error in some bond documents that allowed her company to charge higher rents for a newly acquired property—but once she had proven her case, complete with letters from city hall, the company's (male) lawyer got all the credit. Being denied recognition means being denied promotion and fair pay.

Women like the property manager know that their paychecks are smaller because they are both working while female *and* working while mother. The property manager was a single mother raising her three kids on her own. She had to grit her teeth when, she felt, her firm's owners tested her loyalty to see whether she was a mother or a worker (as if the two could not be combined). "I worked an hour and ten minutes from home," she said. "They would choose four o'clock to talk with me, you know, 'Come into my office.' Always at the end of the day, when I had to get home to my family. I wouldn't get home until seven or seven-thirty P.M. It would be like a test: 'Are you going to choose your family or are you going to choose me?' "

The property manager was quite certain that her wages were less than those of the men around her. "I'm very good," she said. "If I wasn't very good I would not have been employed. I was one of the best in the firm." And yet her male peers "always made more money, at least ten percent more." Routinely, she was ordered to give bonuses and raises to the men who worked for her because, as she was told about each of them, " 'He has to support a family and so we're going to have to pay him more money.' " She did too. They knew it. Had she been male, (s)he would have gotten that daddy bonus herself.

Apparently, her boss couldn't reconcile the combination of her real talents with her family responsibilities. In his mind, women could do one or the other: work *or* raise a family. "I knew it was prejudicial," she said, with a combination of resignation and bitterness, "but I wanted to stay employed." Her paycheck (and her kids' lives) suffered just because she was Working While Mother.

Has a similar indignity ever happened to you? If it has, you're almost certainly earning less than what's fair.

Some high-performing and high-earning women, faced with a series of such insulting situations, seethe so much that they do "choose" to jump ship—because they can afford to. That's what one health company executive did. "Ask anyone: if you need something done, give it to a busy person," she said, still angry that her situation had been so irritating that she felt she had to leave to save her sanity. "The busiest people get things done. So why not give it to a working mother! I loved working. But I got tired of seeing deadbeat guys getting promoted while I wasn't, because I was willing to take on extra responsibilities but I wanted flexibility in my schedule. Like other highly productive women, I was condescended to. I just did not want to put up with that anymore. I needed to be respected more. It's not worth it to me, good-bye!"

Few women can afford to parachute out of the workforce, as she did. But many mothers will instantly understand how that health executive felt. Stories of similar indignities are scattered throughout this book. In chapter 5, we saw a pregnant cop was denied overtime pay and the use of her official vehicle simply because she *would* be having a child; she sued, and won. At Rent-A-Center, once managers found out women were pregnant, they routinely forced them to go out on immediate leave and then ended their jobs; the EEOC won a class action settlement on their behalf. In chapter 8, the woodworker was supporting two kids when she routinely saw less qualified men paid as much as twice her wages and felt she couldn't challenge that unfairness precisely because she had to keep a roof over her sons' heads. And in that same chapter, the transportation manager was supporting two children when she left a job with a salary of $28,000—only to see her male replacement paid twice as much, $56,000, an inequity she felt she would do better simply to ignore than challenge. All those actions were equally unfair. But they happen nevertheless.

Until now, our society has tackled these issues as questions of "work family" balance, as if women were making personal choices to be underpaid in order to be happy. But women who are now hitting the workforce know that that's not so, and they're outraged at getting shunted aside just because they have a child at home. An earlier generation of women, who were just entering the workforce, pushed the discussion of equality as far as they could. Fixing this illegal treatment of mothers as lesser workers is an essential part of getting women even.

It's essential—because all these women needed every penny they could bring home. Surely their bosses did not intend to force families to forgo music lessons, to get by on rice and beans instead of roast beef, or to skip contributing to Mom's retirement account in order to pay for braces. Those employers' stereotypes probably clicked in without reflection. And as we'll see in the next section of this book, that's the problem: the failure to examine and flush out outdated stereotypes. Until we make sure that "working mother" is no longer heard as a synonym for "frazzled" and "unreliable," hardworking mothers (and their children) will continue to pay the price.[12] And the wage gap will continue.

Tale of a Mommy-Pink Paycheck: "Buy Yourself Something Nice"

Over and over, the women in this book said that their field hadn't seen much progress for women—unlike law. More women than men enter law schools; women and men enter major law firms in equal numbers. As a result, many women who aren't attorneys see law as the shining example, the perfect model, the occupation that has fully embraced gender equality. But many female lawyers say that equality exists only until they get pregnant—at which point they're set back by Working While Mother.

"Studies involving thousands of lawyers have found that men are at least twice as likely as similarly qualified women to obtain partnership," according to a 2002 American Bar Association report. Full-time female lawyers earn 76 cents for each full-time male lawyer's dollar—no worse, but no better, than the overall wage gap. Like academia, law has a tightly timed (almost medievally tight) up-or-out system for young professionals. Newly hired associates work until midnight and through the weekends for the first few years while earning a regular paycheck, often with a year-end bonus. By year seven, they've either been promoted to "partner"—which means earning a salary *and* taking home a percentage of the year's profits—or they're no longer employed. Often, the standards for making partner are subjective and somewhat mysterious. And having a child doesn't help.

Unable or unwilling to work around the clock after having a child, many female attorneys step off the seven-year track to partner and step down to part-time status. Or they take less demanding and lower-paying jobs in government, nonprofits, or smaller firms or as in-house corporate counsel. Some pundits insist that these women "choose" the lower-paying positions because they're more humane and sensible than men, too smart to make their whole lives revolve around the firm. But are those choices freely made—or would these women have preferred another option? Either way, women are losing money—just because they are women.

In 1989, one woman—call her "Mary"—graduated in the top 25 percent of her law school class. Discrimination was, she believed, a thing of the past. "I just thought that we were done with all that," Mary said. "This was the 1990s, not the 1950s! I had all the same expectations as any of my male counterparts." And for her first few years at work, nothing ruffled that belief. In her first job, she earned $66,000 per year (exactly what was earned by the other two newly hired associates) at a top corporate law firm in a major city. She worked until 1:00 A.M., earned stellar reviews, saw her salary increasing steadily each year—and assumed that, in a few years, she would be promoted to partner, and therefore paid both a higher annual salary and a percentage of the firm's annual profits.

But in 1993, Mary had her first child. She asked for a part-time schedule, assuming that it would take her a little longer to make partner, which would be only fair. "Part-time" in a law firm can be a somewhat theoretical concept: although she made only 75 percent of her full-time salary, she still went into the office five days a week and worked from home in the evenings. Then she found herself pregnant again.

That summer she had her first less-than-pristine review. "I was told," Mary said, 'You're doing great, but you're up against a roadblock by having another child. Having another baby is really going to hurt you.' " Mary was shocked to hear something so clearly illegal expressed so openly. "I wanted to say, 'Can you speak into the microphone? Your employment lawyers would be having heart attacks if they heard you say that!' " Her employers were smart enough never to be so forthright again. But when Mary came back from her second maternity leave, the chill was unmistakable. Her assignments were fewer, and she was no longer given complex and specialized work for which the firm could bill clients large numbers of hours at high rates, as she had before. "One partner said outright, 'I won't work with you anymore, because you're not here 24/7,' " she said. "It was very, very, very difficult."

It's not that her performance had lapsed. She never missed a deadline. "I used to take my laptop home every single night. When the kids went to bed, I would sit and do my work until eleven o'clock. I mean, I was very conscientious. I would never leave anything undone, because that's my nature."

The following year, she was told that she would not make partner and would have to leave.

Mary had been a high achiever and hard worker all her life. This first rejection stunned her. "I was pretty distraught, I have to tell you," she said. She decided to make a dramatic change and move to a resort town that was a vacation spot for the wealthy, hoping that the improved quality of life would make up for her lost paycheck. There she found a job in a small firm run by two older men. She and another lawyer—Bob, who'd gone to law school midlife and had lots of local connections but very little legal experience—were both hired at $75,000 per year.

The lifestyle change was indeed satisfying. The resort town was beautiful; the partners left the office promptly at five o'clock; Mary could be home in five minutes; and her specialty—real estate—was in great demand during the 1990s boom, as multimillion-dollar houses were bought and sold. When Mary had her next child, she asked once again for a part-time schedule and was given a three-quarters salary for what quickly turned into full-time work. One year later, Bob was made partner. Mary was not.

Mary was livid. That year, she'd had more billable hours (and therefore made more money for the firm) than Bob or either of the partners. Nevertheless, the two senior partners told her that they would not discuss partnership while, as they put it, she was putting her family obligations first. The deep-pink mommy stereotype was blinding them to the facts. They couldn't see the real lawyer: a high-billing, fast-climbing asset who in just a few years would be still more valuable to the firm, who was conscientious to a fault, who was paying her own expensive cell phone bills so that she could work while ferrying her children to and from after-school activities, who was developing a sterling reputation as someone who never dropped a stitch. They saw a "mother": someone with conflicting loyalties, someone who could not be relied upon, someone who would need to run out for pediatric crises and leave others holding the bag—even though that never happened. They cut her to a half-time salary of only $42,500 a year.

With three small kids, a developing clientele, and a family dependent on her medical benefits, Mary felt spread too thin to look for a job. Although outraged, she bit her tongue and kept going.

By 2003, Mary's clientele had ballooned so much that, during the busy summer and autumn months, she was working ten- and twelve-hour days. Her children were finally all in school. She asked for a full-time salary. The partners agreed—but said they'd pay her only $70,000. For Mary, that insulting offer was the last straw. That was $5,000 less than she'd made when they had first hired her. Another female lawyer in town heard the story, and offered to match her salary at $70,000—but at least giving her the hope of being treated fairly in the future. Mary agreed to jump ship.

News travels fast in a small town. Before Mary could resign, her firm offered to make her a partner. "I think they knew they were losing a cash cow," Mary mused. Her clients were clearly going to follow her out the door. But it was too late: she was seething after years of mistreatment. They kept upping their offer. To their disbelief, she kept refusing. "At one point," Mary said, "[one senior partner] came to me and said, 'We don't want you to leave upset. It's a small town. Why don't you go out and buy yourself something nice.' " Mary was appalled at being patronized in such stereotypical terms. She didn't want a parting "gift." She wanted her well-deserved bonus. " 'Buy something nice for yourself, honey.' You've got to be kidding me! I went back to them and said, 'Look, that was insulting. I want money. This year I got paid $70,000—that was less money than I made six years ago!—and I made you $200,000. I am sure we can come to some agreement in between.' "

Mary's supervisors had badly miscalculated and let a valuable worker slip away. After just seven years of highly effective and profitable work on a barely-less-than-full-time schedule, she was ready to go back full-time—and to increase her contribution to the earnings of the firm almost exponentially, as a hard worker with a rich network of appreciative clients. But Mary lost more than her bosses had: she lost her opportunity to be fairly paid.

Did Mary "choose" to leave both the high-pressure corporate world and the partnership track of a small established firm so that she could put motherhood first? You could say that she did and that she became a lower-earning pink-collar lawyer of her own free will. But you could also say—and it would be more accurate—that she was given unfair and shortsighted choices. If she had been paid fairly, rewarded for the work she actually accomplished, and promoted in proportion to her achievements, Mary would still be at the high-end law firm, earning at least

$250,000 a year—as she had intended and expected all along. Instead, Mary was penalized enormously for Working While Mother.

So how much money did this lawyer lose? It's impossible to come to an exact figure. The difference between $70,000 per year and $250,000 per year is easy enough: that's $180,000 per year. But then consider the fact that Mary is starting that far behind at age 40, just as she heads into her prime earning decades. How do you figure out the difference in her next two decades' earning prospects—between the reality of being a modestly paid partner in a small-town law firm, on the one hand, and the quarter-million-dollar income at a sky's-the-limit big-city firm that she might have achieved had her law firm managed to respond to her actual productivity and potential? While there's no way to calculate Mary's losses with any precision, it's easy to see that she and her family lost millions.

But there's a good-news postscript to Mary's story. When I first spoke to her, she had just agreed to change firms. Months later, she let me know that, when she started working for her new female boss, her paycheck was larger than expected. She went to her boss and explained that she had agreed to come over for $70,000. "Oh, that's just ridiculous," Mary's new boss told her. "I'm paying you what I pay myself, $104,000 a year." That wasn't enough to bring Mary's salary back to where it should have been. But it was a sign that some bosses *do* believe in keeping women even—and that it's possible for an individual business owner to make sure that there's no unfair wage gap under her own roof.

The (Extra) Mommy Wage Gap

Unfortunately, none of these women is unusual. Average together the paychecks of our lawyer, woodworker, transportation manager, doctor, pipefitter, property manager, and all those other women who are working while mothers, and then compare it to the average of all those full-time working men who've received their "daddy bonus." Here's what you find: mothers who work full time earn only 60 *cents* to a working father's dollar.[13]

Overall, working mothers earn 73 cents compared to the average male dollar. That means they're missing another 4 cents—money that's badly needed by their families.[14] Imagine the hardship divorced moms face: trying to pay for rent, food, child care, and clothing with that much less in every dollar to cover these basics.

The "mommy wage gap" is commonly accepted by women and men alike as the price women pay for juggling their work and family responsibilities. A whole consulting industry has grown up in the last dozen years to help companies design "family-friendly" benefits for their employees. The hitch is, with rare exceptions, that only women use these. Men know that they're just too costly in real wages; taking the "family-friendly" track would disproportionately hold back their careers.

Over the last twenty years or so, social scientists have tested their favorite theories about why working mothers earn much less than other working women. Their theories are based on their own assumptions about how working moms should reasonably behave. For instance, they presume that mothers choose less demanding (read: lower-paying) work so that they have more energy for their family responsibilities. Or they propose that women choose to drop in and out of the workforce to have children, setting back their experience and seniority. Or that mothers choose to earn less than their husbands, because the pair has sensibly divided up work and family responsibilities, assigning him to bring in the higher paycheck while she brings in the groceries and laundry. Or that mothers choose flexible hours instead of higher pay. All these assume that women knowingly set themselves back financially in order to be mothers.

But is it so? Or are working mothers coerced—forced off the job when they get pregnant, treated as if they've had a lobotomy when they come back from maternity leave, condescended to insultingly no matter how well they perform, passed over for promotion without being told? Their "choices" are so bad as to fail to be real choices at all.

If there's a choice to be made, *the working mother* is the person who should make the choice. Ask yourself or ask a few working mothers you know whether their dollars-and-cents options were laid out to them fairly or they simply realized one day that they'd been financially mommy-tracked. Too often, bosses unilaterally—and patronizingly—

decide to "accommodate" mothers instead of paying them equally. Women's wallets suffer as a result.

Sometimes employers, supervisors, or managers think that paying mothers less is fair because those moms just aren't putting in the time at work that it takes to get ahead. Don't believe it. Time at work is falsely considered a proxy for ambition and dedication. Some men put in extra hours just for others to notice. This overtime may not be especially productive. Maybe a man will drop by the boss's office at the end of the day or go out for a drink after hours with colleagues—in theory to "discuss work" but in practice just to socialize. Maybe he'll return a low-priority telephone call after hours (since important ones would have been returned during the workday). Maybe he'll just stop by another over-timer's office to commiserate about their awful work hours.

Rather than hang around at work late to be seen, many women take work home. They may leave the office precisely at 5:00 or 6:00 to pick up the dry cleaning, shop for groceries, pick up children, and cook dinner—while returning phone calls on the way. Then, after the kids are in bed, they'll pull out the computer and finish a spreadsheet, catch up on e-mail, or finalize a report. Maybe they'll even have *more* measurable productivity than the guys, as happened to the lawyer who wasn't put up for partner even though she had more billable hours than her male colleague. But even extremely hardworking moms lose "credit" because they're not hanging around after hours—the kind of credit that registers in the boss's mind as round-the-clock dedication—even if they are actually contributing more to the bottom line. If pay and promotion decisions are being made subjectively, based on "gut instinct"—the famous "tap on the shoulder" method—guess who will be paid more?

In the chapters to come, I'll look at how women can overcome these mistaken and subjective beliefs—and at how we can overcome *all* wage discrimination. The point now is simply to recognize that financial "mommy tracking" is usually anything but voluntary—and that it may be happening to you. Employers make a host of everyday decisions based on their "instinctive"—read "stereotypical" and often "discriminatory"—notions of what mothers can and cannot do. All those biased decisions take a financial toll on working mothers. That's the mommy wage gap.

Why would a full-time worker—especially one whose time is strained by her efforts to care for her family, both emotionally and financially—choose to be paid less than a man doing the same work? She would not. She accepts less than other working women because she needs to feed her family—and because, far too often, employers *illegally* get away with paying her unfairly.

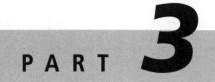

PART **3**

Getting Even

CHAPTER 10

No More Excuses

By now you've seen how much money the wage gap is draining away from each individual working woman over her lifetime. You've seen that the wage gap isn't going away on its own. And you've seen that discrimination—some of it overt, much of it unconscious, all of it costly—is rife in the American workplace. There's plain old discrimination, which openly bans women from hiring and advancement. There's discrimination by sexual harassment, which humiliates women and drives them out of jobs. There's discrimination by sex segregation or by slotting women into job categories that are consistently underpaid. There's working while female, that everyday discrimination by which women are dismissed and paid less than their male peers. There's discrimination against mothers, which forces women (and not men) to pay for parenting. All this scrapes away women's earnings, day after day, year after year, throughout our lives.

Now, what are we going to do about it?

All that *Getting Even* has laid out so far is meaningless unless it motivates women to act on our own behalf. That's what I was told by a longtime champion of working women and good friend, Carol Goldberg.

Carol is a keen, knowledgeable observer of corporate (and human) behavior. She used to be the president and COO (chief operating officer)
of the Stop & Shop Supermarket Companies, a multibillion-dollar
New England grocery store chain, making her one of the ranking corporate figures in the country for many years. She's sat on the board of directors for such major companies as Gillette and Lotus Development
Corporation. She's gained tremendous savvy and invaluable leadership
skills through her career. So I listened carefully when she gave her
straightforward advice on what to do about the wage gap.

"You can show people all the statistics and gut-wrenching stories and
discrimination analysis you want," Carol told me. "That's important.
But it's not enough. If you don't get women to act, we'll always be paid
less than men. To rouse large numbers of women into action—and it
will take a mass movement—you've got to give women two things. First,
you have to give them reasons to act. And second, you have to point
them to actions that will help, not hurt, them."

She's right, of course. So let's start with her first charge: reasons
to act.

By now you know that women have been acting—or rather,
reacting—in response to discrimination on the job for decades. Women
have coped by cramping their financial lives, making do with less, and
leading second-class lives. Some women have reacted by complaining
to the boss and, when he or she doesn't respond, complaining all the
way up the chain of command—and, finally, suing. These women
don't storm into courtrooms using the lofty language of social justice.
Rather, they become so fed up with persistent prejudice and mistreatment that they just have to do something to maintain their health and
self-respect.

But here's what's complicated these reactions. For the past twenty
years or so, most women have had to face the wage gap on their own.
There was a lot of energy and interest in closing the wage gap in the
1970s; then the public discussion moved on. When surveyed, women
say that equal pay is their most important issue. We know we are paid
less than the newly hired young men whom we are assigned to train. We
want our daughters and granddaughters to be treated better than we
have been. But without the focus of a social movement or the rein-

forcement of media attention, women have been left to simmer in silence.

And because we have been on our own, most women have chosen not to act. Much of the reasoning for holding back is based on faulty assumptions about what causes the gender wage gap. Let's look at those reasons, and see whether they hold up when examined closely—or whether they're excuses that we can brush out of our way.

Excuse 1: I'm too busy, and besides, I can't change this alone.

Some women (and men as well) have realized that the wage gap is unfair, not just to them but to most women. But, overwhelmed by the demanding current of day-to-day life, few have the energy to tackle a major social injustice alone. It's hard enough to deal with the day's e-mail, phone calls, and deadlines, to make sure there are groceries in the house and dinner on the table, and to pitch in at the school fundraiser. Figuring out what to do about the wage gap seems just about as doable as eliminating disease. In order to stay sane and reasonably functional, they have had to brush their knowledge of the unfair wage gap to the edge of their minds. Harboring resentments about things you can't change doesn't get you very far in life. So they try to stop thinking about it.

But the knowledge that you're living with injustice never does quite go away. Suspecting that the whole structure is stacked against them, some women give up believing they can eliminate even their *own* personal wage gap. They don't investigate their peers' compensation packages, lest they find out they're outrageously far behind the guys. They don't ask for as much as they deserve when it's time to negotiate a salary, promotion, or raise.

Answer 1: You're no longer alone.

Yes, it's true; the issue of equal pay disappeared from serious public policy discussions in the last decade or so. Women who remember those "59¢" buttons have had to put that issue on a mental shelf; younger women, who believed that there was no more discrimination on the job, have been on their own when, shocked, they realized that things are still unfair.

But now the *Getting Even* campaign is taking this reason away. You are joining thousands of other women and men who, upon reading this book, now know that closing the wage gap is your shared responsibility. From now on, you will no longer be acting alone.

Excuse 2: I'll lose my job if I sue.

Many women who know that they're facing blatantly unfair and illegal discrimination are worried that, if they take a hard line, they'll lose their jobs and never work again. Remember the property manager who, for several years, was a single parent with two children to support? That fear of being indigent stopped her from going to a lawyer. "They [her bosses] had me," she said. "They knew I needed a paycheck. I knew I had a legal claim because I was not being paid fairly, but I couldn't risk losing my job if I sued." Other women have seen friends or coworkers file complaints, only to be fired or forced to quit—and then lose the lawsuit or win so little that they would have been better off keeping their mouths shut and holding on to the job.

Answer 2: You don't have to sue.
You have other options as well.

Throw out this concern. You have many options before litigation. Chapters 11 and 12 will explore and explain those options in some detail.

Excuse 3: I'm not comfortable asking for more money for myself.

I hear this one over and over, and social science research [1] shows that it's true: a lot of women hate to ask for money. They worry that being "pushy" or "greedy" will upset their working relationships. They believe that their good work should be recognized and rewarded, just as their teachers and professors rewarded their schoolwork with good grades.

Answer 3: No one is comfortable at first. You learn.

Here's the dirty little secret about negotiating. Nobody's comfortable doing it—at first. Men learn how to do it. Women should too.

Unfortunately, the world of work is very different from school or family life. Most employers won't reward or promote you *unless you ask for it.* Fortunately, it's not really as hard as you fear. Asking for and negotiating to get paid fairly involves a set of skills and techniques that you can practice and master. In chapter 12, I will point you toward helpful resources. You and your friends can learn together. Negotiating is like riding a bicycle: you may wobble a little at first, but with practice you get so good that it feels natural.

Excuse 4: The wage gap is going away on its own.

Some women tell me that, slowly but inexorably, sex discrimination is going away. Things are getting better each year. All women have to do is be patient, avoid causing a fuss, and wait.

Answer 4: No, it's not.

Throw away this worn-out belief. For more than a decade, the gender wage gap has stagnated around 77 cents. Closure is not inevitable. Even the cockeyed optimists (who say that the gap may have stalled for a decade, but will soon start closing again) predict that it will be gone in *fifty to one hundred years.* Not one public policy organization in America, including the conservative think tanks, predicts that the wage gap—not just the entry-level gap, but the gap for all working women—will vanish any time soon.

So here's a note to the women who let weeks, months, and years go by without challenging their unfair pay because they believe it will all even out someday: you're wrong. As we saw in chapter 3, the wage gap is costing you a fortune *right now*. It's not going away in your lifetime unless you do something. So do it not just for yourself, but for your daughters and granddaughters. Those younger women could earn a decent living all their lives—because of you.

Excuse 5: Women leave the workforce to have kids.

When I ask women and men why they think there's still a wage gap, many say, "Oh, isn't it because women drop out to have children—and then never catch up when they go back to work?"

As *Getting Even* discussed in chapter 9, there have indeed been a steady stream of newspaper and magazine articles about highly credentialed women leaving fast-paced jobs in business and law to raise families. These "stop-outs" are the lucky few: well-educated women with husbands who earn so much that their families can live nicely on his paycheck alone. But since by far *most* families in this country depend heavily on women's paychecks, the media emphasis is misleading.

And even women who *aren't* wealthy decide to work part-time during their children's earliest years. Doesn't that drag down women's average earnings?

Answer 5: That doesn't affect the wage gap.

No. The gender wage gap (as you may remember from chapter 4) is figured by comparing the earnings of all women who work full-time with the earnings of all men who work full-time. *If you are not working full-time, your wages (or lack thereof) are not included in wage gap calculations.* Someone who leaves the workforce or goes part-time doesn't bring down the earnings of that sex; he or she is *removed* from the count. The non-wages of unemployed women *or* men—whether they were fired, quit, decided to stay home with kids, are desperately pounding the pavement, or never worked at all—simply aren't counted in the wage gap. Neither are the partial wages of part-time or seasonal workers, whether those are teenagers flipping burgers after school or new-mom doctors earning an 80 percent salary because they work "only" forty hours a week.

The 59-cent figure in the 1960s wasn't dragged down by stay-at-home moms. Their non-earnings weren't counted. That's also true for today's 77 cents.[2]

Excuse 6: Working mothers choose to earn less in exchange for flextime and "family-friendly" benefits.

Many women and men tell me that, during their children's early years, many women stay in the workforce full-time—but that they choose lower-paying jobs that are located close to good day care facilities, or that have predictable schedules, or that allow them to leave at five and then work from home after the kids go to bed.

Answer 6: Yes, they make less—not by choice, but because of discrimination.

Motherhood does affect the gender wage gap—but it's not voluntary. As we saw in chapter 9, there are a "mommy penalty" and a "daddy bonus" imposed on working parents, often without their knowledge. Sixteen million women are full-time working moms with children and a working husband. They put in a full day's work. They drive their children to sports games and after-school lessons. And then they do the grocery shopping, and the cooking, and the laundry, and whatever cleaning they can squeeze in.

In order to hold jobs that allow them to juggle their work and family responsibilities, they pay a price—a price that's commonly accepted by women and men alike. Employers say that mothers "choose" to earn less in order to have flexible hours, child care benefits, telecommuting days, and other options that let them manage. But with rare exceptions, only mothers—not fathers—use these benefits. That, in itself, should tell you something about the biases hidden in the seemingly gender-neutral "family-friendly" benefits: In today's workplaces, these "benefits" involve real financial losses. And men know it. Women who use them are shunted off the promotion track, get lower raises, and are used as the office mules while men get ahead.

Do mothers accept a smaller paycheck *gratefully*, so that they can work while taking care of their families? No. They grind their teeth and do it because they don't see another option. Why would any hardworking, able woman willingly forgo making as much money as she possible could? If mothers could *choose* to be paid the same amount as a man doing the same work, they would (and that dull roar you hear is the sound of exhausted and underpaid working mothers all over the country cheering).

Working moms earn only 60 cents for every working father's dollar. There's only one word for that: discrimination. And we'll tackle it in chapter 11.

Excuse 7: Women don't want to do the dirty work that makes more money.

When I talk about why there's still a wage gap, some women think for a while and then speculate that it exists because *other* women (not themselves, certainly) won't do the kinds of work that make more money. Maybe, these women say, most women don't want to get dirty and sweaty or do the dangerous, risky work that brings in the big bucks.

Answer 7: Yes, they do.

Throughout this book, you've heard the stories of ordinary women who threw themselves fully into work they loved—but were treated unfairly. You've heard the stories of a pregnant cop, a midwestern firefighter, an assistant district attorney, an academic historian, a fine cabinetmaker, an airline executive, an elevator technician, a high-tech salesperson, a doctor in an advanced medical specialty, a real estate lawyer, an ambitious shop floor manager—and many others. These women were passionate about the work they did—or they wouldn't have felt so angry and betrayed at how badly they were treated.

For every job that was once held only by men, there are plenty of women who are ready, willing, and eager to take it on. Government attorneys, juries, and judges alike have heard these cases—and blamed the employers. Women have plenty of willpower, courage, smarts, and ambition. So throw away this excuse. Women want those jobs. They just don't believe for a minute that they have to look or behave like alpha males to do those jobs well.

Excuse 8: Women aren't as ambitious as men; they want more balanced lives.

Here's the other thing I hear when I ask people why they think there's a wage gap: Women speculate that maybe *other* women (again, not themselves) just aren't very ambitious, or have priorities other than work. If the cost of being, say, CEO is working twelve hours a day, seven days a week, and being available for emergency calls at night or conference calls while on vacation, well then, these women decide to just say no. They'd rather have a high quality of life than be the top dog. They'd rather have Sunday mornings playing with the kids than make partner by playing golf.

Answer 8: Who said all men were ambitious?

The strangest thing about this excuse is that I usually hear it from women who are themselves highly competitive, high-achieving, fast-track people. They've got a couple of graduate degrees, or they've worked their way up through the ranks of their job. And still they're speculating that *other* women are wired for feeling rather than achievement, for mothering rather than mastering, for cuddling rather than competing—that, in other words, most women (though not they themselves!) really do fit the cultural stereotype. It's essentially the same argument that employers make when they say that they simply can't find women who want to be, say, forklift operators or bank managers.

But who said all men were ambitious? Sure, some women tell me that they don't want to work sixty or eighty hours a week. Guess what? Neither do many men. Men simply don't talk about their reluctance (or unwillingness) to let work take over their lives. They know their bosses don't want to hear it. Plenty of women *and* men just want to put in their time, do a good job, get paid and promoted fairly, and go home. And plenty of men *and* women are ambitious, talented, and driven enough to reach the top—where men have an unfair advantage.

Tell any one of the 24 million single, separated, divorced, or wid-owed women now working full-time that she's not as motivated to get ahead or to earn money as the men working alongside her. She'd laugh in your face. She wants and needs to earn as much as she possibly can. Common sense and common conversations with working women con-firm that working women are just as motivated as working men. Not every man—or every woman—aims for the very top. But they all expect to go as far as they can, in line with their own abilities and efforts.

The point is that there should be fair opportunity for both the hard-working homebodies and for the potential high-fliers, whether female or male.

The Employers' Excuse: "It Just Happened"

Many, perhaps most, employers today believe they behave fairly toward women and men. They believe and say that they hire, pay, and promote each individual worker according to her or his education, experience, capacities, and merits. And yet I've heard of very few employers racing forward to prove that no wage gap exists under their corporate rooftop or to audit the books to see if such a gap is there—or, if they notice that a wage gap does exist, examining and fixing personnel practices to get rid of it. Many employers do know that the men are getting paid more than the women. But not a single boss would blame himself (or, for that mat-ter, herself).

Remember the female middle manager from chapter 8? She said that, soon after she had joined one company, that company's only other high-profile female manager quit. Soon afterwards, our middle man-ager found herself at an executive team meeting. "They had this dis-cussion: 'Are we a sexist organization?' " she said. "And I'm looking around the room, and except for me—and I had just joined the company—it's all guys. I'm thinking, the answer is right in front of you. But they said no! 'Oh, no, it's really hard to get qualified people,' and so on!"

When she told that story, we laughed out loud at the male execu-tives' glaring blind spot. But of course the guys were being honest: they truly believed they weren't biased. Americans want to think of themselves as open-minded and fair, because fairness is one of our cardinal virtues. And so to explain the gender wage gap on their own payrolls, employers have had their *own* explanations for what's going on. But are they reasons—or excuses?

Consider the "reasoning" you've heard in the court cases mentioned in earlier chapters. At Home Depot, which had an enormous wage gap, the owners and managers denied that there was sex discrimination in their stores. They said it just *happened* that women remained at the bottom as cashiers while men advanced up through the ranks of store manager. They said it happened because they hired from the construction trades, where women were rare. Or it happened because women preferred to be cashiers instead of sales staff. Or it happened because women didn't like to "mix it up with customers," "throw freight," "get dirty," or climb ladders or because women are "better with their fingers." It just happened naturally; no illegal sex discrimination was involved. And yet they settled that case for millions and accepted years of court oversight.

Grocery stores such as Publix, Ingles, and so on said the same thing. It just *happened* that only men got the promotion-track jobs such as stocker and meat manager because women were *choosing* to stay at the bottom and get paid less. Or because women didn't want to travel or work late. Or because women simply liked being underpaid cashiers, while men liked moving up.

We've seen exactly the same "reasoning" in nearly every kind of employer: in manufacturing, government agencies, sales, academics, restaurants, finance, the trades, advertising, engineering, real estate, retail, medicine, carpentry, and more. At top universities, it just *happened* that male assistant professors were always approved for tenure while women were denied two times out of three. It just *happened* that male professors were paid more in such female-heavy specialties as English, art history, history, religious studies, writing, and communications. It just *happened* that, at Dial, women were shunted into the low-paying production-floor jobs while men were hired into better-paying slots as mechanics and supervisors. It just *happened* that male janitors made more than female janitors in the U.S. Capitol. It just *happened* that, in the Santa Barbara Police Department's 102-year history, not a single female police officer had ever been promoted. It just *happened* that, until the lawsuit, women never got to be traders at J.P. Morgan Chase.

Let's give employers like these the benefit of the doubt for a minute, and say: Maybe it's true. Maybe those organizations (or their hiring managers) never consciously intend to discriminate. Too bad. In law, that's no excuse. The end result would still be illegal. One Rutgers study examined employers' EEO-1 filings of hiring and employment data, and concluded that more than 60,000 employers met the prima facie judicial standards for *intentional* sex discrimination. The study anticipated employers' usual excuses, such as "we can't find qualified women," or "women don't want to do these kinds of jobs," or "no women applied." These researchers meticulously checked and measured to see which employers had a *significantly lower* proportion of women to men that were qualified, interested, and available to work in that job and region. Barring extraordinary circumstances, the report suggests that all 60,000 of those employers would lose (or, more likely, settle) if sued for sex discrimination. When they extrapolated their findings to all American employers, these researchers estimated conservatively that *at least two million women* work for intentional discriminators.[3]

But as employers well know, it's very unlikely that they will be sued. Local, state, and federal antidiscrimination agencies aren't going to come after them unless some individual woman or women rise up with pressing complaints. Such agencies are swamped with a backlog of discrimination complaints, and almost never go searching on their own for employers who discriminate. Unless women bring complaints, these business and organizations face no pressure to mend their ways. And so they keep ignoring their blatantly unfair gender imbalance—because there's no cost to continuing.

The picture isn't uniformly bleak. A few (albeit very few) American employers do revamp their employment practices in response to carefully argued complaints. After all, there's plenty of research into what works and what doesn't. We'll look at those hopeful examples in the next chapter. But when did you last meet someone willing to change if there was no cost to doing things the same old way?

Here's the point. Employers—those unaware of their biases, those who don't care about their biases, and even those who want to do the right thing but don't believe they have a problem—have no reason to root out unfair treatment of women employees. They don't feel any pressure from inside or outside. They don't believe it is going to cost them money. They don't realize that many or most of their female employees are quietly simmering with resentment. They don't have anything to lose in community standing. Until women themselves insist on change—systematically, thoughtfully, and carefully—employers won't re-examine and revamp their own behavior.

And women won't get paid what they're worth.

A Legitimate Academic Excuse: They Don't Have the Data

There's one last excuse that working women should understand. Many social scientists, especially economists, just don't have the data to conclude that the wage gap is due to discrimination. Every one of us should understand, in nontechnical terms, how these academics come to their conclusions. Otherwise, we can be too easily puzzled by their tendencies to underestimate discrimination's damaging effect on our paychecks.

Most social scientists, especially economists, divide the 23-cent wage gap into two parts: the first part, which they call "explained," and the second part, which they call a "leftover." For the first portion, economists compare male and female workers' characteristics—such as levels of educational achievement and years of work experience—to see whether there are any differences that could "explain" the wage gap. If women have fewer years of education than men do, economists believe that this educational difference "explains" a portion of the 23-cent gap. They don't mean it *causes* that difference; they mean that it *correlates with* that difference. So, for instance, if women with law degrees earn on average a certain amount more than those women who do not, that degree "explains" the difference in their paychecks.

But if you read their technical articles carefully, you find that social scientists acknowledge that even these "explained" characteristics may actually be caused by discrimination. For instance, a social scientist may calculate how much of the wage gap is "explained" by women having less workplace experience than men. As you've seen in this book, that lesser amount of on-the-job experience actually may exist *because* a significant proportion of working women have been forced off the job by sex discrimination, sexual harassment, and all the rest. Maybe, in academic terms, "less workplace experience" can be said to "explain" women's lower pay. But in real-life terms, discrimination could still be the root explanation for that lesser amount of experience. So how much of the wage gap do social scientists say has been "explained" by those sorts of educational and experiential differences? About 7 cents—or a little less than one third of the 23-cent gap. And remember, some of that 7 cents might really be due to discrimination.

Even so, that leaves a whopping amount of the wage gap—more than two thirds of it—potentially as the "leftover." And so analysts continue to try to find different characteristics that could explain that large gap. Economists note, for instance, that certain industries and occupations are paid more than others—and that men are more likely to work in those higher-paying industries and occupations. This theory "explains" another 7 cents of the wage gap. But of course, as we saw in chapter 7, sex segregation is often due to discrimination. Just ask the women who've been forced out of police work, firefighting, stock trading, law firm partnerships. Amy McKinney, our ex-firefighter from Muskogee, would certainly agree. And other women feel that their pay in "pink" occupations—secretarial work, for instance—is lower only because those are women's job. So those 7 cents could *also* be due to discrimination.

Still another 9 cents of the wage gap remains as the unexplained "leftover." To social scientists, this term is a catchall, which might include discrimination but might also include any other theory they might someday think up. They're holding this open in part because many economists are predisposed to believe that discrimination is fading. First, they believe that it must be true, simply because it has been illegal for so long. Second, traditional American economists are trained with the idea that every human being behaves rationally in the marketplace: decisions about buying, selling, earning, and paying can all be explained because they are all made with enlightened self-interest.

That underlying thesis leads such economists to believe that *irrational* behavior—discrimination, for instance, which would *not* maximize productivity—can't really exist over the long run. For the last forty years, however, most of us have known otherwise.[4]

It's important for working women to understand how and why social scientists understate the effects of discrimination on our paychecks—so that when you hear or read their conclusions, you can remember how much discrimination is hiding inside their figures.

That's not intended to dismiss academics' conclusions entirely. Some differences in pay—pennies' worth—may be due to American women, as a group, not having quite as much experience on the job as American men, as a group. (Of course, that's like saying that American women as a whole aren't as tall as American men as a whole: individuals differ.) Even if up to 5 cents of the wage gap were due to such unvarnished differences, then women should today earn at least 95 cents for every dollar men earn. That's a far cry from the 77 cents we're earning. So don't let the number crunchers talk you out of the facts. The wage gap measures discrimination.

Redress for Success

Here's the important lesson for women—and for men who want to see women get paid fairly: Your suspicions have been right. You *are* underpaid because of discrimination. All those little slights, those moments of having some guy take credit for your work, those experiences of being passed over while some guy was pushed ahead: You share those with millions of other working women. You can talk to your boss about your paycheck with quiet confidence—free of fault, blame, and excuses.

And now that you know what's wrong, you're responsible for doing something about it. When you do, you won't be alone. From here on in, every step you take—whether that's figuring out how to negotiate for more, or tackling *all* the suggestions in this final section—is taken on behalf of millions of women. You're not being demanding or whiny or greedy or aggressive; you're aiming for rightful redress. It may take a couple of years. But we're going to do it together. Together, we're not going to settle for anything less than success.

CHAPTER 11

Starting to Get Even

So what can American women and men do to close this decades-old *illegal* inequity? Is it possible to win fair pay—equal pay—for every American woman worker? Let me answer with a resounding *yes!* In the rest of the book, I'm going to explain how.

First, let's look at why past efforts have failed. Then I'll give an overview of the *Getting Even* plan. Then I'll tell a few success stories that will illustrate how some employers have used this approach (or elements of it) to start closing the gap. These stories will reveal in more detail how the *Getting Even* approach can work—and will help me explain why this is the surest way to get our wages even. Then, in the next chapters, we'll step down from this aerial view, and look at some practical steps by which each of us can carry out the plan.

Why Have Past Efforts Failed?

Before looking more closely at the solution, it's important to examine past efforts to make a fairer workplace for women and to think about why these initiatives failed to close the wage gap. Each was an important step: social transformations do not come easily. But these well-intentioned efforts were not designed explicitly to close the wage gap. And so—no surprise here—they did not. Knowing that, it becomes easier to see that the task must, and can, be tackled head on.

Family-Friendly Policies and Diversity Consulting

Over the past two decades, many reformers have tried to lessen workplace discrimination by educating the organization's bottom and middle rungs. They've conducted diversity trainings for employees and midlevel managers. They've offered assertiveness training to help women make themselves heard. They've delivered sexual harassment trainings so that employees can draw the line between appropriate and illegal behavior. They've won flextime, part time, maternity leave, and other "family-friendly" benefits.

These efforts often resulted in far more livable workplaces for women. But none has closed the wage gap.

You can see this in the lists that rank the "best" places for women to work. The nomination form for the annual list issued by the National Association for Female Executives (NAFE), for instance, asks for information about women's advancement: how many women are senior managers with profit-and-loss responsibilities; whether managers and executives are accountable and rewarded for recruiting and advancing women; whether the organization has work/life initiatives, and if so, what kind. But here's what they don't ask: What's your company's wage gap? How much does the average female employee make compared to the average male employee? Are the female executives paid as much as the male executives? NAFE—one of the best public interest outfits that's checking on company practices—doesn't ask. And so even the "best places for women to work" haven't felt the pressure to examine or report their internal wage gaps.

Why Didn't Those Efforts Close the Wage Gap?

Here's why both these efforts failed to erase the wage gap: it wasn't their goal. They helped some working women not with wages but with working conditions. They weren't designed to end wage discrimination. And they didn't.

You can't close the wage gap just from the bottom up; you also have to work from the top down. As important as both have been, "lifestyle" workplace reforms and diluted and underfunded government enforcement efforts are not enough to close the wage gap. Let's aim directly at the bottom line: equal pay.

A Sketch of the Solution

To get paid like men, women and men must put pressure on chief executives—their bosses—to make women's pay fair. That's it. It's simple. Social scientists already agree that, in the past years, they've figured out what mechanisms are effective in stopping discrimination. What's missing is the top-down commitment to do it. To get that commitment, all it will take is for women and the men who care about them to act together.

Doing this will involve three parts. First, working women must start documenting our experiences of discrimination (and improving our negotiating skills)—in order to prove to the boss that discrimination exists. Second, CEOs and other organizational top dogs must commit themselves to closing the gap—and to motivating and monitoring changes within their organizations. And third, all of us must build a grassroots campaign that will keep the pressure on employers and policymakers to do the right thing. Each part is equally important, and may not be accomplished in any neat order. But here's what's crucial: women must act, or CEOs will not react by closing the wage gap.

This action plan puts the squeeze on wage discrimination from three sides. Employees will attack their employer's wage gap from the inside up. CEOs will attack it from the top down. And public pressure groups will attack it from the outside in. This "pressure triangle" will inspire and reward changes in the day-to-day behavior of employees, supervisors, managers, executives, and everyone else who has an influence on women's wages. When pressure comes from below, above, and outside, the push toward fairness will be unstoppable.

In this chapter, I will give an overview of how this approach works.

Then, in the next three chapters, I will explain in more detail exactly what *you* can do to carry out this approach in *your* company or organization. But first, let me explain the concept.

Step 1: Women, working from the inside up. Women employees (and their male supporters) have to advocate for themselves individually and for all women where they work.

Within each employer, women must collect data on pay, promotions, compensation packages, and any and all other measures of equity or discrimination that they can find. They must take this data to the *top executive*. Then they must personalize that data by telling stories about how discrimination (conscious or unconscious) has held them back. Neither data nor stories will be enough alone—but the combination is very powerful, as you'll see in the stories to come. And yes, they have to convert the person in charge—not the vice president, not the senior manager, not fellow workers, but the big kahuna who's at the very top of the organizational pyramid.

Step 2: CEOs, working from the top down. CEOs must commit themselves to closing the wage gap within their organizations.

The heart of the *Getting Even* plan is this: persuading each and every CEO to close the wage gap within his or her organization, whether that person is called the chief executive, president, governor, managing director, publisher, maestro, or union leader (which I'll simplify to just "the CEO" from here on). CEOs are the only ones who have the authority and power to ensure that all the women they employ are fairly paid. CEOs can get women to one dollar. Their own female employees will show them that they *need* to take action. Outside pressure will help make them *want* to take action. Social scientists, consultants, and their own internal talent can help them see *what* actions are essential. (I'll lay out some suggestions in the next chapter, but each organization will have to adapt those to its own culture.) But only the CEO can decide that it must be done.

Some readers will believe I'm dreaming. Why should CEOs care—and not only care, but shake up their companies until women are equally paid and promoted? As you'll see in the stories to follow, sometimes moral suasion is enough: convinced that it's the right thing to do, some head honchos throw themselves into ending discrimination and the wage gap. Not all CEOs are moved by righteousness alone. But if employees bring pressure from inside, and boards of directors peg the CEO's bonus to wage equity—well, you see where we're headed, but I'll save more on that for the next chapter.

Converting the CEO is central. Without commitment from the top, nothing will change. When there *is* commitment from the top, that priority gets accomplished.

Step 3: The rest of us, working from the outside in. American women must hold every employer accountable for closing the wage gap.

Of course, not every CEO will be convinced by his or her employees alone that the company's wage gap must be closed. And even if an individual CEO is converted, no boss stays on top forever. So the third part of this triangular model is this: outside pressure.

Companies dread bad publicity. The ugly taste of shame lingers in their executives' minds. Any plunge in sales, profits, stock price, or reputation, which are all tightly linked, hurts just as memorably. And the possibility of civil lawsuits or federal action can pummel all the above. The contrary is also true. Companies love good publicity. They know that civic and community recognition improves the brand's image—and therefore sales.

Which is why American women (and our male friends) must keep an eye on every CEO's efforts to close the wage gap—and must report on those efforts' success through statistics, documentation, and individual stories. In theory, this is the job of the EEOC, the Equal Employment Opportunity Commission. But the EEOC is stretched very thin, underfunded, and overextended. It will take a citizens' uprising to put that external pressure in place.

And that's what we'll do. As I'll explain more in the next chapter, a nonprofit organization dedicated to closing the wage gap within the next ten years has been launched. The WAGE (Women Are Getting Even) Project will gather documentation and report on discrimination against working women—and will aim the bright glare of nationwide activity on every CEO in the country.

Fortunately, to carry out this plan, no individual woman will have to put her job on the line. From experience, I know that once broad-based action gets going, it develops its own life: people leap in to apply their own talents and energy to build toward the new vision. That's what must happen to get women even. Women across the country—and men who care about the women in their lives—will have to get involved.

Employers' Attempts to Get Even

Described from above, this "pressure triangle" might sound very lofty and academic. So now let's take a look at some employers that have in fact tried to close the wage gap. What worked? What didn't? What lessons can we take away?

After reading more than two hundred pages of stories about employers behaving badly, you may want some good news. Here it is: A few (albeit very few) employers have openly acknowledged that their female employees are discriminated against and underpaid—and have actively worked to treat and pay them equally. MIT, Mitsubishi, and the state of Minnesota—each for different reasons, and in different ways—committed themselves to treating women workers fairly. Below are their stories.

We've already seen how unreflective (not to mention downright illegal) is the discriminatory behavior that slows down women's advancement and cuts into their pay. Closing the gap requires doing exactly the opposite: staring discrimination in the eye and holding *everyone* accountable for ending it. (As it happens, the tools available to end discrimination for one group work for all—sometimes unintentionally, as when Home Depot's gender-blind hiring and promotion system also became blind to race, ethnicity, national origin, disability, and religion.)

Those employers that are already tackling gender wage discrimination are pioneers. If you find any others, let me know. They deserve praise and recognition. For now, let's learn from a couple of employers who are leading the way to one dollar—and one employer who's all but there.

MIT: *Professor Nancy Hopkins Working from the Inside Up*

Reaching Professor Nancy Hopkins's narrow office, squirreled away in the mazelike MIT campus, requires navigating unprepossessing corridors and passing lab rooms stacked with hundreds upon hundreds of gurgling aquariums filled (as you can see if you peer closely) with tiny, swimming, wriggling zebra fish. Studying how zebra fish develop— what chemical signals tell its embryonic cells to become fins, eyes, gills, or some other part of the body—is how, in 1994, Hopkins expected to be spending her life and furthering her already stellar reputation. But then she reluctantly started to see that she was being held back by sex. By now, almost against her will, Hopkins has become equally famous for forcing higher education to ask: Do male and female academics have the same chance to advance? Or is much of academia a men's club, with subjective standards and old boys' networks that are unconsciously keeping women down, out, and underpaid?

Such thoughts were anathema to Hopkins when she joined the MIT faculty in 1973. Back then, "I absolutely believed that civil rights and affirmative action had solved the problem of gender discrimination," she said. "I was absolutely certain I would never encounter it in my lifetime." As a graduate student and postdoctoral fellow in biology at Harvard, she'd been mentored by James Watson, who with Francis Crick had won a Nobel Prize in 1962 for discovering the structure of DNA. Hopkins had always believed that science was, above all, fair. Who could argue with a great experiment? Science was about truths that could be measured, facts that could be demonstrated, hypotheses that could be proven either true or false. She believed that any female scientist who complained about discrimination was more than a little pathetic, her complaints proof that she simply wasn't brilliant enough to cut it.

But as she moved up the ranks at MIT, Hopkins occasionally noticed that women weren't taken as seriously as their male peers. "The women were undervalued in terms of their scientific contributions," she said. It was painful to see that "men of lesser accomplishment scientifically were treated as more valuable, had a greater say in the department, were really listened to. At faculty meetings some woman would speak up, and there would be like a silence. Then we'd pass on as if she'd not spoken. I spoke once when I was young and gave up. I never spoke at a faculty meeting again, for twenty years."

After all, in Hopkins's mind, having a voice in the department wasn't what *really* counted: what counted was the caliber of her scientific work. And so, like many highly driven people, she put her head down and concentrated on investigations, experiments, hypotheses, papers— and results.

But in 1994 Hopkins decided to shift her research. She wanted to stop investigating tumor viruses, the area in which she'd made her name, and start examining how zebra fish develop. To do that, she needed a little more lab space. "I wanted two hundred square feet of space," she explained in her rapid-fire but very quiet voice, "which is a very small amount. I mean, that would be a closet, like these two of- fices," gesturing at her own and her secretary's offices combined.

But when she asked for that 200 square feet of space, she was, re- peatedly, told no.

Hopkins couldn't quite believe this annoying refusal. She knew exactly where the 200 square feet of space was; she knew it was avail- able. Still, being a scientist, she checked the facts. With a tape mea- sure she mapped out her research space and compared it to her fellow biologists' square footage. What she found made history. Male junior faculty—assistant professors and associate professors—had, on average, 2,000 square feet. Male senior faculty—full professors, with tenure, like herself—had an average of 3,000 square feet, and sometimes as much as 6,000 square feet. To her shock, Nancy Hopkins—a full professor, who is now a fellow of the American Academy of Arts and Sciences, a mem- ber of the National Academy of Sciences and of its Institute of Medi- cine, and one of the authors of one of molecular biology's essential textbooks—had 1,500 square feet of research space. Men with much less stature and experience had one third *more* space than she did. Her equals had between one-and-a-half and three times more space. And in biology, size matters. More space means you can do more experiments. Less space, fewer results. Hopkins was appalled.

Which isn't to say that her measurements made a difference right away. "I went to the man in charge of space, and I would say, 'Look, I've got less space,' " Hopkins told us. "And he would say dismissively, 'Oh no, you know you don't have less space! Why do you say such ridiculous things?' And I would say, 'Come see and I'll show you, because a five-year-old can tell!' He refused to come upstairs and look."

For months, Hopkins said, "I would just go home tearing my hair out. Every day, I would get up in the morning and say, 'What can I do to get those two hundred square feet of space today?' That took about fifty percent of my time and energy." Frustrated, Hopkins talked to a lawyer, who told her to leapfrog the hierarchy and speak directly to her provost, MIT's second in command. She did. "I took this bag of paper full of my credentials to show him I'm a real card-carrying scientist, that my work is in great demand, that I'm getting all these accolades and grants. And I've got my floor plans, and everything's colored in to show who has what space, and how much less I have, and how I want the two hundred square feet, and that out there in the corridor there are coat closets available, which I could use."

Her provost was stunned. After listening for an hour, she recounts, "He said, 'I just don't understand this. People who come to see the provost want whole buildings. And you're asking for two hundred square feet of space? I never heard of somebody wanting so little!' " The provost sent her back down the hierarchy to her dean, who reluctantly leaned on her department's administrators, and eventually, Professor Hopkins had her new, storage-closet-sized lab space. "It had taken me ten months to get two hundred square feet," she said, still appalled. But not long after, she told me, a male colleague arranged to have her pushed out of a course Hopkins had helped to develop.

That was Nancy Hopkins's road-to-Damascus moment, she said. "I finally realized that I'd had it. I came to an end of the line." It was the final insult that shattered her belief that science was built entirely on merit. She suddenly started to see all the other moments in her past in which she'd been overlooked, shoved aside, demeaned, diminished, credit for her work denied—just because she was female. In other words, for the better part of a year, most of her attention, energy, and time had gone toward securing lab space—attention, energy, and time that she therefore could *not* spend thinking up and carrying out brilliant experiments, building her reputation, and establishing the objective merit on which scientists are judged.

The idea that, even in science, you could be held back just for working while female was a painful revelation. Hopkins, like other scientists, had had a nearly theological belief that "pure science is a rational thing: if you discover the structure of DNA, they give you the Nobel Prize, and people respect you. Isn't that the way it works? Isn't it truly merit-based? It's so hard to part with that idea! I truly believed that women who thought they had been discriminated against must not be able to make it on their own merits. You've got a lab, you've got graduate students, you go in there and do a great experiment, and what are they going to do? They can't prevent you from succeeding. But they can!" If you have less money, less space, less energy, less time, and fewer assistants, how can you do the same caliber of work as your male peers? "First, they can prevent you from doing the work, and then they can prevent you from getting credit when you *have* done the work!" She had already sensed that all this was true for the women around her. She had wanted to believe she was the exception. "I just didn't *want* to believe it. It took me twenty years to see what was going on."

Hopkins realized that, if she were to continue to work at MIT, she had to take this insight to the top: to MIT's President Charles Vest. She wrote a letter to Vest. But she worried about being dismissed as shrill and crazy. So she asked another professor—a woman she didn't know well and who had a sterling reputation—to read it. She waited anxiously while her fellow professor read the letter. The other female professor said she agreed with every word and asked to sign on.

"I thought, 'This is power. Now we've got power.' We both thought the other person was a highly respected scientist—although that's not how we felt about ourselves, because that wasn't how we were treated," Hopkins explained. If one female scientist was complaining, she might just be a troublemaking crank. But if *two* accomplished female scientists were complaining, they had to be listened to. "So we thought, 'My God, could there be other women who think the same?'" The two made a list of the other women in MIT's six science departments, intent on contacting them all. They were shocked to find only 15 tenured women—alongside 194 tenured men. "I hadn't even known it! I hadn't thought about it! There was about the same number as when I came to MIT twenty years before. That percentage of women faculty had not changed."

All but one signed the letter.

Then came what Nancy Hopkins calls "a miracle": both the dean of science, Bob Birgenau, and President Charles Vest took those fourteen senior scientists seriously. Even better, when the MIT women professors asked if they could start an investigative committee to look into the problem, Birgenau helped them to shape the committee and to persuade all the departments to cooperate. Had MIT's administration not backed them, Hopkins believes, nothing more would have been done. "Some department heads did not want the women to have their committee and look into this. The idea that women were going to look at data and get information was very frightening."

Even with the administration's backing, getting that data wasn't easy. Salary data, for instance, was private to a nearly sacred degree. "Nobody wanted to tell me their salaries," Hopkins explained. "They were too scared. Nobody, men or women. People are so sensitive about this because they don't want to find out what people really think of them." And this was within the investigative committee itself, made up of six women and three male department heads! Determined to break the logjam, "I took my salary and put it on the table and gave it to everybody. It was very hard to do! It was very hard!"

But that's what it took to prompt her peers to open up. "Gradually, people came to me individually," Hopkins explained, "and told me their salaries. Men even told me. We would compare raises every year, year by year by year, so we could learn from them. But still—the dean refused to let us see the primary salary data."

Despite the occasional snag, two years later, the committee returned with a 150-page report that demonstrated discrimination in meticulous detail, comparing such things as lab and office space measurements, salaries, key committee and departmental appointments, grant sharing, numbers of research assistants, numbers of hours of secretarial help, and all the other administrative minutiae that can boost or hold back research's depth and speed. They examined the cycle of marginalization: the support women felt early in their careers and the strange sensation of being slowly elbowed aside, which led women to doubt themselves. They documented the "leaky pipeline," which showed women steadily being pushed out of science, making up 50 percent of undergraduates majoring in biology, 45 percent of Ph.D. students, 35 percent of postdoctoral students, but only 15 percent of the biology faculty—and as little as 8 percent in all six fields of science at MIT and other high-end institutions. They examined how men understood salaries to be markers of each others' relative importance and used outside offers as leverage to negotiate larger salaries, while women professed a lack of interest in money and refused to bring up other offers in salary discussions, believing that approach to be distasteful. And perhaps they were right to refrain; a few women who had tried that approach had not received counteroffers. They looked into how arbitrarily department heads made decisions about whose scientific "merit" (or family demands, or promise, or prominence) deserved a raise and whose income could be left as is. And they delivered the report to the president, for his review.

In other words, at MIT the first side of the "pressure triangle" was in place: respected women who worked within the institution had carefully documented discrimination, and made the case to the CEO.

Then came the second miracle. Dozens of schools have produced similar studies with similar results, Hopkins says—but those studies were buried in a file drawer somewhere. President Charles Vest had the opposite response. Several years later, when a summary of Hopkins's report was made public, Vest wrote a preface to the report that said, "I have always believed that contemporary gender discrimination within universities is part reality and part perception. True, but I now understand that reality is by far the greater part of the balance."

The full preface, and the summary of the report, were posted on the MIT Web site—and shook up not just MIT but hundreds of schools around the world.

MIT: *President Charles Vest,*
Working from the Top Down

I went to talk with Charles Vest, wondering: What prompted him to
own the problem at MIT?

Vest struck me as a genuinely modest man. He kept trying to extend
credit to the dean of science, Bob Birgenau; to Professor Nancy Hopkins; and to all the faculty women and men who had presented their
findings so clearly. Birgenau, Vest explained, had worked carefully with
Hopkins to select an investigating committee that would have maxi-
mum political credibility within MIT. That hadn't happened easily,
Vest acknowledged. "There was a lot of resistance among some of the
department heads in the School of Science. I like to believe that was not
because they wanted to discriminate, but because salary's always been
an extremely private matter."

Once he saw the study, Vest said, he was impressed. "I'm going to
sound like I'm engaging in normal MIT arrogance here, but if you pull
any twelve or fifteen tenured senior faculty members at MIT, you're
going to have a bunch of very bright, accomplished, intense people.
These were serious people! They all had quite solid scientific and
academic credentials." Because the committee was credible, so were
the data. "At MIT, we do like numbers," Vest explained in his serious
and straightforward (if slightly self-deprecating) way. "It sounds funny
to other people, but going in and looking at lab space is a very smart
thing to do. I don't think that that had ever actually been done before.
So they presented to me a very credible case based on a variety of actual
metrics."

Still, Vest acknowledged, the facts alone hadn't been enough to
convert him. What really moved him was listening to the women themselves. "We were sitting, a few of us, around this table," Vest said, gesturing to a large coffee table, "and the statement was made by one of
the women faculty that most of the young women are pretty happy:
they feel supported, they're getting the same kind of treatment in
startup funds and teaching and so forth, they're feeling pretty good.
Whereupon one of the more senior women in the group said, 'I felt that
way when I was that age too.' " Here Vest paused, as if struck again by

that comment. "And we're now a little bit into emotion here, but that statement—that just grabbed me in some deep way that almost none of the other conversations did."

Vest's moment of insight didn't come out of the blue. He had started with an open mind, encouraging the committee to do its research—an approach very much in keeping with the pragmatic, fact-based spirit of MIT. He had pored over the data. He had spoken to many on the science faculty, both male and female. And so, when he heard that off-hand but honest comment, he grasped what lay behind such quiet, re-signed anger. As a result, he said, "The combination of reasonably hard data that shows that something is statistically going on, and listening face to face with people's experiences—between the two of those it was crystal clear to me that we had a serious problem."

Vest isn't naive: he knew that a lawsuit was possible. Nevertheless, he sat down and wrote a statement that urged MIT faculty to take the study seriously and consider what they should do. "I tell people somewhat facetiously that MIT doesn't have a general counsel," Vest explained. "I did *not* go to a general counsel and say, 'Am I going to get into trouble if I say this?' I'm old-fashioned enough to believe that if you're dealing with the truth, somehow, it's not going to come around and bite you." It was that simple. Charles Vest decided to do the right thing. "I was not intending to do anything that was going to create national waves; I was primarily making a statement to our community, but to me it was a sim-ple statement of fact. Nothing more, nothing less."

But what he did *was* something more than just a statement of fact. As Hopkins put it, the president had declared, "We are never going to have a measurable inequity in my school again. He said, 'That we can fix. It's very difficult to fix the underlying attitudes that produce it, but we can control it, keep track of it, and fix it as it goes.' "

When I spoke to him, I had the very strong feeling that Vest's mod-esty wasn't for show: he had seen a problem, decided that it had to be fixed, and acknowledged it openly. (Or as MIT Provost Bob Brown, a chemical engineer, told Hopkins, "We're engineers. We solve prob-lems.") In simply confirming what these women scientists had carefully documented, Charles Vest told his university and the public that MIT treats women unfairly and that it had to stop. No other CEO of a private corporation or nonprofit institution has been so publicly forthright in recent times.

The second side of the "pressure triangle" was in place: The CEO had declared that there was a problem that had to be solved, and started to insist that every subordinate fix that problem.

As a result of Hopkins's committee and Charles Vest's leadership, MIT began to systematically look at how to undo its own sex discrimination. That's what happens when the boss says there's a problem. Department leaders started to change their ways.

"The dean got religion," as Hopkins put it. The first to do so was Birgeneau, dean of science. Next it was Tom Magnenti, dean of engineering. "Magnenti said, this is unacceptable, we're going to work on this. And he got together with his department heads, and they worked together on it." For instance, she explained, "They would do things like call up schools and ask for outstanding young people. The schools would name some men—and [the department heads] would say, Do you have any outstanding young women?" Surprise! Asked specifically about women, the men at the other end would say, " 'Oh, yes, I forgot about Betty.' " It wasn't that Betty (or Lakshmi or Jamila) was any less qualified than Ben (or Vijay or Marcus). It was that their minds automatically tossed up a stereotyped response about what made a "good MIT candidate." When they were prompted consciously to look beyond that circumscribed description, Betty suddenly came to mind.

Provost Bob Brown asked the dean to ask department heads to rethink their hiring and promotion practices—and ask specifically about those who might be unintentionally forgotten. It wasn't long before a significantly higher percentage of women were being hired into the School of Science.

That's all it took. Once they gave it conscious attention, MIT managers found ways to make sure hiring and promotion were closer to equitable. As Vest put it, "I believe that [discrimination] is almost exclusively unintended. I don't think you can find any faculty member at MIT who would say, 'I believe we shouldn't all have equal opportunity.' It's just that some of us may be blinded to where opportunity really isn't equal, and then may unknowingly contribute to that level of inequity. If one becomes convinced that there is an inequity, something that's not right, simply saying in straightforward simple terms in one or two declarative sentences can make a huge impact. I guess that's the primary lesson I learned."

MIT: *Attracting International Attention*

But declarative statements and informal approaches aren't enough. Hopkins and her group had documented discrimination. With the initial report in hand, MIT had to institutionalize that same investigation—and monitor constantly whether women and men are *still* being treated fairly. Getting there required the third part of the Getting Even triangle: outside pressure.

In 1999, MIT was preparing to post the School of Science report's summary and Vest's remarkable preface. Just before it did so, as Hopkins tells it, she was being interviewed by some reporters about science at MIT. One of them asked what it was like to be a female scientist at MIT. Hopkins mentioned the report and Vest's impressive preface, thinking no outsider would be able to understand how much such a statement meant. Hopkins said, "The next thing I know, standing in my office is a nice young woman from *The Boston Globe,* and shortly thereafter there's a phone call from a nice young woman from *The New York Times.*" The MIT report became front-page news.

"It was astounding what happened next," Hopkins recounted. "I mean, absolutely astounding. It was like standing in the path of some avalanche. For several days, first of all, you have nothing but cameras up and down the halls of your place, and people thrusting microphones in your face. The most astounding thing of all was the e-mail that came from women all over the country, saying, 'Thank you, thank you, thank you. You're not going to believe this, I have exactly the same problem in my institution. Let me tell you about it.' The dean was deluged; I was completely deluged; the president was deluged. Universities don't tend to put out reports that get this kind of reaction."

Vest agreed, using almost the same language. "I've never seen anything like it," he said, clearly still amazed. "The letters, the e-mails, the instant reactions all around the country, and really all around the world: I've just never been through anything like it! It was absolutely astounding. They were just kind of pouring in. It was all with a single message: 'This is my story, too.' That's what they all said one way or the other. And I bet half of them said it in those words: 'This is my story, too.' That gave huge reinforcement that this really was a powerful, powerful thing."

Vest, Birgenau, Hopkins, and others were already thoroughly committed to fixing its endemic, if unintentional, sex discrimination. But that outside scrutiny—which included eighteen months of nonstop letters, e-mails, and requests for Hopkins to speak on campuses across the continent—also heightened their attention and commitment. The entire academic world was watching. The third part was in place: outside pressure.

Because of that enormous publicity, Hopkins says, still more doors started to open. "MIT tried to fix it in a very systemic way," she explained. For instance, payroll data became available for scrutiny. "They made the gender equity committees in science and engineering into permanent committees, and women faculty openly review the primary salary data. I see it for all of MIT now. If there's anything that looks odd, we go to the department chairman, discuss it, and corrections are made." That's no small step forward, especially when you understand how secretive academic institutions are about paychecks. That's produced results. Hopkins agrees that "This is not an MIT problem. This is a universal problem in science and engineering. MIT is actually ahead of most places; it has gone from eight to fourteen percent women in engineering in the last four years."

This approach—requiring conscious attention to equity and measuring to make sure no one's lapsing back into their ordinary habits of mind—is exactly what social scientists say is needed. "You never say, 'Now everything's even, and things will naturally evolve in an equitable way from here on out,' " explains William Bielby, professor of sociology at the University of California at Santa Barbara. Rather, he explained, you need "constant and routine monitoring." He was talking about consent decrees in class action cases, but he agreed that the same was needed for any attempt to overcome stereotyping.

None of this is to say that MIT has yet closed the wage gap between women and men. "It hasn't gone away completely," Hopkins said. "Is it better? Yeah. It's different."

So what now? Will MIT's pay equity reforms (and all its other efforts against unconscious sex discrimination) stick? That's an especially important question, given that Charles Vest left MIT in 2004. Will the new president, the neurobiologist Susan Hockfield, be as committed to an effort that will forever after be attributed to her predecessor? "I sure want to believe so!" Vest said. His optimism, he said, comes from the fact that the results haven't entirely been left to chance: he and others at MIT have built in institutional safeguards. "There is a much greater awareness of the issue. We try very hard to make this an issue for the deans. We've got a very committed provost and deans out there. It's not going to go away."

Hopkins is also cautiously hopeful about the future. Realizing that Vest and Birgenau would not be there forever, "We raced to put in place committees and rules and whatnot, committees to check on committees, and the whole system," she said. "But it still requires women and top administration to be committed."

MIT: *The Lessons for the Rest of Us*

So what should we learn from MIT's transformation? For one thing, one woman can make a difference. Nancy Hopkins got fed up. She stopped being able to believe that her employer or her colleagues were treating women fairly. The results made history.

But it's just as important to notice that Hopkins was careful, even strategic, about how she confronted this systematic inequity. She slowly and steadily collected data—first on lab space, then on percentages of qualified women hired and tenured, and finally on salaries. She used that data both to check her own impressions and to persuade others that those inequities were real. She documented what she had experienced by writing a formal letter about it—a process that forced her to clearly articulate what was wrong, to marshal the evidence and explain its consequences. Before sending off that document, she checked its conclusions with her colleagues, a process by which she built allies. All along the way, she collaborated with others who cared about the institution. And she was open with outsiders about what she had found.

In other words, Nancy Hopkins made change much as she had pursued scientific truth: regularly checking her facts, reviewing her data with others, and rigorously testing her conclusions. She worked with women and men, with peers and superiors. And she's committed to this course of change—reviewing this process of change for as long as it takes to transform the institutional culture.

That's one model of making change. As we'll discuss in the chapters to come, each person will tackle the wage gap in her (or his) own way. But no one should risk her whole career by tackling the issue all alone, or all at once. Nancy Hopkins's lessons are clear: Inform yourself fully; build a group of female allies who also know they've been treated unequally; keep researching as you go; collaborate with women and men throughout the institution; and keep your focus on fairness.

But Nancy Hopkins and her female colleagues were only one side of the pressure triangle that made change. The larger lesson of MIT is this: Fixing the wage gap requires women to be committed. It requires top executives to acknowledge inequity and make a commitment to ending it. And it requires the rest of us to keep watching, and to cheer (or boo) as needed.

Brigham and Women's Hospital: Once Is Not Enough

So does MIT really need to have a committee that reviews hiring, promotion, and pay each year? Couldn't an institution just adjust once— and then, having brought everyone even, let women and men compete on their own terms?

No. That's the lesson to be learned from Brigham and Women's Hospital in Boston. There, led by Carol Nadelson, a Harvard clinical professor of psychiatry and director of the Partners Office for Women's Careers at the hospital, an informal assortment of female physicians persuaded the dean of the Department of Medicine to review and equalize salaries.

At Brigham and Women's, the situation was and is genuinely complex. Each physician and researcher has joint appointments at the hospital and at the medical school. Salaries and other compensation come from a variety of sources: research grants, clinic or medical group sal-

aries, bonuses for seeing more patients, or sometimes a portion of patients' insurance or Medicare reimbursements. A variety of direct and
dotted-line managers weigh in on an individual physician's salary and
compensation package. And those creative compensation packages can
be negotiated so as to include surprising extras: research assistance,
extra administrative support, parking spots (which can be quite expensive in Boston), malpractice insurance payments, mortgage and reloca-
tion assistance, and more.

Nevertheless, in 1998, "the department of medicine did look at all of
the jobs," explained Nadelson. It created a complicated ranking for-
mula that included such elements as specialty and subspecialty, rank,
length of employment, and so on. Using that, the department drew a
line for median compensation, and graphed who was above and who
was below that line. "And guess what? There were more women below."
The hospital equalized the salaries for all those doing comparable
work—and far more women received increases than did men.

But here's what they discovered: it's not over until it's over. Because
of complicated market dynamics (including real estate markets, higher
pay for physicians in private practice, insurance reimbursements for a
particular specialty, and so on), every time a new person is hired, the
scale has to be adjusted again. Usually the new person must be hired at
a higher rate than what those already at Brigham are making. Since that
breeds resentment among all those already at work, the hospital must
readjust salaries each time there's a new hire. "And that became a very
complicated problem, very expensive," explained Nadelson.

Nevertheless, a couple of years later, the same committee urged the
dean to do a review. Here's what it found: when they drew the median
line, once again, many women had dropped below it. All the discriminatory dynamics that had been in place before—those unconscious
stereotypes that leave women reluctant to negotiate and uninformed
about what's fair, that prompt men in positions of power to pick other
men and overlook talented women, and so on—were still in play.

Nadelson's conclusion is this: "You have to keep reviewing salary
equity episodically." Once is not enough. You have to adjust—*and* pressure for behavioral changes, *and* keep that pressure on by measuring
regularly—and adjust and adjust until the American culture has *com-*

pletely changed. Handling the matter once just doesn't fix it. Sustained attention and ongoing monitoring will.

When Pressure Starts from the Outside: Change at Mitsubishi

Nobody loves a lawsuit. You've seen that in the previous chapters. Women bring them only when they feel pushed to the wall. Employers fight them tooth and nail. They're enormously expensive for everyone involved, both financially and emotionally. The aftermath can be nasty as well. After years of legal wrangling, everyone—employer, plaintiffs, fellow employees—has an entrenched point of view and more than a little anger left over from the fight. The organization has been through a civil war—and now has to repair both the damage *and* the discrimination.

So lawsuits always leave a question behind: Once the court award or settlement money has been paid out, will the company change? When, and how, can a lawsuit get women even?

They don't always. I talked to a number of EEOC attorneys and plaintiff bias lawyers. All agreed that a consent decree with court supervision can change employers only if (like the therapist's lightbulb) those employers really want to change. For instance, the National Center for Women and Policing reports that consent decrees have indeed dramatically increased the numbers of women in law enforcement—but that the numbers drop again, almost as dramatically, "as soon as the consent decree expires or is otherwise lifted by the courts."[1] More than one employer, having signed a consent decree that allows the government to monitor its behavior for three or four years, does absolutely the minimum required until the decree expires and then returns to its old ways.

Nevertheless, frustrated by wrongdoers that would rather pay out millions of dollars than change, government and plaintiff bias lawyers have come up with some very creative and effective consent decrees in the past decade. Before signing on the dotted line, employers must agree to some far-reaching structural changes—changes that go much deeper than simply publicly posting job openings or promoting a few token women. Many financial service companies, for instance, were forced to create objective measures by which new and old accounts would be distributed. Rent-A-Center's consent decree required the creation of a human resources department that would write and enforce fair employment policies, and whose vice president would report directly to the CEO. Home Depot agreed to create an online job application system that enables anyone who's qualified to apply for jobs and promotions, without having to know the "right" manager. And always, an effective consent decree imposes outside monitors who review reports, check on the climate, and measure compliance.[2]

When you boil down the most effective consent decrees to their essence, here's what you find: all three parts of the pressure triangle are in place. Women have already documented the discrimination thoroughly; otherwise the company wouldn't have lost the case (or settled before that could happen). There's certainly outside pressure, in the form of court oversight requiring organizational changes. And those changes take root *only* if the third part of the triangle is in place: if the CEO has agreed that the organization must be transformed.

All that was in place at Mitsubishi, site of one of the most notorious sexual harassment cases of the 1990s—which transformed itself into a zero-tolerance employer.

On April 9, 1996, the EEOC filed a sexual harassment suit against Mitsubishi Motor Manufacturing of America and UAW Local 2488. According to the EEOC, sexual harassment pervaded the 4,000-worker plant in all the ways you remember from chapter 7: obscene drawings and sexual graffiti on walls and on cars moving along the assembly line; air guns and wrenches shoved between women's legs "in fun"; groping, fondling, and daily obscenities. More than 300 women were joined in the class action complaint against the 4,000-person assembly plant in Normal, Illinois.

The plant was run by Diamond Star Motors, a joint venture of Mitsubishi and Chrysler Corporation. Diamond Star (and many of its employees) fought back ferociously. It chartered 59 buses to send more than 2,500 workers and managers to picket the Chicago EEOC office and installed phone lines to let them make free calls to their Washington representatives. Employees' jobs were threatened. One plaintiff found a note pinned to her locker that read, "Die, Bitch, you'll be sorry." Others got threatening calls at home.

But Diamond Star found itself in the middle of a media tornado. Both the National Organization for Women and Jesse Jackson's Operation PUSH and Rainbow Coalition organized boycotts of Mitsubishi and Chrysler. Thirteen members of Congress, led by Representative Patricia Schroeder of Colorado, sent the company a letter saying that American women were watching Mitsubishi's behavior toward its female employees. Both the plant's and the parent company's reputation were badly damaged.

The judge sent the parties to mediation under Abner Mikva, former chief judge of the U.S. Court of Appeals for the District of Columbia. On June 23, 1998, the EEOC and Mitsubishi (joined by the UAW's Local 2488) emerged from mediation with a signed consent decree. Mitsubishi agreed to pay out $34 million to the harassed employees — eventually paying $10,000 to $300,000 each to 486 women in the largest sexual harassment award ever resulting from Title VII of the Civil Rights Act of 1964.

The money was only the beginning. The comprehensive twenty-four-page decree required far-reaching and detailed changes to the plant's policies and procedures — including the appointment of three monitors who would oversee the Normal plant for three years. One monitor was appointed by the EEOC; one was appointed by Mitsubishi; and one was appointed by mutual consent. These monitors were responsible for reviewing and revising all of Mitsubishi's sexual harassment and employment policies and practices. The goal: a zero-tolerance policy toward sexual harassment that would stop problems long before they got out of hand.

On the day the consent decree was signed, no one involved with the case would have predicted a happy outcome. Anger still crackled in the air. "When I walked into that plant the first day," said Nancy Kreiter, the EEOC's appointee and research director of the Chicago-based organization Women Employed, "the daggers that were being thrown my way, especially as a representative of the government! There was just so much hostility among the parties. They had been through years of litigation. It was awful! Employees all hated each other. I thought, 'Oh my God, this is going to be impossible.' "

Mitsubishi already had much of the first part of the "pressure triangle" in place: the sexual harassment had been thoroughly documented. But if needed changes were to take hold, more documentation was still needed. The monitors had to find where the policies and procedures were broken, so that they could be fixed. What happened when someone complained? How quickly was the complaint investigated? How well did employees understand what was acceptable and what was beyond the pale? Did supervisors and managers keep an eye out for harassing graffiti or obscene comments or nasty attitudes, even before they were reported?

Within a year the monitors had conducted on-site interviews with key managers and more than one hundred randomly selected employees. They surveyed the attitudes of five hundred employees; observed sexual harassment training for supervisors and associates; reviewed procedures for filing and investigating complaints of sexual harassment and retaliation; and looked into all the investigative reports in the company's files. The monitors walked the entire production line, learning the minutiae of spending a workday making a car. They wanted to know for themselves whether a worker might feel isolated in the paint shop, for instance, or how close workers stood on the assembly line. They walked from the factory floor to the complaint office, to see whether a woman who filed a sexual harassment complaint could do so privately—or whether she risked retribution simply for heading in that direction. "We did whatever it took to feel what it would be like to work there," Kreiter said. "You can't regulate civility, but you can create the right conditions for it."

The monitors got down into that level of detail. They translated sexual harassment training out of legalese and back into plain English. "It came down to saying in training," explained Kreiter, " 'You can't do this! Clean up your language. Clean up your attitude.' They needed to know what was acceptable behavior and what was unacceptable." They ensured that the office charged with investigating sexual harassment complaints was physically separated from employee and labor relations, to make it clear that it wasn't treated as a collective bargaining grievance. Disciplinary measures were made consistent, no longer subject to favoritism. "The guidelines became so clear, the results of discipline became so clear," said Kreiter, because the monitors forced Mitsubishi to "come up with and document very, very consistent investigatory processes."

One thing that helped, said Kreiter, is the fact that the consent decree imposed three outsider monitors, not just one. Working as a team gave them several advantages. For one thing, they had the benefit of one another's professional perspectives. "Having outsiders in there was significant," she said. "We had to have a consensus in order to go forward. By the end you couldn't tell who represented whom. We would laugh when we were writing the reports. I would be sitting there arguing for what the company's appointee was supposed to advocate. We really, truly worked as three unbiased people." And having a group of three, Kreiter said, gave their recommendations much stronger moral force, making them harder for management to dismiss or pick apart: to do so would require dealing not just with one person but with all three.

But as effective and as well informed as their pressure was, said Kreiter, the monitors couldn't have succeeded alone. "A consent decree alone cannot do it [make institutional changes]; a consent decree absent monitors probably can't do it at all," she said. "It's all about management."

Mitsubishi: Commitment from the Top

Mitsubishi had plenty of documentation about what was wrong; it had plenty of outside pressure. But what really transformed Mitsubishi was top management's decision that there would be no more sexual harassment at the plant, ever—just as Charles Vest decided there would be no more sex discrimination at MIT, ever.

"I never thought the Mitsubishi plant was going to be a place free or relatively free of sexual harassment," said Noelle Brennan, an EEOC attorney who litigated the Mitsubishi case, "and they really did, from all accounts, turn it around." In her opinion, "What made the difference is that their general counsel—who fought us tooth and nail during litigation—decided after losing that that wasn't an effective strategy."

His new attitude, Brennan said, was "I'm going to now cooperate with these people."

When I asked Gary Shultz, the Diamond Star general counsel, why he'd done such an about-face, his answer was straightforward: Mitsubishi had been battered in the media; its reputation among consumers, especially women, was lousy. So it might as well transform its organizational culture. "We were at the bottom of the barrel here with regard to respectability. We needed to rise from that. And we needed help. The monitors were there; we were going to have to take them whether we wanted them or not. So when you're given lemons, you make lemonade." Instead of stalling and resisting, Diamond Star threw itself into the consent decree. As it selected its monitor and nominated a joint monitor, Diamond Star chose "people who were going to challenge us. We needed to improve. The best way to do it was to have tough schoolmasters."

Diamond Star didn't sit back and wait to be told what to do. The company charged aggressively into implementing the consent decree. First, it created a credible investigation department, as the consent decree required—and it did that as quickly as it could. As Shultz put it, "There was a very low confidence in being able to resolve this through our human resources department, because they had been so tainted." The plant's official human resources organization was clearly part of the problem, not the solution. A new and independent department, named the Opportunity Programs Department (OPD), was created. Its newly hired director had run a similar department at a local university. As her deputies, she hired former Illinois Department of Human Rights complaints investigators. That gave the department both much-needed experience *and* much-needed credibility.

Why did Diamond Star embrace the transformation so wholeheartedly? "Well, I think that when you're so far down, the only place you can go is up," Shultz explained dryly. "And so why not aim high?" To its surprise, improvements in employee morale and on-the-job behavior also led to an improved product. "As we clawed our way out of this employment situation, we noticed also the improvement in our manufacturing quality," Shultz added. "As we saw the effects coming about, we kept aiming higher."

That came naturally, Shultz believes, because Diamond Star was already dedicated to a manufacturing process called "continuous improvement," or *kaisan* in Japanese. This continuous improvement process was transferred over to its sexual harassment and antidiscrimination policies as well. "This became one of those projects where we took an introspective look at ourselves, our employees, and how we manage our employees, and we improved it. The monitors were right there with us with regard to discrimination claims, to help us grow. That was the stimulus."

Nancy Kreiter, the EEOC-appointed monitor, agreed that Mitsubishi's management team had been terrific. "We had a fabulous general counsel. The OPD [Opportunity Programs Department, created to investigate sexual harassment and discrimination claims] person was good. The HR person bought into it. Everybody we dealt with bought into it. Once they saw that we were there to help, that we were a very united team and wanted to work *with* them, not against them—one by one, they were basically the biggest promoters."

But Kreiter put the final responsibility for the turnaround even higher up than the senior management team. She and the two other monitors had been anxious when, midway through their term, the plant's top manager changed. Progress had been made. Would it continue?

Yes, it would. "This guy, Rich Gilligan, came in as executive vice president," said Kreiter. "He seized this zero-tolerance policy and just went after it with a vengeance, and started communicating with his hands-on style. [He] actually increased the progress. It went from resistance, to gradual acceptance, to an outright decision: Get us to the best place. They bought into the notion that instead of just being in compliance with the consent decree, they wanted to be a model company." Mitsubishi's attitude became " 'We want the best training, the best policy, the best investigations, the most thorough tracking of charges, the best follow-up, the hardest discipline.' It was like 'If we're going to do it, if we're forced to do it, then let's come out looking better than any company.' I don't think that it would have happened without Gilligan. His role was monumental. And he's still there."

At the end of three years, in their final report to the EEOC, the court, and the company, the monitors wrote:

The Normal plant in many ways is a different place than it was three years ago. MMMA [Mitsubishi Motor Manufacturing of America, Inc.] has complied with its obligations under the Consent Decree and deserves credit for its efforts. There has been a significant change in the "culture" on the plant floor. . . . [T]he evidence strongly suggests that serious incidents of sexual harassment at MMMA have become rare. Offensive sexual talk and disparagement of women . . . are now understood to be impermissible and are avoided by most employees. . . . MMMA's procedures for investigating and disciplining sexual and sex-based harassment generally work as intended. . . . At present, employees who violate the "Zero Tolerance Policy" (ZTP) are likely to be reported, investigated, and disciplined. Serious transgressions can and do result in terminations. . . . [F]ear of retaliation for reporting sexual and sex-based harassment to the company has also decreased markedly.

When I spoke with Gary Shultz, I asked him what he'd recommend to other companies. "I get asked that all the time," he answered. "It's real simple. Just don't do what we did! Open yourselves up before you get opened up! Why not call in experts now, and be proactive instead of reactive?" He compared Mitsubishi's old policies to a messy garage, with hoses and rakes thrown everywhere. "It's not so obvious to you because you're here all the time. But an outsider is going to point out that you have to clean house. Auditing or monitoring is essential! No matter how good you think you are, it's always nice to have an outside person gauge it. Call in somebody else that might have some expertise or ideas."

That's hardly the attitude he would have taken before the lawsuit. But "we had our wake-up call," he explained. "Because before we were charged by the commission, we were very closed. And now we're transparent. We saw what happened." According to Kreiter, by the end, Shultz had said, "I think every company should have monitors in them whether they have a problem or not." Can you imagine a company lawyer advising employers to bring in outside snoops? Such a statement says a great deal about how much an outside eye can help in reforming any organization's policies and operations.

Diamond Star Motors' transformation—from harboring some of the country's most egregious sexual harassment to becoming a zero-tolerance model—has apparently continued. The government remains a source of real outside pressure. Had the company relapsed, say both Kreiter and Brennan, the EEOC would be seeing a rise in complaints. That hasn't happened. Kreiter said that she's had enough ongoing contact with the executives to feel confident that Normal, Illinois, remains dedicated to having one of the best plants in the country.

"It was a huge, huge win for everybody," said Kreiter. "It was a huge turnaround. I give everybody credit in it. I give the company credit. I give the government credit for writing an absolutely brilliant consent decree with every conceivable thing that could pop up."

Has women's *pay* gotten even at Mitsubishi's Normal, Illinois, plant? I doubt it. Wage disparities weren't on the list of charges; getting rid of unequal pay was not among the monitors' responsibilities. And since it wasn't tackled directly, I'd bet that female and male workers at Mitsubishi aren't yet even, dollar for dollar. But sexual harassment, as you saw in chapter 7, steadily drains away women's paychecks. Getting rid of it is an enormous step—if not toward equality, than at least away from the worst sort of *in*equality.

So what can we learn from Mitsubishi? That the three parts of the pressure triangle worked together to force change. Women's sexual harassment charges were thoroughly documented. Outside pressure forced Mitsubishi's policies and procedures to change. And then management ensured that change really took hold throughout the plant, wholeheartedly supporting those changes not just in the letter but in spirit. "It worked at Mitsubishi because it came from the top down," said Kreiter. "The mandate came from the top."

The North Star Guide to 100 Percent: Minnesota

All right, so it's possible—with a concerted and ongoing effort from below, outside, and the top—to tackle discrimination on the job. But is it possible for women to get to one dollar?

For an answer to that question, let's go to the North Star state: Minnesota. In 1982, when the movement for "comparable worth" was at its height, Nina Rothchild was the director of that state's Council on the Economic Status of Women; Linda Bergland was a state representative. Bergland and Rothchild were shocked to find that some of the state government's female employees—such as clerical workers and nurses' aides—qualified for food stamps. Working for the state was supposed to be a secure post—but these jobs didn't pay single, divorced moms enough to feed their kids. Bergland and Rothchild did a study and found that the state's predominantly female job categories were paid significantly less than the predominantly male categories—and that even within categories, women were regularly paid less than equally qualified men. And so they launched a campaign to evaluate and adjust state government workers' pay until it was equitable.

The comparable-worth campaign had several things going for it. First, its backers had concrete evidence that state government was going to pay the money one way or the other: either upfront in wages or out back in food stamps and housing subsidies. Second, the western state of Washington had recently been charged with systematically underpaying women compared to men in comparable jobs—and had lost in court. Similar winning court cases looked inevitable. "We took the position that we can either do it right up front," explained Rothchild, "or we can resist and fight, and it will cost us a gazillion dollars later on in back pay. The women's movement was much more visible and active then. There was a sense of inevitability at that time: sooner or later that things were going to start getting better for women."

Third, the inequity was obvious. Minnesota had recently started using the Hay job evaluation system. Many people in corporate America know about the Hay evaluation system and other similar human resources evaluation systems. These methodologies enable employers to systematically assess and compare every job by a series of measurements in order to come up with a pay scale that will rank and reward comparable jobs fairly. Points are awarded for various aspects of the job, such as its degree of complexity, danger, responsibility, and so on, as well as what levels of education and experience are required. Equipped with these point systems, human resources departments and executives can then come up with rational job grades and accompanying pay scales. In theory, these systems are sex-blind, along with being blind to race, religion, age, disability, and other factors that might incur discrimination. Because the Hay system and some others were created in an earlier era, they often need to be fixed to drain off some residual bias, but that can be done. For instance, Ronnie Steinberg, a sociology professor at Vanderbilt University, has been a pioneer in removing sexism from job classification systems.

The state of Minnesota took the results from its Hay evaluation, and compared men's and women's pay in government jobs at all levels of skill, effort, and responsibility. The results were stark. "The Commission on Women got the listing of job classes," said Rothchild, "and saw an absolute, consistent pattern of disparity between men's jobs and women's jobs. These were not fancy statistics! I used little Magic Markers to make red lines and blue lines. There were such glaring disparities. [The Hay system is] really an establishment system. And you find this absolute pattern: When women predominate in a job class, it's paid less than its points would indicate."

The legislature was surprised by the gross gap between pink and blue pay, explained Rothchild. "I can remember being before legislative committees, and they'd say, 'Well, what about the ones [the female-dominated job classes] that are higher?' And I'd say, 'There are none.' The pattern was absolutely consistent. There were *no* places where female jobs were rated equal to men's, and got paid either the same or more." Ignoring critics who warned that the effort would bankrupt the state or that it was interfering with the free market, the legislature passed a bill requiring that all salaries would be evaluated and adjusted to ensure equal pay for comparable work. But while they had passed the idea in principle, they didn't yet have money budgeted to implement that effort.

The equal-pay forces had documentation. They had outside pressure: both the threat of a lawsuit, and the morally abhorrent fact that female state workers qualified for relief. What they needed next was support from the top. That came the following fall, when a populist Democrat, Rudy Perpich, was elected governor. Said Rothchild, "He felt strongly that women's rights were high on his agenda." The monies were budgeted, the system was put into place, and Perpich appointed

Rothchild to be his Commissioner of Employee Relations, the state agency in charge of implementing pay equity.

"I must say that I did run into a fair amount of resistance in the beginning," explained Rothchild. "Staff said it was too hard to do, that we really needed to look at the job evaluation system again, and all that stuff. But I was the boss, which is always nice! And I said 'Nope. We can do it.' " As at Mitsubishi and MIT, Minnesota had committed leaders who refused to back down.

Commissioner Nina Rothchild and her small staff took the state's job evaluation report, which assigned points to every job based on skills, responsibilities, experience, and work conditions—in other words, what it took to do the job, rather than *who* was doing the job. They found in 1984, for instance, that the experience, responsibilities, and work conditions of the categories (all-male) delivery van drivers and (99 percent female) clerk-typists II were comparable. But the female job earned only 80 cents for every dollar the male job earned. Similarly, (all-male) radio communication supervisors' jobs required skills, experience, and responsibilities that were comparable to those of (all-female) typing pool supervisors. But these women earned only 75 cents for every dollar their male counterparts made in radio communications.

Men's salaries were never lowered; rather, women's salaries were raised to match. About 8,500 employees got pay equity raises that averaged $2,200, which took effect over a couple of years. No one got rich. But thousands of women got well-deserved raises that boosted their badly needed take-home pay.

Faith Zwemke is the one-woman bureaucracy now responsible for implementing the state's pay equity laws. She explains that the law's cost "was carefully estimated to be two to four percent of payroll. It came out to be 3.7 percent when it was fully implemented. It was done in a very orderly, phased-in, manageable fashion." Let's look at what that meant in real figures. In 1983, legislators voted to earmark $21.7 million (1.25 percent of the payroll) for pay equity raises; in 1985, the legislature earmarked another $11.7 million to complete the task. Since then, the legislature has continued to vote small financial increments to correct for slippage.

Unlike Brigham and Women's Hospital, the state of Minnesota continues to evaluate women's and men's jobs for equity every year. "It's an ongoing process," said Zwemke. "Jobs do change. Administrations change. You have to keep adjusting every couple years. But it doesn't require much money after awhile. The tools of analysis stay the same."

"Maintaining a system is really simple," Nina Rothchild explains, echoing Zwemke's sentiment. But it's necessary. Usually, she explained, wages are set by looking at the market rate. "You look around and see what everybody else pays! And that does nothing but perpetuate three hundred years of discrimination. By forcing people into setting wages in a different manner, you give them a new way of looking at wages. That new way maintains itself if they have to look at it every two years."

How well has the system worked? Twenty years later, women who work for the state of Minnesota earned 97 cents for every dollar men make. And the state's bond rating was AAA, the highest bond rating possible: bankruptcy was nowhere on the horizon.

That's an extraordinary feat. State agencies are full of laws and rules passed when an issue is hot—but left unfunded, or buried in a file cabinet, or inadequately implemented because legislators never followed through. Minnesota legislators have kept their integrity on women's pay: for years, they've allocated the money needed to get women to 97 cents. What's more, they've loaned their system to local governments as well, which wouldn't have been able to get women even on their own: using the same point system, Faith Zwemke evaluates and adjusts women's pay for 1,500 towns, cities, and counties as well.

The state of Minnesota has shown the nation that a large employer can pay female employees just as much as men in similar jobs. It has demonstrated that it's possible to raise women's wages without draining men's paychecks. It has shown that large employers can lead the way for smaller employers. And it has proven that all this can happen without financial ruin or large social costs. As Faith Zwemke puts it, "The law was implemented without lawsuits and without bureaucracy."

If only things were just as fair for *all* women who lived in Minnesota, and not just those who worked for the state! But that's not so. In 2002, Minnesota women who did *not* work for the state earned only 73 cents to a man's dollar. Its private and nonprofit employers continue to set wages through salary surveys and other such tools, paying market rates for each job. But the methodology that the state of Minnesota used can easily be adapted by any employer. "It would work *easily*," explains Rothchild. "In fact, most large employers do have job evaluation systems. All it would take would be somebody who says 'We're going to do it,' somebody who has the power to make it happen." In more practical terms, Zwemke explains that any employer, large or small, "could use that statistical analysis that we have on our Web site and punch in all their data." Documentation, outside pressure, leadership, practical approaches, and ongoing commitment. Minnesota has shown that women's wages can get—and stay—(almost) even.

So how can we get *every* American woman even in the next decade? For that, let's turn to the next chapters.

CHAPTER 12

Women, Working from the Inside Up

Step 1: Women working from the inside up. Women employees (and their male supporters) have to advocate for themselves individually and for all women where they work.

The wage gap is not women's fault. It exists because of discrimination. At the same time, each woman *does* have a responsibility to act. Without your efforts, the wage gap will never close—and the next generation of women will be stuck with that gap as well.

So how can *you* convince *your* employer—and American employers as a whole—to close the gender wage gap, once and for all?

By standing up for yourself. You must make sure that you are paid fairly. It's that simple. Doing so can be straightforward. You don't need to have a Ph.D. in statistics to get paid what you deserve. You don't have to sue your employer. You don't have to get mad and act so aggressively that you become someone you don't like. You must simply take five steps: document, research, collaborate, ask for fair pay, and celebrate.

In this chapter, we'll consider why each of these steps matters, and how each step can be carried out. But let me be clear: This chapter offers a vision and an outline, not a detailed map. Your job is to be creative in how you carry out these steps. Do it in a way that best fits your situation, your character, your industry, your job. This isn't a one-size-fits-all self-help book; it offers a diagnosis of, and set of prescriptions for, fixing a national social ill. In addition to getting yourself paid fairly, maybe you'll also pressure one man to do the right thing. Or maybe you'll organize a conference for an entire industry. Maybe you'll add or advocate for a "wage gap" report about your own company's pay scales in its quarterly documents, internal bulletins, or newsletters. Maybe you'll start a petition to your CEO or write a letter to the editor of the local newspaper. Maybe you'll read about and learn from what other women are doing at www.wageproject.org (see next paragraph) before deciding on your own approach. Each of us will, in her or his own way, keep the pressure on employers, the media, and our politicians to ensure that women's wages are fair.

Whatever you do, know that you are not alone. What *can* help all of us is information about and communication with each other. As I've mentioned in previous chapters, while you're reading this book, a national nonprofit organization called the WAGE (Women Are Getting Even) Project is being launched. The WAGE Project can be a communications hub for all of us who are working on closing the gap, whether in our own personal lives, in our companies, or in larger communities. WAGE has one purpose: to support those working to end sex discrimination in the American workplace in the near future—and to make sure women and men are paid equally. There will be a bit more about the WAGE Project's plans in this chapter and in chapter 13, but for the most current information, check our Web site at www.wageproject.org.

The WAGE Project is a resource, offering important information about the gender wage gap, and a watchdog on progress. Women must act on their own. So please, while you read these steps, do so actively. Think about how you can apply them in whatever way you can do best. And let WAGE know when you have successes or ideas that might inspire others.

Among other efforts, the WAGE Project will support women who launch WAGE Clubs. A WAGE Club is a cross between a book group and an investment club. They can be groups of women who work for the same employer, who live in the same neighborhood, or who know one another socially. At their inception, WAGE Clubs will be women coming together to work their way through *Getting Even* (with a reading and discussion guide posted at the WAGE Project's Web site). Next, WAGE Club members will work through the action steps below. They will support, critique, supplement, and celebrate one another's efforts to win fair pay, both individually and alongside other women. As they do so, they'll be a key source of ideas and feedback for the national WAGE Project. If you want to plunge in this way, be sure to register your club at the WAGE Project Web site, where you'll find suggestions and resources.

But launching or joining a WAGE Club is not mandatory. Closing the wage gap will take a national effort involving many individual women (and male supporters) working in concert. No single individual can do *everything*. That's the point: we have to work together.

1. Document every incident of discrimination — and of defeating discrimination.

Back in the late 1990s, when I first started asking women what they thought about the wage gap, *every* woman had a story about how her earning power had been set back. And here's what really grabbed my attention: their stories weren't about long-ago difficulties, but about recent setbacks. Even now, several years into the new millennium, I'm still hearing the same stories over and over again. Now is the time to turn those anecdotes into powerful, persuasive documentation. Using thousands and thousands of stories of women's experiences as evidence, we will demonstrate that most, if not all, of the lost 23 cents measures wage discrimination. We will drag the unconscionable gender wage gap into the public spotlight, and into employers' consciousness. The glare will be so strong that employers will be forced to do something — lest courts and legislators do it for them.

But we need to record those stories first. Right now, women have a credibility gap. Almost no one in business, the media, or public policy realizes the extent to which women are discriminated against — in the wallet, where it counts. Too many chief executives flatly deny such discrimination exists within their operations. They believe it's not their problem. And even if they do suspect that some sex discrimination might exist, they worry that any formal recognition might lead toward costly litigation.

As long as the full picture of women's wallet discrimination does not exist, employers can and will get by with ignoring this problem. In Part II, I documented and told the stories of as much discrimination as I could find. But that's just a beginning. We need more evidence. And we'll have enough only when women everywhere write down all their experiences.

That means you. Every single time you think you're treated unfairly on the job—even if you're not 100 percent sure it was discrimination— document it. Just found out that the man who replaced you was hired for much more than you ever made? Appalled that a man with less experience gets on the payroll while you're still a consultant? Sick of being told your promotion is coming, when the men around you have all moved up? Furious that the shy woman down the hall quit because her manager wouldn't stop pawing her? Appalled to see, in the payroll data, that women make less than comparably (or lesser-) ranked men? Angry that certain job categories—or promotion-track projects—are somehow never open to you or your female coworkers?

Write it down. On paper or on disk, track your own encounters with discrimination. Measure and document whatever unfairness you see, wherever and whenever you see it. I'll discuss what to do with these documents later in the chapter. But for now, think of Nancy Hopkins measuring her own and her colleagues' lab space or the history professor in chapter 5 comparing the numbers of women and men in her department who'd been tenured. Keep a log with dates, times, and facts about each incident and—this is important—calculate what that incident cost you, both at the time and projected into your future. If you absolutely cannot stand writing things down, do this step with a partner. Have her interview you and write down your experiences, and then do the same for her. The point is to go beyond simply steaming privately or pushing things away, and to look at discrimination coldly and precisely. It's one thing to suspect that you're being treated unfairly; it's another to examine your evidence in black and white, as objectively as you can. If you have a WAGE group or a WAGE buddy, go over each others' evidence. Ask: Does this sound like discrimination to you? How much did this bite into my paycheck?

In addition to keeping track for yourself, please send your story (or stories) to www.wageproject.org. One of the WAGE Project's main efforts is building a national database of just how much sex discrimination is costing working women in America. We will guarantee your anonymity. On the Web site, you'll find an explanation of how we'll keep your story confidential. Your privacy will be *paramount*. The WAGE Project is dedicated to helping equalize women's wages, not to helping women lose their jobs. We will make sure that, when you add your story to this archive, you won't be putting your paycheck in danger.

A national archive is needed for two reasons. First, individual women often doubt themselves. A single incident can be confusing: there's no way to know whether there's a pattern of discrimination. Second, those who are mistreating women *may not recognize that they're doing it.* As we saw in earlier chapters, discrimination is often happening thoughtlessly, through unreflective stereotyping. As a result, if you bring up your concerns with your coworker, or manager, or human resources department, you might get brushed off as an oversensitive troublemaker—even if you're right.

In their book *Legalizing Gender Inequality*, law professors Robert Nelson and William Bridges[1] found that, within any particular company or institution, the decisions that nick women's pay may be made by many different people—none of whom intends to hurt women's earnings. But, they explain, when women show that all these little nicks are part of an employer's normal operating procedure, and when the women themselves tell personal stories about how that financial loss has hurt their lives, their lawsuits can win large sums of money.

I'm not suggesting that you should race off to court. But what works in the courtroom will also work in the boss's office. Remember President Charles Vest at MIT—what moved him was carefully documented data showing that female scientists systematically received less support than their male counterparts—combined with those women's personal stories about being worn down by everyday discrimination.

That's what the WAGE Project archive will do—document that everyday discrimination on a national scale. If all women record these moments, the WAGE Project will be able to show whether, and where, there's a pattern. And we can show these systematic patterns to anyone who needs the proof: employers and their boards, reporters and their editors, corporate and plaintiff employment lawyers, and local, state, and federal government agencies. When combined with those of others, your story—your testimonial—will show employers that these patterns of "disparate treatment" exist right under their noses. Believe me, they'll get the message: if they don't do something to eliminate the stereotypical behavior that results in unequal pay ("disparate treatment"), sooner or later, some of their disgruntled women employees will decide they've had enough—and drag those employers into settlement negotiations or, ultimately, court. Adding your story to the WAGE Project archive will help *all* working women shine a glaring spotlight on discrimination and its costs.

And please, send WAGE the positive stories too! The WAGE Project will be thrilled to hear about your discrimination-busting employer, your successful negotiations, your transformed workplace. Show others that it can be done!

2. Do the research.

Find out what men with your experience, performance record, education, or other qualifications get paid for doing jobs like yours. Research your industry, region, and job title. Look at the gender composition of different job titles to see whether female employees are clustered together in a lower-paid "ghetto" with no way out. With people you trust, brainstorm strategies to find out more about your workplace's salary scales, compensation packages, and policies and practices. While you're at it, learn how to benchmark your salary against your coworkers' and against your peers in similar companies nearby.

You can use a number of resources for this pursuit. Check commercial Web sites such as www.salary.com (or do your own Internet search to find a similar calculator) to compare your salary to those of others in your occupation, industry, and region. If you get stuck during your research, ask your local librarian for help, lean on your WAGE Club, talk to trusted colleagues within your employer or industry, call a favorite old professor, talk to your brother or spouse or mother, or check the WAGE Project's Web site for others' suggestions. Notice that, at this stage, you're not necessarily comparing your salary to those of your male peers within your company. You're trying to get a general sense of what your skills, experience level, and responsibilities are worth on the job market in your industry and region.

Here's the point of your research: Figure out what you *should* be getting paid. If there's a gap between what you're making today and what you *would* be making if you were an equally qualified, equally experienced, equally responsible man—you need to know that. Because in the next step, you'll figure out what to do about it.

As you do this research, guard against two common tendencies: either despairing ("I'm afraid to find out how underpaid I am!") or downgrading your own worth. Unless you have a lot of confidence, it would be wise to have, if not a WAGE Club, then at least a WAGE buddy who'll talk you through any interior roadblocks. Research is essential. Unless you know what your personal wage gap *is*, there's no way you can be sure you've closed it. Think of MIT professor Nancy Hopkins telling others her salary so that she could find out theirs. Your research will take persistence, creativity, and collaboration. Think of all the other women across the country who are doing this too. Together we're tackling this not just for ourselves and each other but for the next generation.

Remember that this step is ongoing. Keep researching as you go along—and as you figure out what else you need to know. Next, you need information about what's fair within your company. You might not be able to get internal salary information right at first. So start with what you *can* measure. What's important on your job? For some, that might be having the most current safety equipment or software upgrades. In others, you might see whether men and women have the same amounts of administrative or research support. Does everyone have the same opportunities for training, or the same budget for industry travel—or are some of your colleagues more equal than others? How are decisions made about who is allocated new clients, assigned parking spaces, or re-location money?

Even if you can't find information about others' salaries today, you might figure out how to do so tomorrow. Many employees find this data—and without being either devious or confrontational. Sometimes it's handed to them accidentally. There was the purchasing agent who found her predecessor's time cards and pay stubs in her office, back in chapter 3. Sometimes employees know what others make, and see the pay scales every day. They don't have to go sneaking around or violate any confidentiality obligations, in order to realize—or even mention to others—that pay is unfairly skewed by sex. Sometimes women ask their male buddies, colleagues who have heard on the grapevine who makes what. Men often know what their peers earn. It's their way of keeping score.

But even before you have found out about salaries within the company, calculate what the wage gap means for you. Go to the Web site www.wageproject.org. Use the wage loss calculator to see for yourself what discrimination is costing you. How much will you be losing—not just this year, but for the rest of your life—because you're missing two, or five, or fifteen thousand a year? What's the cost of *not* getting that promised raise or promotion? What are all those moments of being marginalized doing to your *lifetime* earnings?

While doing these calculations, figure out what you're missing right now: the vacation *you* can't afford next summer, the college tuition money *you* could have set aside, and the contribution *you* could have made to your retirement nest egg. Once you add up the actual costs to *you*, the wage gap gets very personal. When that happens, I have no doubt that you will be fortified for the next step: pressing your employer for the pay you deserve.

3. Collaborate and build allies.

When MIT's Nancy Hopkins became so frustrated, so fed up with knowing that she was being mistreated and not being heard, she decided to write to MIT's president, carefully detailing how female scientists were being held back. But before she sent that letter, she paused. Worried that she could be too easily brushed off as a crank, she decided to show it to one other female scientist. To Hopkins's immense relief, her colleague agreed with her conclusions—and wanted to sign on to the letter. Then the two of them wondered whether MIT's *other* female scientists agreed. All but one signed on. Hopkins no longer had a personal complaint; she had a movement.

You must do this as well. Find some other women who work where you do. If they've already discovered their own wage gap, suggest that you band together. If they haven't, encourage them to do the research by discussing your own.

Talking with others in the company is a good idea for two reasons. First, it brings you information you might not have known you were missing, information about compensation extras that you didn't even know were up for discussion. Second, and just as important, you find allies among both women and men. These are the people who will help you later on. Be sure that when you do this, you do it in a smart way. For instance, don't start your search by raising this issue in a staff meeting, where others might be embarrassed. Instead, start these conversations by being open, welcoming, and thoughtful, with a constructive approach that won't be perceived as undermining your colleagues or the company. Talk about everyone's shared belief that wages that should be fairly earned, and rationally and equitably distributed. Practice talking about this with your WAGE group or someone else you trust, to be sure that you're comfortable enough to be confident and open. When you're at this step, be sure you do it wisely.

It's important to do this even if you're not a "joiner." MIT's female scientists certainly weren't; before Hopkins's now-famous letter, they had never talked to one another about what it felt like to be a woman at MIT. Yes, there are some things you will have to do alone. Still, collaboration is important for effectiveness. Working together reduces the risk of being ignored as individual troublemakers or ridiculed as malcontents. And lasting organizational change is best accomplished collaboratively.

Consider collaborating on efforts outside the company, too. Maybe you'll be getting together with civic leaders to focus local media attention on your region's wage gap. Maybe you'll be offering pro bono services to WAGE or your regional EEOC office. And maybe—this is my favorite prediction—you'll come up with something better than I can picture today. Whatever it is, please let the WAGE Project know how it works out!

When you collaborate, include men wherever possible. Men's help and support are critical to getting women paid fairly. Not just men who are bosses and chief executives, but also the men who work beside women in every plant, store, and office. These men can be natural allies. And only with men's help can women get even.

Nothing in the *Getting Even* plan means men have to take pay cuts for women to get paid fairly. Companies will threaten this as an excuse. Don't listen to them. The state of Minnesota didn't cut men's pay: it raised women's. Men won't lose. And they have a lot to gain. Wives who bring home bigger paychecks help the whole family live better. When men see women who work alongside them get treated and paid fairly, they'll know their employer intends to treat *every* employee fairly— including men, even the men who aren't special favorites on the inside track. And men who see employers paying women what they're worth can breathe a little more easily about their sisters' and daughters' and nieces' futures. Men have a direct and personal stake in seeing women get even.

There are many ways men can help women. For instance, they can be solid mentors. They can include women in the informal networks that explain how things get done and that share information about one another's bonuses or benefits. They can coach women in negotiating. They can listen seriously when women charge discrimination, and dive into investigating, documenting, and ending it—without the kind of defensiveness that forces a lawsuit. They can help create a corporate climate that refuses to harbor excuses for discrimination in hiring, paying, or promoting women.

You've read about such men throughout this book. Men have stood up to discrimination when they've seen it. They've filed EEOC charges or testimony on behalf of women. Some are even willing to suffer career setbacks rather than sit idly by and watch women be mistreated. That's what happened when Rent-A-Center managers quit rather than throw away women's job applications or fire women just for being women. And it's what happened when a recruiting firm head refused Hyundai Semiconductor's order that he stop referring women and African Americans for its jobs. In interviewing women for this book, I've heard about appalled husbands who urge their wives to stand up to unfair treatment and who back them when they do. I've heard about fathers who take a stand because they're eager to make a better world for their daughters. MIT President Charles Vest, for example, said that, among the men involved in MIT's pay equity effort, "all have daughters. And we do absorb things from a totally different perspective."

Women need working men as allies in the campaign to get even. Just ask them to help. Many will gladly step up to the challenge and opportunity.

4. Learn to negotiate: it's just asking the boss for a fair paycheck.

> At one point I saw a printout—I wasn't supposed to but I did—so I knew what everybody was making in the department. Now, my boss is the kind of guy who wants to be fair. He says, "You're the best engineer I ever had." He doesn't have that blindness that women are inferior. So I say, "How come I am getting paid less than _____ and Anne is getting paid less than so-and-so?"
>
> He was being very honest with me. He said, "If they're not asking for more, I am not going to give it to them." That's what he said to me.
>
> This is what I learned: That any boss will pay somebody the least amount of money they can to keep them. He knew that Anne was willing to make fifty thousand, but the guy sitting next to her wants fifty-five or he was going to look for another job. And if you look at women's statistics, we're not jumpers. We get in a company and we stay. I had *never* negotiated for my salary.
>
> —Environmental engineer

I had my annual review with my executive director last week. I asked her for $65,000. I had looked around and compared my job with similar jobs. I got a four percent raise, to $57,000. She did what she could. She has to justify pay changes with the board.

The whole point is that the level at which you start determines your fate.

—Nonprofit executive

The next step is one that many women say they dread: asking for more money. One female economist, when she heard my prescription, asked skeptically, "Are you suggesting women put their jobs on the line just to get paid a little more? Women won't take that risk."

So let me be clear. You don't want to make demands on your own, angrily, full of outrage, charging into the boss's office and sounding unreasonable. But if you *don't* ask, you *won't* get paid what you deserve; you can be sure of that. With facts and reason, with support and suggestions from your allies, you can ask your boss to correct the unfairness that's in your paycheck today.

Remember what you found out from your research in the last section. You probably found a difference between what you are paid and what's being paid to a man doing similar work, with similar experience and responsibilities. And if you did, you found out why there's a difference in pay: because he was promoted while you are still waiting; or because the company gave him more resources to bring in business; or because your boss thought you couldn't handle any more work because you have family responsibilities. Whatever the excuse, the real reason is that you're a woman. That gap is due to discrimination. It is both unfair and illegal. And you're the one who's paying the price, in weekly, monthly, and yearly income lost.

Prepared with your documentation and with your research, you're almost ready to negotiate with your boss. Don't flinch at the word "negotiate." It doesn't have to mean confrontation or conflict. The dictionary definition of "negotiate" is quite moderate: "To confer (or, exchange views) with another so as to arrive at a settlement of some matter." You're going to confer with your boss about facts and information that reveal your paycheck to be unfair. You're not accusing anyone of being evil; you're laying out the objective facts as you see them.

But don't leap into the conversation with the boss too soon. First, prepare thoroughly. Learn the skills of persuasion and negotiation. Like everything else about your job, persuasion and negotiation are learned skills. Repeat this out loud: *I can learn how to persuade. I can learn to negotiate.*

There's no such thing as a "born negotiator" or a "natural persuader." They learn. That's true for men too. Ask some of your male friends and family. Here's the evidence: Walk into a bookstore and look at all the advice books about persuasion and negotiation on the business shelves. Who do you think is buying all those books? Most people, men and women, sweat the first time they have to persuade their boss or client to do things their way or negotiate a big contract. But they learned how, just as you learned how to get good grades, how to come across well in an interview, how to dress in a style that's appropriate for your workplace, or how to behave in a way that fits the organization's culture.

How can you learn? Go to the bookstore or library and look through relevant books until you find a few that speak to you. Ask friends or family members how *they* learned to negotiate or what tips they might have for you. There's no correct blanket recommendation; you'll have to find a guide whose style suits you personally. Don't just rush in and ask for more money *today*. If no one is a born persuader or negotiator, then everyone has to practice. Practice—out loud—with a trusted friend, in your WAGE Club, or in your mirror. If you do belong to a WAGE Club, consider inviting expert guest speakers who will talk with you about wages, salary negotiations, compensation packages, and career ladders. Trust me, these professionals will leap at the chance to give their best advice—for free. They'll hope that some of your club's members will pay them to be coaches or advisers sometime in the future. Or perhaps they'll jump at this chance to help women close the wage gap.

Most important, be sure that this step is part of your group's research effort. You'll do a much better job if you've been swapping ideas, tips, resources, and mistakes, and if you've spent some time practicing together and critiquing each other (constructively, of course). I know I'm beginning to sound repetitive, but this is important: Don't tackle this all alone.

Too many women get halfway and then stop. They think that if they work hard enough to earn a raise or promotion they'll be treated fairly and that raise will automatically show up in their paycheck. Many women believe that salaries should be handed out like grades: if you work hard, your worth will be recognized. They pretty much assume, as Professor Nancy Hopkins put it, "that there was a system that was fair." But in reading this book, you've learned that that's not true. Wages and promotions aren't grades, which are awarded on merit. You have to persuade someone to give them to you. No employer willingly pays workers any more money than they have to. You have to both earn it—and ask for it. If you don't, your pay will remain unequal. You have to advocate for yourself. You have to make your case for being paid fairly now—and later. Once you get even, you must remain vigilant. You must insist on being treated and paid fairly, for the rest of the months and years that you work.

If you're reluctant to ask for more money, it's not your fault. You've been pressured *not* to ask. Gender stereotypes aren't just *outside* of us, prompting men to undervalue women; they're also *inside* us, prompting women to feel that it's not "right" to ask for money for themselves. Just as it feels "natural" to men to automatically think of another man for the job, so it feels "natural" to women to wait until someone thinks to reward them for their good work.

But it *is* your responsibility to buck those pressures—and to stand up for yourself. After all, if women are asking men to override *their* internal stereotypes, it's only fair that we must also override our own. If men must change, then women must change too. We're all in this together. If *you* don't do it, you're reinforcing the guys' ingrained beliefs that they *can* take advantage of women—and they'll treat the next woman (and the next generation of women) the same old way. So when you learn to ask for fair pay, it's not just for yourself: you're doing your part to get all women paid fairly.

Asking for a fair paycheck doesn't have to be like pulling teeth. You don't have to confront your boss. You don't have to act like an arrogant, cigar-chomping jerk. You don't have to become so nasty that you wouldn't invite yourself over for dinner. It's better to ask in a style that's comfortable and that fits your personality. In fact, there's growing evidence that that's much more effective. For instance, negotiations coach

Lee Miller, who cowrote *A Woman's Guide to Successful Negotiation* with his daughter Jessica Miller, suggests trying to convince, collaborate, create—hardly a combative, testosterone-driven style.

5. Talk to the boss.

If you've done your research well, the chances are good that you'll be able to respond intelligently to any questions—and that your boss will accept your facts. Be sure you've lined up your allies first. Be sure they've helped you check your research, examine your facts, investigate the company's wage and compensation packages, and practice your negotiation techniques. Now you are ready for the next: Ask to be paid fairly.

Many women will begin with individual conversations with their own managers. This might come as part of an annual review, or while discussing a possible promotion. And some women will immediately get even. Hard to believe? Let me tell you the story I heard from one engineer—who had to get even twice. Late in the 1980s, this engineer accidentally ran across another engineer's pay stub. The two of them had been there the same amount of time and were ranked as equal on the company's internal "order of value," a printed document. And yet she was making $28,000 and he was making $34,000. She immediately understood that the percentage difference was quite significant. So she pointed this out to her boss. "They immediately rectified the salary discrepancy. Like that. And we only got raises once a year. This was like 'Oops, she's got us!' "

The engineer didn't stop there. She told two other female engineers to check their own salaries—and both got salary increases of their own. "None of this was retroactive," the engineer explained. "It was just at the end of that day when we were making more money. But then I could take it with me." She could negotiate her next salary from a much stronger base.

Nevertheless, a decade into her *next* job, this engineer found herself in precisely the same situation. "At one point I saw a printout—I wasn't supposed to but I did—so I knew what everybody was making in the department," she said. Her boss thought of himself as a fair guy. "He says, 'You're the best engineer I ever had.' But she was *still* getting paid less than her male peers. When she asked why, he explained that when she had been hired, she hadn't negotiated for a higher salary—while the male engineer had. "This is what I learned: that any boss will pay somebody the least amount of money they can to keep you. . . . I had never negotiated for my salary."

Finally this engineer had learned her lesson. When she moved to her next job, "I went from $100,000 to $140,000. I went in as cocky as I could possibly be, [saying] 'This is what I am looking for; this is what I need to come over here.' And you know what? They gave it to me! If I had only known this twenty years ago! I was sitting around waiting for it to come to me."

So ask. Few, if any, bosses want to be known as unfair. Demanding, yes. Hard-driving, sure. They want to be known as high performers, talented, and creative. But unfair? Nope. Especially when they know that beneath the label "unfair" may hide the word "illegal." You never have to use that word. Few bosses respond well to direct threats. Challenges, yes; threats, no. When you present the facts in a reasonable way, you will have conveyed your message.

Of course, you might not have as much luck as this engineer. Your manager may not be willing or able to get you even or fix unfair organizational practices. What now?

Here's where your allies are absolutely essential. The cliché is true: there's strength in numbers. You don't want to go any further alone. That might put your job at risk. So here's the next step: As a group, meet with the CEO, the top dog. Tell your stories—just as the female MIT professors did with President Vest. Let your CEO know that these stories may signal a larger, systematic pattern of wage discrimination throughout the whole company. Ask the CEO to do a gender wage analysis like the one that the state of Minnesota does. If that study shows a pattern of underpaying women employees, press the CEO to eliminate the wage gap by raising those women's wages, which will save the company a lot of bad publicity and costly litigation.

Once you've done this, your group has triggered the second part of the pressure triangle: CEOs working from the top down. When you make a sustained, solid case about your unfair pay to the boss, he'll be hard pressed not to make amends.

Sure, you may nevertheless run into a stone wall with the CEO. But armed with the facts and your new sensibility, you and your allies still have other options. You might get the attention of board members or the business's owners—using whatever method seems the most sensible course, given your group's situation—and ask that they hold the CEO accountable. You might come up with a strategy that would work still better within your organization. Be creative and thoughtful about how you approach this. But do get yourselves even.

The point is this: You must make insisting on a fair paycheck a part of your workaday thinking and behavior. Do your research to make sure you're being fairly paid. Hone your styles of persuading and negotiating. And then, to borrow the slogan, just do it. With your allies, act as if you're calm and confident. Ask for fair paychecks as if your group were asking on behalf of all women. Because you are.

For instance, remember B. J. Wilkinson, the highly skilled and underpaid woodworker from chapter 8? Not long after being interviewed for this book, Wilkinson started thinking harder about fair pay. She went to www.salary.com to find out her region's salary range for the kind of work she did—and discovered that it ran $45,000 to $60,000. She was being paid $30,000. That did it. She quit her company and started her own Web-based business, Flying Horse Woodworks, which designs precision plans for any custom woodworking project, including detailed instructions for specialty carving. She sounded proud and delighted as she described her new business. "Give me a couple of dimensions and a picture—kitchen cabinets, you name it! I can draw up computer-routed plans for it and tell you how to make it." When she was asked whether she would make more money, you could hear Wilkinson's grin over the telephone lines. "Yeah! Oh, I'm going to make more money. Definitely." She's doing her bit to help close the wage gap.

6. Celebrate!

Take pride in your moments of wage-related success! Every time you— or one of your female friends, colleagues, or WAGE Club members— gets a raise, a promotion, more benefits paid by employer, or some unforeseen extra, anything that fattens her paycheck and gets her closer to even, take time to salute her accomplishment. The wage gap is made up of lots of small nicks and cuts. Wiping it out will require many small efforts—and a lot of stamina. So let's celebrate every time we move forward even a notch.

Not just for you, but for *other* women as well. So be sure to tell the rest of us about it. Post your successes on the WAGE Project Web site. As you'll see, you won't have to link individual names to specific salaries. But when women throughout the country see the paycheck gains made by other women, they'll celebrate too. Others can learn from your tactics how to get better pay.

All that goes triple for your collaborative efforts. When it's appropriate, boast about your organization's successes to the WAGE Project and to the media. That will push your company to do more—*and* put pressure on *other* employers to get their women's salaries even as well.

Hopelessness is solitary; success is infectious. Every one of us will get better at getting even when she hears about other women who are doing so as well.

Now what?

Here's what will happen when large numbers of working women document their experiences in wage discrimination, research their own wage gap, collaborate with each other in standing up for equity, and ask that they and other women be paid fairly. Their employers are going to feel pressure. When employers see that the women who work for them are informed about what they're due and are making the cases for their own pay, employers will feel heat to reexamine their entire operations. That's exactly the pressure women *must* put on their employers to be paid like men. Women must *act* to get bosses to *react*.

Many individual women will realize that what they are asking for is simply fairness for themselves and all other working women. They will see that they are not alone. Other women will catch the spirit—and women will act en masse to get even.

CHAPTER 13

CEOs, Working from the Top Down

Step 2: CEOs, working from the top down. Bosses must commit themselves to closing the wage gap within their organizations.

Chief executive officer. President. Boss. Whatever the title, in the American workplace, the person at the top has all the power necessary to make sure that female employees are fairly paid—today. Not next year. Not ten years from now. Now. I've sat on enough corporate and nonprofit boards to know that when a strong chief executive decides something will be done, his (and it's usually his) leadership team single-mindedly gets it done. Not only does he (or, far less often, she) have the power, but he also has all the authority he needs. He certainly doesn't need any more laws. Discrimination at work is already illegal. He doesn't need a vote by his board of directors. They assume he's running the operation within the letter of every law and will judge him harshly if they see any hint that he is not.

Most important, he has the responsibility. If there's any pay inequity within the organization, it's illegal—and it's his job to fix it. No other employee but the chief executive bears the ultimate responsibility for today's pay equity—or, I should say, pay *inequity*. When women are not paid fairly, far too often the chief executive is either ignoring this *illegal* problem, denying this *illegal* problem, or hoping this *illegal* problem will go away before his company gets sued. If the top boss isn't tackling pay equity head-on, he's failing one of his key job responsibilities: obeying the law.

Discrimination and stereotyping are so deeply embedded in most workplace cultures that only the chief can fix it. Even those a level or two lower in the organizational pecking order cannot erase inequity on their own. Some of these employees, wittingly or unwittingly, are part of the problem; others simply lack the authority to be effective.

When I talk to people about wiping out the gender wage gap, some object that CEOs are responsible only for their own square inch of territory: their own employees. According to this line of thinking, bosses can't do much about the larger marketplace. That means they're not responsible for sex segregation, which crams women into pink-paycheck occupations such as waitresses, teachers, and nurses. They're not responsible for the fact that the "market" offers higher wages to blue-paycheck production supervisors, maintenance workers, truck drivers, and electricians. If the market offers higher wages to one group than the other, it's not the CEO's fault—or problem.

But this objection is faulty. After all, women in sex-segregated occupations aren't employed by that *occupation*. They work for some corporation, business, government agency, or nonprofit institution. And CEOs oversee all kinds of employees. A hospital president is responsible for approving the wages of both nurses and maintenance workers. An auto manufacturer's top boss is responsible for approving the wages of both production workers and janitors. A mayor is responsible for approving the payroll for both teachers and truckdrivers. It's up to those CEOs to ensure that their wage scales are fair. CEOs must take responsibility for paying women fairly. If the state of Minnesota can do it, so can every other employer.

So here's the bottom line for this book: ***Chief executives officers, individually and as a group, must be accountable for eliminating what each one of them contributes to the nation's 23-cent gender wage gap.***

It may not be due to malevolence. "We may be blinded to where opportunity really isn't equal, and then may unknowingly contribute to sustaining that level of inequity," says MIT President Charles Vest. That's understandable. But it's not excusable.

Here's the corollary to that bottom line: ***Without CEOs' action, the problem will not just fade away. Every top boss must insist that pay inequity is erased within that organization.*** In Part II, we've already seen the multitudinous evidence of discrimination, and learned about insidious stereotyping. To undo such unthinking behavior, CEOs have to assign rewards for fixing it, and penalties for failing to. They may well hand off the day-to-day tasks to a vice president of human resources, ethics officer, or chief counsel—someone who reports to them directly. But the rest of us mustn't lose sight of who's responsible for the wage gap, and who must therefore be held accountable: the chief executive.

Motivating CEOs

Until now, CEOs haven't been clamoring to close the gender wage gap. What will it take to motivate them now? The most straightforward motivation is this: pressure from their female employees (and male allies). When bosses read this book, or when they hear about the WAGE Project's national archive of women's discrimination stories and wage data, they will feel pressed to look long and hard at their own operations. Knowing that women are documenting their personal experiences with wage discrimination and asking for fair treatment, many CEOs will begin worrying that their organizations could be legally liable or vulnerable to negative media attention.

Some CEOs will eliminate their own wage gaps just because they've read (or heard about) this book or the WAGE Project. I know. While writing *Getting Even*, I spoke to top bosses who decided on the spot to eliminate their organization's wage gap. Sure, they told me at first that they didn't believe they had a wage gap. But they agreed to analyze their employees' wages—and, if they discovered that they were systematically underpaying women in "women's work," promised that they'd raise those wages pronto. When they do it—and an outside audit confirms that they've closed that in-house wage gap—you better be sure that the

WAGE Project will loudly trumpet their successes. Good publicity can be its own reward.

As women make this a national issue, some chiefs will realize that it would be cheaper to tackle this problem from the inside out than to risk a multimillion-dollar lawsuit, or even unflattering news stories about their treatment of women—since merely the accusation of unfairness can taint the company, whether or not a lawsuit is ever filed. Prompted by pressure from women inside and outside of the company or by growing public attention to this outrageous inequity, many chief executives will calculate that it's in the organization's best interest to close its own wage gap—before someone else decides to force them to do so. As Mitsubishi's general counsel Gary Shultz advised, in reflecting how much the Normal, Illinois, plant had benefited from fulfilling not just the letter but also the spirit of its EEOC consent decree, "Just don't do what we did! Open yourselves up before you get opened up. Why wait?"

There's a third important incentive for CEOs, one that shouldn't be overlooked: money. I've spent a lot of time with CEOs, and I know that they are straightforward creatures. They do what they're rewarded for doing. If their bonus is tied to revenue growth, they'll see to it that sales grow. If their bonus is tied to profit growth, they'll drive the company to increase profits. Every year, CEOs and their directors agree on a couple of clearly articulated, measurable goals. The chief and his or her leadership team achieve these goals because their bonuses—which can be as big as a year's salary—depend on these performance measures. But in well-run companies, directors hold their CEOs accountable for more than just numbers. So here's what should be done: Boards of directors should peg a hefty portion of the CEO's bonus to closing the wage gap—not for one year, not for two years, but for as many years as it takes until the annual wage review shows that the gender gap hasn't come back. That will be the proof that the organization has changed its culture and discrimination is gone.

Why should boards bother? Because eliminating sex discrimination is part of the directors' fiduciary responsibility. Giving the CEO an incentive to drive sex discrimination out shows that directors have recognized the potential cost to the company's reputation—and therefore, the bottom line—if biases are not rooted out. Directors have a powerful hammer: they can hire or fire the CEO. When those directors make it *financially* clear that sex discrimination must not be tolerated, the CEO will know that his job is on the line—and he will close his company's wage gap.

Those boards can act, in other words, as the third part of the "pressure triangle": the outside pressure. Because of insider malfeasance at Enron and other companies, there has been public pressure to add truly independent outsiders to many boards of directors. Of course, some boards still include directors who have no ties to the company, but whose close relationships with the CEO may cloud their judgment. Nevertheless, as they exercise their trust obligations to the stockholders, all directors know they face intense scrutiny by public officials and the media. As they realize that discrimination is rampant in the American workplace, and as women make clear that we will no longer allow ourselves to be underpaid, boards of directors will be forced to ask: Could *this* company be vulnerable in the court of public opinion? Is *this* company breaking the law? Or is this company a community model of respect and fair pay? They will—and must—raise these questions in board meetings. Since these directors decide how long the CEO will stay on, the CEO will be forced to respond with serious and substantive action.

Boards can and must hold one person accountable for answering those questions correctly: the CEO.

Does it sound crass—or utopian—to recommend tying the chief's bonuses to compliance with the law? Well, then, it does. I'd like to think that most CEOs are, as MIT's president Charles Vest describes most people, "fundamentally good. Most people *want* to do the right thing. If one becomes convinced that there is a problem, an inequity, something that's not right, whether it's gender bias or something else, then simply saying that in straightforward simple terms, in one or two declarative sentences, can make a huge impact." I hope he's right. I hope that, after reading this book, chief executives will make pay equity one of their organization's top goals, simply because it's the right thing to do. To outsiders, this may seem hopelessly naïve. But most CEOs think of themselves as decent men and women who are doing a civic service by providing jobs and income for their employees. They think of themselves as fair and want their companies to be fair—especially when, as with closing the wage gap, the pursuit of fairness does not compromise the pursuit of profit.

Still, I am a realist. I want to see working women get even with working men in my lifetime. If that means tying the top boss's bonus to organizational pay equity for five years, then that's what it takes. Millions of women will be better off for it.

So here's my message to directors and CEOs: Pay for it and get it done. Take the advice that Gary Shultz, Diamond Star's general counsel, gave in chapter 11. It'll cost less to do it on your own than it will cost to be forced by bad publicity or a lawsuit or strike.

If you're sure that your business or organization is already fair to women, prove it. Analyze all your employees' wages by gender. Bring the WAGE Project the results. Your analysis can be confirmed (without divulging confidential company information) through an impartial assessment; you'll find the analytic tools and resources you need at the WAGE Project's Web site. If you don't have a wage gap in your company, or if you are committed to closing that gap, trust me, we will publicize it to the skies.

Below is a checklist of *exactly* what head honchos need to do to close their organization's wage gap.

1. Adjust pay scales throughout the company.

Examine how much men and women with comparable education, experience, working conditions, productivity, and responsibility are being paid. Compare pay in job categories that are dominated by women with those dominated by men. Where women are systematically being paid less, give them raises. Get them even. And get an independent audit to ensure that the gap has been closed. You may hear "We don't have a gender wage problem" from your subordinates, not because that's true but because those directly under you don't want to tell you a costly truth or reveal what they may have overlooked for years.

Adjusting pay scales isn't hard to do. As described in chapter 11, Minnesota did it with its 38,000 state employees. Brigham and Women's Hospital's Department of Medicine did it. Businesses can do it, too. Here's one of the reasons it can be straightforward: because many employers already use some point-based job evaluation system, as Minnesota does, to classify jobs and compare salaries. At companies that use such a job evaluation system, bosses need only adjust their reports and databases to rid job classes of any lingering gender bias, and then compare salaries by gender. They'll quickly be able to see where pay is systematically skewed by gender, and calculate the appropriate adjustments. The guiding principle is simple: Pay for the job, not for who's doing it. I asked Faith Zwemke, Minnesota's one-woman pay adjustment office, whether there was any reason companies couldn't use Minnesota's methodology to eliminate its own gender wage gap. "Absolutely not," she said. Any company "could use the statistical analysis that we have on our Web site and punch in all their own data. It's a Web calculator, just like the loan calculators banks provide on their Web sites."

If the employer doesn't have the internal expertise to get there, there's plenty of help available. Many existing consulting firms already offer such services. Other companies can also use the Minnesota system, says Zwemke. Minnesota's job match booklet includes its 1,800 titles, ratings, and job specifications, and it's freely available online. Go to the WAGE Project's Web site for instructions and a link. There employers can figure out which mostly female job classifications (say, administrative assistants) are underpaid compared to mostly male job classifications (say, maintenance staff). All they need to do is set aside some of the company's budget for raises and give these women pay equity raises. There are no intellectual or methodological breakthroughs required. All that's needed is a chief executive with backbone.

Audit pay annually.

That initial pay equity adjustment patches up the problem—but it doesn't get rid of it. Every year, the CEO will need to audit pay patterns within and among job titles, adjusting for managers who've slipped back into undervaluing women. Minnesota does regular audits. So do MIT and Brigham and Women's Hospital. Ongoing auditing—built into the regular processes of the company—shows whether you're making progress, and where you need to pay closer attention.

Listen closely when individual women complain
about unfair treatment.

Individual women will tell you about their experiences with unfair treatment. Listen carefully to them. Make it clear that you welcome their stories, respect their concerns, and are committed to solving those problems. Make financial amends when they have reasonable claims, without making them wait for a total company reform. Especially avoid forcing them toward demoralizing formal charges and investigations. Buried in those individual stories may very well be the clues to organization and managerial behavior that causes systemic discrimination. You can learn a lot from the female employees who have the courage to come to you to make well-reasoned cases that their paychecks have been unfairly clipped.

While you're at it, check the WAGE Web site to see how, under the force of consent decrees, other companies have vaulted forward. Learn from those companies that have been forced to change—and borrow that creativity to improve your own. Find out how your company can alert women to chances for promotion, investigate and prevent sexual harassment, fairly treat pregnant employees and those returning from maternity leave, and pay women and men equally.

2. Insist on zero tolerance for overt discrimination.

Next, chiefs need to show all employees that discrimination won't be tolerated one bit. Annual pay adjustments are just a stopgap. If the wage gap measures discrimination, then discrimination must be eliminated to enable the company to close the gap *permanently*. Top bosses need to investigate each and every accusation and rumor of sexual harassment and other sorts of discrimination. The organization must stop shuffling harassers and misogynist bullies from one protected spot to another, the way the Roman Catholic Church did.

Investigating doesn't mean judging in advance. If the charge isn't valid, that's a relief. But if it is, the organization must swiftly and firmly take disciplinary action—and show everyone in the company that misbehavior is strongly and appropriately punished. CEOs must then follow up to make sure that the whistle-blowers aren't punished later by colleagues sympathetic to the wrongdoer. Employees know when disciplinary action has been meted out. They take that warning very seriously when it comes from the top. The reverse is also true: If the warning doesn't come from the top, they know it can be ignored.

Chief executives must take personal responsibility for these investigations. The CEO should designate someone—human resources, corporate counsel, a grievance or ethics officer—to report each quarter on discrimination and harassment charges. The responsible officer must report those charges directly to the CEO *and* the board of directors, without any intermediate hierarchy, reinforcing the message that driving out discrimination is a top-level priority. The CEO's job is to see that, quarter after quarter, those numbers go down steadily. There might be a spike at first, once women realize they can report in safety. But over time, numbers should go down—not because women are afraid to report, but because discrimination and harassment are chased out.

Of course, no organization will ever get to zero. Some people behave badly. There's no psychological screening test for outrageously intractable bigots. But most employees respond to their corporate culture. The person at the top can make sure that others know there are consequences for harassing, mistreating, ignoring, or underpaying women. Chief executives could help themselves by taking a lesson from Mitsubishi's experience. Once management swallowed hard and paid $34 million for sexual harassment and agreed to overhaul its harassment procedures, the plant set out to have the best systems anywhere: for reporting harassment charges, for investigating charges, for tough, no-nonsense punishment when charges were proven. "Zero tolerance" at Mitsubishi became more than words in a corporate policy document; it became a daily reality.

Once again, employers can find plenty of help in accomplishing this. Some corporate consultants have made this a specialty. I have no doubt that, as this movement gets going, various specialists—legal academics, social scientists, human resources magazines, business school case writers, EEOC officers, and others—will outline best practices and profile model companies. There can be no excuse for failing. If the top boss wants to get this done, it *will* get done.

3. Use objective measurements for hiring, raises, and promotions.

As mentioned above, adjusting pay is an essential and extremely important first step. But it simply patches over the problem. And erasing overt discrimination gives women a chance to shine. But neither of these *ends* the subtler, daily problem of undervaluing women.

Fortunately, there is a fix. After decades of research and careful studies, social scientists today agree about what it takes to override mindless and systemic discrimination. Employers must eliminate stereotyping *behavior* of individual employees and group managers—which excludes outsiders, such as women and nonwhite men—at every stage in the work life cycle.

Some of you are rolling your eyes at this. End stereotyping? Shut down power cliques? Why not just announce that we're going to end war, hunger, and disease while we're at it? It is true that stereotyping often happens without explicit thought. It's also true that power cliques often don't realize that their unfair discrimination is hurting others financially. That's the point: you can't stop those stereotyping thoughts. As we saw in chapters 7, 8, and 9, that mental habit is deeply ingrained in our brains. But you can stop the *behaviors* that result. By making stereotyping explicitly conscious, and by letting people know that their behavior is being watched, you can end discriminatory *behavior*. You can retrain people into *behaving* fairly. And eventually, what employees *do* will alter what they *think*.

Start by articulating objective performance measures everywhere in operations, at every stage of the work life cycle: hiring, raises, promotions, and any extra step that's significant in your industry. (For financial services firms, for instance, the extra steps would include distributing leads and accounts; in science, allocating research assistance and lab space; in light industrial and the trades, deciding who gets sent to which

job site.) What exactly is required to do the job? What are the requirements to do the *next* job up the ladder? How do you measure a good
year, a mediocre year, and a bad year? When there's more than one
qualified candidate, how do you decide who moves up and when?
Write it down, make it clear, and make it fair.

Almost every employer says that it can't be done. But when forced,
they figure out how to do it. Home Depot said it couldn't be done—
until, under the pressure of a multimillion-dollar lawsuit, it came up
with its computerized hiring and promotion kiosk. Universities regularly insist that outstanding scholarship can't be measured—yet they do
it every day, when they decide on hiring, tenure, and promotion. "Every
single large defendant claims, 'Oh, it can't be done, it's too cumber-
some,' " William Bielby, a sociology professor at the University of California at Santa Barbara, notes—but then they figure out a way, even
where creative genius is the job's essential ingredient. "Lawrence Livermore Labs insisted that every single organizational unit was different,
that there was a different science involved. Fine. We're not saying there
has to be a single performance evaluation. But there needs to be a set of
standards that are measured in a systematic way in every unit." Guess
what? Lawrence Livermore figured out a way to measure geniuses!

"Even if the criteria and standards are complex, and require exercises in judgment, and can't be rated easily on a scale of one to ten,"
Bielby says, "you simply insist that they be articulated and written down.
You insist that a mechanism be put in place to apply them systematically. And then you monitor that."

Here's why this works. When managers are forced to write down reasons for their hiring, pay, and promotion decisions, they must think
about those decisions consciously. That's how you override stereotyping: by making decisions consciously, instead of on the more comfortable but biased measure of "gut feel." "Gut bias" happens not just to
women: many groups (notably, but not only, African Americans) know
what it feels like to be held back by stereotypes, evaluated by superficial
group characteristics rather than individual evidence about skills and
effort. The "tap on the shoulder" approach favors the in-group, whatever that group might be: other white guys, retired military officers,
Tri-Delta sorority sisters, or Notre Dame alums. But the good news, ac-

cording to experts, is that whenever an employer puts into place systems to overcome unconscious bias or in-group favoritism, *everyone* reaps the benefits—and has a greater chance of getting ahead on his or her merits. A manager might still hire or promote exactly the same person. But he or she will have had to think about and articulate the reasons—and make sure that those reasons are the *right* reasons.

The other reason it works is one good CEOs already know: *people live up to expectations.* We all know that expectations are extremely powerful. Knowing—or even suspecting—that the system isn't fair has a corrosive effect on employees' performance. The reverse happens when managers make it explicitly clear that all performance measures *are* fair. More female employees (as well as employees from any other disfavored group) will be freed to live up to their potential.

There's a big bonus to this approach. "The things that affect women are often perceived as unfair generally," Bielby said. Other experts agree. If the measures are objective, it's more likely that not just sex discrimination but *all* discrimination and favoritism are put under the microscope and exposed. Home Depot's approach ended up diversifying the workforce not just by sex but also by race, ethnicity, religion, age, and national origin. That goes for all kinds of diversity, not just multicultural diversity. If a CEO eliminates the stereotyping behavior that sets back women's paychecks and replaces it with objective measures, he or she also eliminates discrimination for all other outsiders—which means anyone who isn't part of the corporate "in crowd." That might be people with disabilities, lesbians and gay men, or older workers . . . or it might be anyone who doesn't belong to the boss's country club. When everyone knows the grading system, it's harder for one person to get an unfair advantage.

Experts warn that there's a danger to watch out for: it's easy to apply objective standards in an unfair way. "There's a phenomenon called the 'leniency bias,'" explains law professor Joan Williams. "Objective rules can be used in an extremely biased fashion. In sexist environments women tend to have the rules applied very rigidly, and men have them applied very comfortably." That happened, for instance, to the pipefitter in chapter 7 when she was docked for taking off her life jacket to use the portapotty—something the men did without repercussions. It happened to the firefighter when she was told she had to wear gloves, even though there were no gloves small enough to fit, and was then chastised for taking too long to unreel a fire hose that had been incorrectly jammed into place.

But a determined boss can make sure this doesn't happen. That's what the next step is for.

4. Monitor and measure progress.

Each CEO must monitor progress on gender equity. "Keep track of what happens," says Marc Bendick of Bendick and Egan Economic Consultants, Inc., "to see if they are making progress over time—and to hold individual managers responsible." Employers must keep tabs on the gender balance in hiring, raises, promotions, and pay every year, measuring each manager for progress. Knowing that they'll be measured forces managers to think about their decisions in a way that they could justify to others. That explicit consciousness of their behavior with regard to gender is what motivates and enables them to catch and fix any bias.

Think about the examples you've read about so far. At MIT, when department heads made recruiting calls and no women were mentioned, they would ask specifically whether there were any outstanding female candidates. Usually the man on the other end had, without malevolence, simply forgotten about "Betty." Being asked specifically for female candidates brought "Betty" to mind. When managers know that they're being *measured* on gender equity, they make a conscious effort to be fair—overriding not only their own but also others' mindless biases. That's why it matters that the CEO proclaims gender equity to be a priority *that will be measured.* If the top boss decrees it's important and insists that subordinates be held accountable, every boss down the line will make it happen.

Each employer will come up with its own way to measure progress on closing the wage gap (and all the misbehaviors that create it, including the hiring, pay, and promotion gap, and the sexual harassment gap). If they need help, many human resources specialists and diversity consultants are willing to offer advice. Corporate personnel can swap ideas with one another at professional conferences. Whatever measurements are chosen must fit the organization's culture. I don't want to crimp organizational creativity by laying out a one-size-fits-all system that *doesn't*, in fact, fit all. This step is not difficult. Organizations figure out how to measure their employees all the time. Only one thing is essential: the CEO must insist that it be done, and done right.

Once bosses up and down the line commit to a disciplined, objective program to drive out discriminatory behavior, employees will take up the cause with enthusiasm. Employees know that fair treatment helps every single one of them. Remember how attitudes at Mitsubishi were transformed from resistance to a desire to be the very best at eliminating harassment? That can happen in many other workplaces as well.

5. Insist on roughly equal numbers.

Finally—and this is essential—chief executives must establish *roughly equal* numbers of men and women at every organizational rank and job title.

Today, in most companies and institutions, women are clustered at the bottom. The higher up you go, the fewer women you see. And those few are often tokens. That must change. Roughly as many women as men should be seen everywhere on the organizational chart, from shop-floor managers to executive vice presidents.

This is not a call for quotas; it's a call for fairness. Women are equally qualified. Women work equally hard. Any organization that can't see highly talented women has to open its eyes.

I wouldn't presume to know what *roughly equal* means for each company or institution. The CEO must figure that out. But I'll tell you what gender balance is not: it's *not* recruiting one, two, or three prominent women when the company has a dozen or more men holding comparable positions. It's become easy for a chief executive to point to a couple of high-level women or board members to show that women can make it if they want. Directors feel relieved by this tokenism. Well-intentioned outsider groups tip their hats to these slight signs of improvement. When picking such tokens, management often looks for women who are not just the peers of those men who've risen through the ranks, but rather women who are *outstandingly* better than their peers and who thus bring real luster to the company. Employers continue celebrating such tokenism year after year, without making real change.

Real gender balance makes a different statement altogether. It says that not just the brightest female stars, but also women who perform just as well as men, have a genuine chance at recognition. And real equality changes things. Once a company has an equitable presence of women and men at all levels, the biases and favoritism of prevailing male cultures will fade. Having one or two women on a large leadership team doesn't change the culture. Even women holding a quarter of the top positions is not enough. Real gender balance ends the isolation of individual women. No longer is each individual woman representing her entire sex, bearing the brunt of all those stereotypes; now she's representing only herself. She's no longer an outsider. She can turn to other women when she suspects that something fishy is going on. Discussions start to take place in executive meetings and boardrooms. Policies and practices are instituted to accommodate family responsibilities without subtracting from pay or advancement chances.

Where there are *roughly equal* numbers up and down the organization, within and among similar jobs at every level, employees and outsiders alike know that this employer genuinely offers equal opportunity, equal treatment, and equal pay.

Not a single Fortune 100 company can make this statement today. Will that also be true ten years from now?

CHAPTER 14

All of Us, Working from the Outside In

Step 3: All of us, working from the outside in: American women must hold *every employer* accountable for closing the gap.

In the previous two chapters, we've looked at how important it is for an organization's insiders—the CEOs, women employees, and their male allies at every rank—to take action to close the gap. But what can *we* do—not just as employees and employers, but as *citizens*—to take on the persistent, unfair, and costly gender wage gap?

Let me offer three actions that all of us can take in the public realm. First, we must vigilantly watch the progress—or lack of progress—of Fortune 100 companies in their efforts to eliminate the wage gap (and we must let them know we're watching). Second, we must insist that the nation's top CEO—the president of the United States—set a shining example by making federal employees even and that Congress strengthen the legal framework against wage discrimination. Third, every one of us must make the eradication of the wage gap our own *personal* project for the next decade.

1. What Fortune 100 companies can do

The Fortune 100 companies are the leaders of the American economy. Many are industry trendsetters. Together, these companies employ more than 5 million people. And they're large enough to have the resources to plan and implement change.

If a Fortune 100 company—say, Ford Motor Company—were to make its women employees even with men, you can bet that the other automobile manufacturers wouldn't be far behind. If AT&T announced that, within five years, it would close its internal wage gap, so would its competitors. They would have to, both to stay competitive in attracting and retaining the best workers and to keep from falling out of favor. If the Fortune 100 companies closed the wage gap, they'd set an example for *all* companies, demonstrating not only that getting women even with men is a legal and moral imperative but that *it can be done*. And whatever those top companies learn about how to pay women fairly can be passed on to smaller companies as well.

From the outside, it looks as if the Fortune 100 have a long way to go. In 2001, only two Fortune 100 companies had anything that even resembled a balanced management team. The leadership in the other ninety-eight companies—98 percent of the Fortune 100—did not even approach gender balance. That's true both for the Fortune 100's senior executive positions and for their boards of directors.

What about their employees' wages? How close to even is the pay of the women and men who work at the Fortune 100? That's hard to say. These companies do not publicly disclose the comparative wages paid to their male and female employees. For now, counting the women at the top will have to be a proxy measure of those companies' commitment to ending sex discrimination.

That's why the WAGE Project will report on how gender-balanced (or far from it) are the Fortune 100's upper-level staff: running lines of business or holding corporate officer titles such as executive vice president, senior vice president, division president, and director. Every year for the next ten years, WAGE will issue a report so that women throughout America can check up on the Fortune 100 companies. Are these companies getting to roughly equal numbers? Has the CEO made a commitment to pay women employees like men—*and* committed the company to an independent audit of its wage equity? Have directors put in incentives to make this a top priority for the CEO?

Silence from these employers will speak volumes; it will be clear that such employers are *not* committed. A CEO who's seriously committed will want to make his or her intent public. When that CEO becomes committed, the WAGE Project will ask for that corporation's wage equity data and include that, too, in its annual reports.

With all this information, all of us will be able to assess whether these leaders care about paying women fairly and equally—and whether we're inclined to buy their products, their services, their shares of stock. To buy or not to buy, of course, is the power that every one of us has. If you see a company making no progress quarter after quarter, you can register your dissatisfaction where it counts: don't buy that brand. You're not just sending a message to the CEO that you want results. You're also telling the women employees of that company that you support their internal efforts to get paid fairly.

Picture it. Women inside the company taking action to get paid fairly. Millions of women and our male allies *outside* the company exercising our buying power, and speaking out about why—to the company, to the media, to each other. With pressure like that, CEOs who avoid making wage equity a top priority will put their organizations' bottom lines and reputations at great risk.

2. What the President and Congress can do

As *Getting Even* has already made clear, the United States has most, though not all, of the laws it needs to close the wage gap. What's needed now is employer commitment, motivated by pressure from within and without—along with renewed pressure from the government.

As the nation's chief executive, the president should set an example for all other CEOs—both by eliminating the gap among his (and, someday soon, her) employees, and by enforcing existing anti–sex discrimination laws. Next, Congress could and should close the remaining fair-pay loopholes in our laws, requiring "comparable-worth" pay by every employer and eliminating financial protections for unfair employers.

Neither the President nor Congress can close the gap by themselves. But all of us can hold them accountable for doing what they can and should do. Let's look at each of these in turn.

Getting Federal (and State) Employees Even

As the nation's largest employer of women, the president of the United States has a responsibility to set the example for every other CEO. One step would be breathtakingly bold, yet quite simple to initiate. The president could declare that the U.S. government will, through an executive order, implement a pay equity program like the one that works in Minnesota. Civil service has had some success in equalizing gender pay within grades. But even within the federal government, some job titles are held overwhelmingly by women and others are held overwhelmingly by men. The rates of pay for those women in sex-segregated job titles must be evaluated—and adjusted to match job titles for men with similar experience, qualifications, and roughly the same responsibilities.

The president could, through the same executive order, commit to roughly equal numbers of women and men at all levels of civil service titles and appointments. Just as in business, women become sparse in the senior civil service ranks, such as GS-13 and above. One signature—accompanied by presidential follow-through—can shatter the governmental glass ceiling. Have you ever seen a picture on the nightly news of people sitting around a table meeting with the president in the White House and seen *roughly equal numbers* of women and men? By eliminating discrimination among federal workers once and for all, the president could set an example for the Fortune 100—and for all American employers. And every governor could do the same.

As thousands of women go public with stories of unfair and unequal pay, they will deserve a presidential response that matches their outcry. The president, like any CEO, already has all the authority necessary to get federal employees even. Such an impressive action would establish a president's legacy—ensuring not just the respect of all working women, but also a place in history.

Enforcing the Law

The other step for the president—enforcing the law—is mandatory. Yet the law has been weakly enforced by one president after another. The nation's chief executive is sworn to enforce and uphold the existing laws against sex discrimination throughout the economy. But president after president has underfunded such efforts. Without vigorous enforcement, employers' compliance becomes "voluntary." And we know where forty years of "voluntary" compliance has gotten us: 23 cents in arrears.

Just how underfunded have EEOC efforts been? Very. When it began in 1965, the nation's top antidiscrimination agency was charged with ending blatant discrimination based on two factors: sex and race. But as the years went by, Congress gave it new antidiscrimination enforcement responsibilities, such as age and physical disability. Despite its expanding mandate and despite the dramatic growth in the number of employers, despite the fact that there are 35 million more people work full-time, the EEOC's budget in real dollars (that is, adjusted for inflation) has *remained the same since 1978*. The same paltry funding afflicts the other federal agency responsible for catching discrimination, the Labor Department's Office of Federal Contract Compliance Programs. An agency can only do so much to increase efficiency before effectiveness starts to go. After a certain point, less means less.

As a result, one EEOC watcher summed up the impact of the agency's activities as not much more than isolated victories. With inadequate budgets, both the EEOC and the OFCC take months and years to process, investigate, and bring charges. That delay has a chilling effect on women who do, or might, bring discrimination charges. If one woman has to wait months before her charges are heard—months during which her employer already knows that she's brought those charges—her work life becomes ever more uncomfortable. Other women around her, quite sensibly, conclude that it's smarter to keep silent.

Does it seem trivial to expect a president of the United States to enforce the nation's laws? Hardly! That's the job description, as written into the Constitution. Every working woman has the right to expect adequate protection and enforcement of antidiscrimination laws. So here's a suggested activity for WAGE Clubs or independent watchdogs: Hold the president accountable for enforcing the nation's antidiscrimination laws. Keep an eye on the president's suggested EEOC appropriations each year, and on how much of it Congress approves. And make sure they know that you're watching. Write letters telling them to fund the EEOC to be a real watchdog. Then make your interest clear where you have the most public buying power: at the ballot box! Vote for a president, congressional representatives, and senators who really do help women get even.

The U.S. Congress

There is one legal loophole Congress can close: Make it clear in the law that employers cannot systematically pay women less for "women's" jobs than for "men's" jobs that require roughly the same skill, experience, and working conditions. As we saw in chapter 7, jobs dominated by women bring in smaller pink paychecks when compared with the fatter blue paychecks offered for jobs dominated by men. That unfair discrepancy is one of the reasons women still make only 77 cents to a man's dollar. During the 1980s, women brought a number of lawsuits against the failure to offer comparable pay for comparable jobs, a concept called "comparable worth." But many federal district court judges said that "comparable worth" failures did not violate Title VII's ban on sex discrimination. Those judicial decisions have closed off comparable worth for now.

Here's their basic reasoning: requiring wage parity inside a company would be government interference with the marketplace. Of course, we know that governments "interfere" with the marketplace all the time: it's called regulation. Doesn't the Federal Reserve Bank interfere with the marketplace when it sets central bank interest rates? Don't the Securities and Exchange Commission, the Environmental Protection Agency, the Food and Drug Agency, the Department of Housing and Urban Development, and so many other federal agencies interfere with the marketplace every day—in order to ensure that the American people (in our capacities as investors, consumers, and citizens) are treated fairly? Why shouldn't women expect the same interference to do what the law requires: eliminate wage discrimination practiced by employers who slot women and men into separate and unequal job and wage tracks in order to pay women less? Nevertheless, the fact that "comparable worth" died in the courts leaves a big legal loophole for unfair pay.

Ideally, chief executives will listen to women's stories and mend their ways—on comparable worth as well as every other kind of discrimination documented in this book. But Congress should find these same stories sufficiently convincing—and pass a law that requires comparable pay for comparable jobs. As I write this, one bill already before Congress, the Fair Pay Act of 2003, would do just that. Another bill, the Paycheck Fairness Act, would remove the arbitrary cap on what women can win in court when their employer has discriminated against them. Why should employers be protected when they break the law?

Let me reemphasize that passing laws will *not* magically solve this problem. The State of Maine has had a pay equity law on its books since 1965. It took thirty-one years—until 2001—for that state's Department of Labor to come up with regulations to implement that law. In that year, Maine's women earned only 72 cents to a man's dollar—a gender wage gap that was much worse than the national average! A new law won't magically erase the wage gap.

But when thousands of women document their experience with sex discrimination, Congress will get outraged enough to pass a law requiring pay equity—and employers will have to worry about still more sweeping government action and judicial penalties, if CEOs themselves don't even up their payrolls. Together, we can all make sure that government does its part to get those pink and blue paychecks even. So along with pressing your employer to pay women fairly, urge the federal government to lead by example—and to pressure CEOs into fairness as well.

Eliminating the Wage Gap: Your Personal Project for the Next Decade

In 1996, our congressman lost his chief of staff. He called and asked if, by any chance, I wanted to give it a try. He knew how much I loved politics. He knew that I was good at what I did. He knew I knew his district and his constituents. So that was helpful.

The funny thing about that jump was that his wife, who is also very assertive, said to him, "You know, you can't pay her any less than you were paying your former chief of staff. People are going to know." So I have his wife to thank: I jumped from $68,000 to $85,000.

—Nonprofit executive

From experience, I know that once a campaign gets going, it develops its own life: people leap in with their own sweat and creativity to build toward the new vision. Each woman (and fair-minded man) will know what she has to do, and what she *can* do—alone or in groups, depending on her time and temperament. That's your project: Find what you can do to close the wage gap, and do it.

Maybe, like the congressman's wife in the example above, you'll pressure one man to do the right thing. Maybe you'll add a "wage gap" section to your company's annual report. Maybe you'll strategize about how to get the president and Congress to close their own organizational wage gaps. No central coordination will be needed. Each of us will, in her or his own way, keep the pressure on employers, the media, and our politicians to ensure that wages are fair.

You know what you can do. And if you don't yet, you will when you see it. Take it as your mission. Look around you in your job, your family, and your community. Find your own ways to get women even. And then chip away at it *every day*.

All this may sound like an ambitious prescription. But Americans have launched other such revolutions. Unions won the eight-hour day. Trustbusters restrained greedy monopolies. Suffragists won women the right to vote. The civil rights movement dismantled Jim Crow laws. Mothers Against Drunk Driving transformed a nation's attitudes, leading to such new concepts as the "designated driver" and barroom liability when serving alcohol to someone too intoxicated to drive.

Closing the wage gap is no different. Solving this problem calls for action by thousands and thousands of people — just as those other movements did. Keep in mind that this movement need not wait for anything or anybody. Getting women paid fairly requires no scientific inventions or new technologies, no costly research trials, no sweeping institutional changes, not even congressional action. That's why this can be done in a decade.

Yes, a decade. Together, we can close the wage gap in ten years. But it will require concerted action — day after day, without letup — by working women and men, focused on the top bosses. Of course, the social undercurrents will at times be tricky to navigate. But there's an extra payoff. When women are paid like men, we will become socially equal as well. Just imagine handing *that* legacy on to your daughters, nieces, granddaughters, and other younger women you love. Let that dream inspire your actions for the next decade.

So here's my hope for this book: From the moment this book is published, every employer will start to feel the pressure to get women even — because women are rising up in enormous numbers. Recognizing our own stories in these pages, relieved that our missing wages are not our fault, and outraged that wage discrimination continues into the twenty-first century, thousands upon thousands of women will say: I have to do something about this.

Women have already been seething privately. With the rank injustice laid out in black and white, women (and men who care about the women in their lives) will use our time and knowledge to rid the American workplace of this inequity forever. My hope is that we will keep our eyes on the wage gap with a passion we never before imagined we could feel about a dry statistical average; that women will take risks and venture into new realms to leave our daughters a work legacy different from the one we inherited.

I hope that once *you've* read this book and decided to do everything you can over the next ten years to end the wage gap, your courage will be strengthened by the fact that you are engaged in a stirring nationwide effort to rid America's workplaces of *all* discrimination. By chipping away at *one* deeply embedded form of discrimination, you will also be tearing down bigotry and bias based on race, religion, sexual orientation, age, and physical ability. You will be doing your part to transform America into a society of people who genuinely value and respect one another.

It's been more than a quarter century since the women's movement brought women fully into the workforce. The time is right for the next step: getting even.

Notes

1: INTRODUCTION

1. IMDiversity.com, as well as the Web sites of the Women's Educational and Industrial Union, the Feminist Majority Foundation, and a business-women's listserv.

2. Calculated from Table 1 in "Highlights of Women's Earnings 2002," Report 972, Bureau of Labor Statistics, U.S. Department of Labor, Washington, D.C., September 2003.

2: WHY NOT A DOLLAR?

1. Policy analysts pinned the explanation of why the gender wage gap widened in the mid-1990s on "welfare reform." Their theory: Since almost all—90 percent—of welfare recipients were women, when these low-skilled, untrained mothers lost their welfare support and were forced to join the full-time workforce in low-paying jobs, their wages dragged the average of women's overall wages down. That explanation sounds plausible. But it's wrong. Women's average wages dropped between 1993 and 1996—*before* Congress passed the welfare reform law in 1996. A number of states experimented with reforming welfare before national legislation took effect. In these states, some welfare recipients did trickle into minimum-wage work before national welfare reform passed—but not enough of them to drag down the overall average of

women's wages. Even in August 1996, when welfare reform passed, welfare recipients still had more time before they had to seek work. Not until 1997, 1998, and 1999 did large numbers of former welfare recipients start working in low-paying jobs. And in those years, contrary to welfare reform theories, average women's wages *increased*—and the wage gap narrowed.

2. Table P-32, "Educational Attainment—Full-Time, Year-Round Workers 18 Years Old and Over, by Mean Earnings, Age, and Sex: 1991 to 2003," U.S. Census Bureau, *Historical Income Tables—People,* Washington, D.C., 2005.

3. Lawrence Michel, Jared Berstein, John Schmitt, *State of Working America 1998–99,* Economic Policy Institute, Washington, D.C., Chapter 1: Family Income.

4. "Educational Attainment—People 25 Years Old and Over by Median Income and Sex: 1991 to 2001," in U.S. Census Bureau, *Historical Income Tables—People,* Washington, D.C.

3. THE PERSONAL COST OF THE WAGE GAP: A SECOND-CLASS LIFE

1. This middle manager asked for anonymity in print. Interview tape and transcript on file with the authors.

2. "Ask a Working Woman Survey, 2002," Lake Snell Perry Associates for the AFL-CIO, www.aflcio.org/issuespolitics/women/report, accessed Feb. 2005.

3. See IWPR Briefing Paper, "The Male-Female Wage Gap: Lifetime Earnings Losses," March 1998, as applied at www.aflcio.org/issuespolitics/women/equalpay/equalpay.cfm, calculated February 2005.

4. Ann Crittenden, *The Price of Motherhood: Why the Most Important Job in the World Is Still the Least Valued* (New York: Henry Holt and Company, 2001), p. 89.

5. National Center on Women and Aging, "The MetLife Juggling Act Study: Balancing Caregiving with Work and the Costs Involved," Brandeis University, Waltham, Mass., November 1999.

6. Joyce P. Jacobsen and Laurence M. Levin, "Effects of Intermittent Labor Force Attachment on Women's Earnings," *Monthly Labor Review,* September 1995, pp. 14–19.

7. Current Population Reports, Consumer Income, Table A, "Comparison of Summary Measures of Income by Selected Characteristics: 1993, 1999, and 2000," in *Money Income in the United States: 2000,* Washington, D.C., p. 7.

8. Adapted from Table A1, "Marital Status of People 15 Years and Over, by Age, Sex, Personal Earnings, Race, and Hispanic Origin/1, March 2000," in *Marital Status, Census 2000 Brief,* by Rose M. Kreider and Tavia Simmons, U.S. Census Bureau, (Washington, D.C., October 2003).

9. Rose M. Kreider and Jason M. Fields, "Number, Timing and Duration of

Marriages and Divorces: Fall 1996," in *Current Population Reports* (Washington, D.C.: U.S. Census Bureau, 2001), pp. 70–80.

10. Under the sponsorship of Wider Opportunities for Women and the leadership of Dr. Diana Pearce, a self-sufficiency standard has been developed for almost all cities and states in the country. This standard calculates how much money working adults need to pay for their basic needs without subsidies of any kind. Unlike the federal poverty standard, the Self-Sufficiency Standard accounts for the costs of living and working as they vary by family size and composition and by geographic location. This standard estimates what wages a full-time worker needs to afford to pay for rent, child care, transportation to and from work, basic necessities like toothpaste and soap, food, and taxes on earnings for his or her particular family. This standard offers a bare-bones existence, no frills. But if a working woman's earnings meet or exceed the self-sufficiency standard, she can make ends meet for herself and her family. For example, a woman with an infant and preschool child living in pricey New York City needs to earn $43,932 to make ends meet, while a woman with the same family living in a less expensive city, like St. Louis, needs to earn $32,165 to make ends meet. According to U.S. Census data and the self-sufficiency standard, single working mothers in these three cities—and many others—have, on average, insufficient earnings to make ends meet. These standards are found in the report "Coming Up Short: A Comparison of Wages and Work Supports in 10 American Communities," Wider Opportunities for Women, Washington, D.C., Summer/Fall 2004.

11. Table 3.7, "Total Money Income of Nonmarried Persons 65 or Older, by Sex and Marital Status," in *Income of the Population 55 or Older, 2000*, U.S. Social Security Administration (Washington, D.C., 2001), p. 59.

12. Ibid.

4: CENTS AND SENSIBILITIES

1. The United States has no coordinated system for reporting, recording, and collecting discrimination statistics from the decentralized maze of local, state, and federal administrative offices, commissions, agencies, and courts that handle such complaints. Doing so meant searching major and local newspapers for reports of court awards and settlements; combing through rulings from the Equal Employment Opportunity Commission (EEOC), the U.S. Labor Department's Office of Federal Contract Compliance Programs, and the U.S. Merit Systems Protection Board; and reading state and local commission and attorney generals' reports. None of these sources was comprehensive, even for its own system. Even the EEOC annual reports gave examples instead of listing the outcome of every case its attorneys had settled or won. Early on I saw that even my most relentless efforts would produce only a partial listing. Nev-

ertheless, I tried to be as thorough as possible, keeping my eye on the goal: to create a database that would give a sense of how much discrimination had been proven in the United States, so that we could see whether that discrimination was enough to account for the wage gap. I was ruthless in refusing to include any charges other than those involving awards or settlements. I didn't want to draw any conclusions from cranky accusations or claims that hadn't stood up to others' careful scrutiny. If I were to measure the extent of American discrimination, I wanted the data set to be populated only by thoroughly documented, reviewed, and declared injustices: those in which judges and juries had made awards or in which companies had paid off female employees rather than air their dirty laundry in court.

2. In all tables, the particular year includes cases resolved in that calendar year and that fiscal year in federal reports. When the public record does not reveal the particular office or site where unfair behavior occurred, the employers' main office is given.

5: PLAIN OLD DISCRIMINATION

1. "Jury Says Caterpillar Retaliated Against Employee for Discrimination Claim," Associated Press, May 22, 2001.

2. "Plaintiffs' Brief in Support of Their Motion for Class Certification," p. 12, *Wilfong et al. v. Rent-a-Center*, filed in the Southern District Court of Illinois, 2001.

3. Ibid., pp. 16, 21.

4. Unless otherwise noted, all individual Rent-a-Center employee quotes are from the *Wilfong et al. v. Rent-a-Center Class Member/Witness Declarations*, vols. 1 and 2, filed along with the brief for class certification, above.

5. Sara Rab and Jerry A. Jacobs, "*Sex Discrimination in Restaurant Hiring Practices*," unpublished manuscript, Department of Sociology, University of Pennsylvania, 2003.

6. David Nemark, Roy J. Bank, and Kyle D. Van Nort, "Sex Discrimination in Restaurant Hiring: An Audit Study," *The Quarterly Journal of Economics* 111, no. 3 (August 1996): 915–941.

7. Nick Ravo, "Caterer Settles Lawsuit Claiming Bias Against Female Waiters," *The New York Times*, August 28, 1998, p. B3; Kirsten Downey Grimsley, "Caterer Settles Bias Complaint: ACLU Accused New York Firm of Discriminating Against Women," *The Washington Post*, August 28, 1998, p. F2.

8. Rab and Jacobs, *Sex Discrimination*.

9. *Highlights of Women's Earnings in 2002*, Report 972 (Washington, D.C.: U.S. Department of Labor, Bureau of Labor Statistics, 2003).

10. Nicole Harris, "Publix: Revolt at the Deli Counter," *Business Week*,

April 1, 1996, available online at www.businessweek.com/1996/14/b346956 .htm.

11. U.S. Newswire, "Lawsuit Charges Ingles Grocery Stores Discriminate Against Women Employees," March 3, 1998.

12. Home Depot Web site, www.homedepot.com.

13. Home Depot statistics are from the *Report of William T. Bielby, Ph.D., on Behalf of Plaintiffs* filed in *Butler et al. vs. Home Depot, Inc.*, and *Frank et al. vs. Home Depot, Inc.*, March 21, 1997, pp. 7–9, 11, 14; see also Tables 1–5.

14. Home Depot quotes from the *Report of Professor Susan T. Fiske on Behalf of Plaintiffs*, filed in *Butler et al. vs. Home Depot* and *Frank et al., vs. Home Depot* in the United States District Court, Northern District of California, March 24, 1997, pp. 8–9, quoting from plaintiff and defendant depositions. Also from *Report of William T. Bielby, Ph.D., on Behalf of Plaintiffs* filed in *Butler et al. vs. Home Depot, Inc.*, and *Frank et al. vs. Home Depot, Inc.*, March 21, 1997, pp. 17–18, quoting from defendant depositions.

15. Cora Daniels, "To Hire a Lumber Expert, Click Here: Home Depot Automated Hiring and Promotions to Settle a Sex-Discrimination Suit. But Guess What? Managers Love It," *Fortune*, April 3, 2000, pp. 267 ff.

16. Bernie Marcus and Arthur Blank, with Bob Andelman, *Built From Scratch: How a Couple of Regular Guys Grew the Home Depot from Nothing to $30 Billion* (New York: Times Business, Random House, 1999), p. 122.

17. Publix Super Markets was not alone. During the 1990s, one grocery chain after another lost or settled enormous sex discrimination lawsuits — paying out millions, adjusting pay scales, overhauling hiring and promotion practices, and accepting ongoing judicial oversight. Those included Ingles ($16.5 million, 1999) in the South and Nob Hill Goods ($1.3 million, 1998), Lucky Stores ($107 million, 1996), Safeway ($7.5 million, 1994), and Albertson's ($32.5 million, 1994) in California. All of them had to pay because they had consistently kept women in dead-end and part-time jobs while men moved into management—in the same passively discriminating mode as Home Depot, with equally costly results.

18. Kirsten Downey Grimsley, "Fla. Grocery Chain Settles Sex-Bias Case," *The Washington Post*, January 27, 1997, p. D1. To readers not familiar with legal grounds for discrimination, this quote may sound harshly dismissive. Lawyers call this classic intentional discrimination.

19. "Jury Awards Nearly $4 Million in Gender Pay Dispute," Associated Press, January 25, 2003.

20. "AAUP and Fair Pay on Campus," *http://www.aaup.org/Issues/ WomeninHE/FAIRPAY.HTM*, updated October 2002. Also see "Tenure De-

nied: Cases of Sex Discrimination in Academia," a report by the American Association of University Women, Washington, D.C., 2004, for some illuminating information about women denied tenure at colleges and universities over the last several decades, including the difficulties these women faced in litigation, and the personal and professional costs they paid in battling for tenure.

21. Michelle Conlin, "The New Gender Gap: From Kindergarten to Grad School, Boys Are Becoming the New Second Sex," *Business Week,* May 26, 2003, www.businessweek.com/magazine/content/03_21/63834001_m2001 .htm, accessed Feb. 2005.

22. Interview, July 12, 2003, tape and transcript on file with the authors.

23. Although the lawsuit of which she was a part is on public record, this officer requested anonymity in this book; tapes and transcript of an interview on August 14, 2003, on file with the authors.

24. All information about Sharon Pollard, including direct quotes, is from the August 20, 1998, opinion of District Trial Judge McCalla in *Sharon B. Pollard v. E. I. DuPont de Nemours, Inc.*

25. District Judge Jon P. McCalla, *Sharon B. Pollard, Plaintiff, v. E. I. DuPont de Nemours Inc., Defendant, August 20, 1998, Memorandum Opinion and Order,* United States District Court W. D. Tennessee, Western Division, No. 95-3010 M1/V.

26. "Waitresses Get Award in Discrimination Case," *The New York Times,* February 7, 1998, p. A13.

27. Tape and transcript on file with the authors.

6: WAGE DISCRIMINATION BY SEXUAL HARASSMENT

1. From an interview and correspondence with Detroit EEOC Regional Attorney Adele Rapport, October 7, 2003, tape and transcript on file with the authors. The case, *EEOC vs. Benchmark Residential Services, Inc.,* subsequently settled with the home accepting a consent decree.

2. All of this teenager's quotes come from a June 21, 2001, deposition taken at Bonanza Reporting in Las Vegas, Nevada, in the case of *EEOC v. Pizza Hut of America, Inc.,* case no. EDCV 00-774 RT (EX). Deposition text on file with the authors.

3. For a more up-to-date listing, check the case database at www .wageproject.org.

4. *Getting Even* will report throughout on how much the jury awarded lawsuit plaintiffs. That number is significant, because it points out what a jury thought the woman's losses and suffering were worth. In some cases these awards were later knocked down by the trial judge or an appeals court—typically, because federal law protects employers by limiting damage awards. In other cases, in order to stop the ongoing appeals process, plaintiff and defen-

dant reached a settlement that was lower than the jury award. Tracking those numbers is not always possible. Therefore, the *Getting Even* charts do not necessarily reflect the amount finally received by all plaintiffs, although wherever I found an amended amount, it is noted in the tables and text.

5. www.washingtonpost.com/wp-adv/classifieds/careerpost/library/harrass1 .htm

6. Susan Antilla, *Tales from the Boom-Boom Room* (Bloomberg Press, Princeton, N.J.: 2002). Antilla scrupulously documents charges of sexual harassment in such firms as Olde Discount, Smith Barney, Shearson Lehman, Merrill Lynch, Rodman & Renshaw, Josephthal Lyon & Ross Inc., Lieberbaum, and others during the 1990s.

7. Antilla, *Tales from the Boom-Boom Room*, pp. 44–45. Antilla footnotes these allegations from *Martens et al. v. Smith Barney et al.*, 96 Civ. 3779 CBM (U.S. District Court for the Southern District of New York, December 8, 1999), "Corrected Memorandum in Opposition to Motion to Enforce Settlement Stipulation," Table D, and "Declarations in Support of Plaintiffs' Memorandum in Opposition to Motion to Enforce Settlement Stipulation," Table D.

8. Iver Peterson, "Sexual Harassment Trial Plumbs 'Atmosphere' in a Trenton Agency," *The New York Times*, July 30, 1998; David Kocieniewski, "Jury Finds Lawyer Was Harassed by Her Boss at New Jersey Agency," *The New York Times*, August 18, 1998; "New Jersey Assistant Attorney General Awarded $350,000 in Sexual Harassment Suit," Associated Press, August 18, 1998.

9. This production line supervisor's story is summarized from a telephone interview conducted on October 12, 2003, with a named Dial plaintiff who asked for anonymity in print. Tape and transcript on file with the authors. No facts have been changed.

10. Telephone interview with Noelle Brennan, October 9, 2003. Tape and transcript on file with the authors.

11. "Plaintiff EEOC's memorandum in Opposition to Defendant Dial's Motion for Summary Judgment," *EEOC vs. The Dial Corporation*, Case No. 99-C-3356 (N.D.Ill., April 29, 2003).

12. Alan Fontana, Ph.D., and Robert Rosenheck, M.D., "Focus on Women: Duty-Related and Sexual Stress in the Etiology of PTSD Among Women Veterans Who Seek Treatment," *Psychiatric Services* 49 (May 1998): 658–662.

13. Heidi Prescott, "Elkhart, Ind.–based Motor Home Maker Settles Sexual Harassment Suit," *South Bend Tribune*, October 11, 2001.

14. Denny Walsh, "Kings, Ex-Execs Settle Suit; Terms Are Kept Secret over Sexual Harassment Allegations," *The Sacramento Bee*, October 3, 2002, page B1.

15. Serge F. Kovaleski, "D.C. Payments to Conclude Suit Against Corrections," *The Washington Post*, January 22, 2002, B1.

16. Not all cases lead employers to mend their ways. In *EEOC v. Sears, Roebuck & Co.*, 1988, statistical and historical evidence of women's exclusions from better-paying sales jobs was countered by testimony that women did not want these jobs. The ensuing debate provided employers with grounds to wriggle out of their responsibilities to give women the same promotional opportunities as men. See, e.g., Vicki Schultz, "Telling Stories About Women and Work," *Harvard Law Review* 103: 1749.

7: WOMEN'S WORK

1. Interview, July 2001, tape and transcript on file with the authors.

2. Interview, July 2001, tape and transcript on file with the authors.

3. Interview, July 2001, tape and transcript on file with the authors.

4. Stephanie Boraas and William M. Rodgers III, "How Does Gender Play a Role in the Earnings Gap? An Update," *Monthly Labor Review*, U.S. Department of Labor, March 2003, pp. 9–15.

5. Interview, December 2003, tape and transcript on file with the authors.

6. "Sex Segregation in the Workplace," *Annual Review of Sociology* 19 (1993): 241–270.

7. See the discussion of the lawsuit against Advantage Staffing, p. 77–78.

8. Blank and Marcus, *Built from Scratch*, 119–120.

9. William T. Bielby and James N. Baron, "Men and Women at Work: Sex Segregation and Statistical Discrimination," *American Journal of Sociology*, January 1986, pp. 759–799.

10. According to Sugerman, she landed her job because President Jimmy Carter's expansion of Executive Order 11246 of 1980 mandated affirmative action for women on all federal contracting jobs—and the local unions were forced to apprentice women.

11. Molly Martin, ed., *Hard-Hatted Women: Stories of Struggle and Success in the Trades* (Seattle, Wash.: Seal Press, 1988), pp. 33–34.

12. Ibid., p. 35.

13. According to its literature, Women in the Fire Service is a nonprofit membership organization based in Madison, Wisconsin. The information used here was found at www.wfsi.org.

14. Table 3, "Median Usual Weekly Earnings of Full-Time Wage and Salary Workers by Detailed Occupation and Sex, 2000 Annual Averages," *Highlights of Women's Earnings in 2002*, U.S. Department of Labor, Bureau of Labor Statistics, Report 972, Current Population Survey, Washington, D.C., Sept. 2003.

15. Information and quotes in this section come from telephone interviews with Tom and Amy McKinney in November 2003 and from contemporaneous

newspaper articles about their experiences. Tapes, transcripts, and articles on file with the authors.

16. Minutes, Civil Service Commission, City of Muskogee, Oklahoma, Special Call Session, Wednesday, July 10, 2002, p. 4. When Captain Doe was contacted for comment on the McKinneys' story, he referred questions to his lawyer, citing a pending lawsuit against the City of Muskogee. His lawyer declined comment.

17. Interview, July 2001, on file with the authors.

18. David J. Maume, Jr., "Glass Ceilings and Glass Escalators: Occupational Segregation and Race and Sex Differences in Managerial Promotions," *Work and Occupations* 26, no. 4 (November 1999): pp. 483–509. This article includes a review and bibliography of the supporting research to that date.

19. Some men even admit to researchers that they chose "women's work" because there they find a faster track into management. See C. L. Williams, "The Glass Escalator: Hidden Advantages for Men in the 'Female' Professions," *Social Problems* 39, 1992, pp. 253–267.

20. Interview, July 2001, tape and transcript on file with the authors.

21. Interview, July 2001, tape and transcript on file with the authors.

22. Mark Jurkowitz, "More Women in J-School Doesn't Translate to Jobs," *The Boston Globe,* August 27, 2003.

23. Deborah Rhode for the ABA Commission on Women in the Profession, "The Unfinished Agenda: Women in the Legal Profession," 2001, available online at www.abanet.org/ftp/pub/women/unfinishedagenda.pdf.

24. Wayne J. Guglielmo, "Physicians' Earnings: Our Exclusive Survey," survey by *Medical Economics*, September 19, 2003, p.71. Total compensation for unincorporated physicians is earnings after tax-deductible expenses but before income taxes. For physicians in professional corporations, it's the sum of salary, bonuses, and retirement/profit sharing made on their behalf. All figures are medians. The data apply to individual office-based M.D.s and D.O.s. The source for this and all following tables and charts is the Medical Economics Continuing Survey.

25. Cheri Ostroff and Leanne Atwater, "Does Whom You Work With Matter? Effects of Referent Group Gender and Age Composition on Managers' Compensation," *Journal of Applied Psychology* 88, no. 4 (2003): 725–740.

26. Interview, July 2001, tape and transcript on file with the authors.

27. Association of Fundraising Professionals, "2000–2001 Compensation and Benefits Study." In the survey of 1,200 association members, 67 percent of the respondents identified themselves as female.

28. GuideStar Nonprofit Compensation Report, 2002, www.guidestar.org/news/features/2002_cr_highlights01.jsp, accessed Feb. 2005.

29. Heather Joslyn, "Charity's Glass Ceiling: Salary Gap Persists for Women

in Nonprofit Organizations," *Chronicle of Philanthropy*, March 20, 2003, pp. 47–51.

30. Interview, September 2003, tape and transcript on file with the authors.

8: EVERYDAY DISCRIMINATION

1. Interview, July 2003, tape and transcript on file with the authors.

2. Interview, July 2003, tape and transcript on file with the authors.

3. Ostroff and Atwater, "Does Whom You Work With Matter? Effects of Referent Group Gender and Age Composition on Managers' Compensation," *Journal of Applied Psychology*, 88, no. 4 (2003):726.

4. Sharon Begley, "The Stereotype Trap: From 'White Men Can't Jump' to 'Girls Can't Do Math,' Negative Images That Are Pervasive in the Culture Can Make Us Choke During Tests of Ability," *Newsweek*, November 6, 2000. See also David M. Marx, Joseph L. Brown, and Claude M. Steele, "Allport's Legacy and the Situational Press of Stereotypes," *Journal of Social Issues* 55, no. 3 (Fall 1999): 491.

5. For a thorough summary of this research, see Joan C. Williams, "The Social Psychology of Stereotyping: Using Social Science to Litigate Gender Discrimination Cases and Defang the 'Cluelessness' Defense," *Employee Rights and Employment Policy Journal* 7, no. 2 (2003): 401–458.

6. Ostroff and Atwater, "Does Whom You Work With Matter? Effects of Referent Group Gender and Age Composition on Managers' Compensation," *Journal of Applied Psychology* 88, no. 4 (2003): 725–740. This quote summarizes a 1997 article by M. Heilman, C. Block, and P. Stathatos.

7. Inspired by a chart included in Joan Williams, *Unbending Gender: Why Family and Work Conflict and What to Do About It* (New York: Oxford University Press, 2000), p. 247. Information and examples drawn from that chart and from Joan Williams, "Litigating the Glass Ceiling. . . ."

8. Ostroff and Atwater, "Does Whom You Work With Matter?" referencing a 2000 article by K. Graddy and L. Pistaferri.

9. Interview, July 2001, tape and transcript on file with the authors.

10. See "Stereotypes, Expectations and Perceptions," Glass Ceiling Commission paper; the fact-finding report, "Good for Business: Making Full Use of the Nation's Human Capital"; and the recommendations report, "A Solid Investment: Making Full Use of the Nation's Human Capital," *Glass Ceiling Commission Report*, Washington, D.C.: U.S. Dept. of Labor, 1995; Douglas M. McCracken, "Winning the Talent War for Women," *Harvard Business Review*, November–December 2000, p. 164.

9: WORKING WHILE MOTHER

1. Samuel E. Joyner, "Pregnant? Congratulations . . . You're Fired! Extending the Burk Public Policy Tort to Pregnancy Discrimination After Collier v. Insignia Financial Group?," *Tulsa Law Journal*, Spring 2001, p. 677.

2. Quoted in Joan Williams, "Litigating the Glass Ceiling and the Maternal Wall: Defanging the 'Cluelessness' Defense."

3. Madeleine Blais, "Who's Got Time to Stay at Home?" *The New York Times Magazine*, April 5, 1998, p. 48; Lisa Belkin, "The Opt-Out Revolution," *The New York Times Magazine*, October 26, 2003, p. 42.

4. Dennis Wagner, "Bias Claims Soar for Mothers-to-Be," *The Arizona Republic*, January 24, 2003.

5. Quoted in Joan Williams, *Unbending Gender*.

6. Information from EEOC Web site and *The Sentinel-Record* (Arkansas), February 17, 2001.

7. Williams, "Litigating the Glass Ceiling."

8. Joyner, "Pregnant? Congratulations . . . You're Fired!"

9. *Trezza v. The Hartford, Inc.*, 1998.

10. Cindy Richards, "Doting Governor Gets Off Easy," *Chicago Sun-Times*, November 12, 2003.

11. U.S. Government Accounting Office, "Analysis of the Earnings Difference Between Men and Women," October 2003 presentation to Representative John D. Dingell and Representative Carolyn B. Maloney.

12. The mommy penalty can strike daddies too, if they try to be caretakers instead of just money machines. The stereotype system for them works this way: A "good father" is a good provider, and a "good man" is a man who does his job. If they try to act like "mothers," they can be hit with the same (or sometimes even harsher) penalties as women do. Consider what happened to Maryland state trooper Kevin Knussman, a paramedic. After twenty-two years on the job, Knussman asked for parental leave when his first child was born prematurely and his wife was too sick to take care of the baby or even herself. He desperately wanted to be there—but his request for federally mandated family leave was repeatedly denied, at every level from his immediate boss to the woman in personnel. Why? Because "God decided only women can give birth," he was told. "Unless your wife is in a coma or dead, you can't be primary care provider." Knussman decided that his place was with his family. He lost his job. In 1999, a jury awarded him $375,000 for sex discrimination, which in 2001 was upheld on appeal. And when a South Carolina state trooper, Lance Corporal David O. Roberts, applied for family leave—his wife hadn't been working long enough at her job to qualify for extended leave, and they didn't want to put their newborn into day care—he was denied. According to the complaint filed by the ACLU, Roberts's boss told him that "in his day, the man

was the breadwinner and it was the man's responsibility to work, not stay home with the kids; and [the boss] had to eat 'beanie weanies' at one point in his life in order to make ends meet, but his wife still stayed home." The boss then asked Roberts "if he understood the meaning of the word 'motherhood' and explained that it means 'mother.' " Suddenly Roberts, who had never before been reprimanded in any way, was being written up for infractions so minor they had never before been mentioned. Not long afterward, he was fired (*David O. Roberts v. State of South Carolina, South Carolina Department of Public Safety, First Amended Complaint and Jury Demand*, June 22, 1999, available online at http://archive.aclu.org/court/robertsvcarolina_complaint.html. According to Roberts's lawyer, Sara Mandelbaum, the case was settled for an undisclosed but "satisfactory" amount before going to trial.)

No wonder so few men ask for parental leave. They're afraid that if they do, they'll be treated like women.

13. Jane Waldfogel, "The Family Gap for Young Women in the U.S. and Britain," *Journal of Labor Economics* 16, No. 3 (1998): 505–545.

14. Jane Waldfogel, "Understanding the 'Family Wage Gap' in Pay for Women with Children," *Journal of Economic Perspectives* 12, no. 1 (Winter 1998), p. 144.

10: NO MORE EXCUSES

1. Linda Babcock and Sara Laschever, *Women Don't Ask: Negotiation and the Gender Divide* (Princeton, N.J.: Princeton University Press, 2003).

2. Some quibblers might wonder: When those high-powered, high-earning women leave their jobs, doesn't that bring down the average earnings by removing some of the highest numbers, those farthest out on the bell curve? Technically, yes, but that effect is almost too slight to measure. Think of it this way. If, after just three years in the workforce, half of all the 1999 female law and business school graduates had quit to have children, that would have removed 9,000 women's paychecks from the average. That's just one tenth of 1 percent of all 40 million working women—not enough to shift the scales very much at all. In economic terms, that effect is trivial. What's more, those new moms are too young to be multimillion-dollar earners—a level that very few people, either male or female, ever achieve. To project that these would be the handful who'd eventually make it to the top is so hypothetical as to be sheer fantasy.

After all, 7 million women of working age are full-time stay-at-home moms. They're drawn from every economic level. Some of them were earning $160,000, some were earning $36,000, some were earning $16,000, and some were never earning at all. At every economic level, some woman's potential wages aren't being figured into the female average, just as, at every economic level, there's always some man who's out of a job, whose nonearnings aren't being figured into the male average.

3. Alfred Blumrosen, Professor, Rutgers Law School, New Jersey, and Ruth Blumrosen, Adjunct Professor, Rutgers Law School, New Jersey, "The Reality of Intentional Job Discrimination in Metropolitan America—1999," sponsored by the Ford Foundation.

4. Outstanding academics have made extremely valuable contributions to analyzing the wage gap, including economists such as Francine Blau, Heidi Hartmann, and Lawrence Katz, and sociologists such as Jane Waldfogel. But as discussed in this book's first chapter, statistical interpretations are confined by the statistics used. The U.S. Census Bureau and U.S. Bureau of Labor Statistics describe working people by their age, race, gender, educational attainment, job earnings—and nothing more. When social scientists try to draw conclusions about the wage gap based only on data about workers' demographic characteristics, they're drawing conclusions from only part of the picture. They don't have the data that would allow them to correlate wages with different behaviors in the workplace—such as discrimination. So they are left trying to measure discrimination indirectly. As mentioned earlier in this chapter, a recent Rutgers study has done some innovative work on this subject with data that haven't been used before, data from employers that peek into workplace biases against women employees. These findings strongly suggest that federal agencies should be collecting more data from all employers about wages and promotion practices. Once that happens, social scientists will be able to measure the effects of discrimination on the gender wage gap.

11: STARTING TO GET EVEN

1. *Under Scrutiny: The Effect of Consent Decrees on the Representation of Women in Sworn Law Enforcement* (Arlington, Va.: National Center for Women and Policing, Feminist Majority Foundation, 2003), p. 2.

2. For consent decree documents signed to settle some cases in this book, see the consent decree file at www.wageproject.org.

12: WOMEN, WORKING FROM THE INSIDE UP

1. Robert L. Nelson and William P. Bridges, *Legalizing Gender Inequality: Courts, Markets, and Unequal Pay for Women in America* (Cambridge, England: Cambridge University Press, 1999), p. 348.

Acknowledgments

This is a book that I had to write. Not one that I wanted to write but had to. Its contents have riled my sensibilities every single day of the seven years that I have been researching and writing it. Along the way, I have been remarkably fortunate that many wise and wonderful people have enthusiastically offered their time and energy to enrich this work. I want to thank them for their generosity.

I am extremely grateful to scholars, activists, and businesspeople who read and critiqued the entire manuscript, page by page, letting nothing slip by their intense scrutiny. In so doing, Michael Ames, William Bielby, Linda Glenn, Jennifer Jackman, Stacey Lauren, Martha Minow, June Rokoff, Eleanor Smeal, and Joan Williams improved this work immeasurably. Randy Albelda, Nina Balsam, Emily Barkin, Christina Crowe, Dawn-Marie Driscoll, Eileen Friars, Shanti Fry, Carol Goldberg, Heidi Hartmann, Victoria Lovell, Jane McBride, Tom and Nancy Rogers, and Ronnie Steinberg reviewed parts of the manuscript and waded through early versions laden with mind-numbing facts and numbers. Each of them made valuable contributions to this work. To all, my profound thanks.

I am indebted to friends and colleagues who gave me forums in which to present my research and recruit interviewees, as well as to those who just listened to me work through the material in my head for years: Shula Reinharz and the scholars in the Women's Studies Research Center at Brandeis University; Mary Lassen and the Women's Educational and Industrial Union; as well as Meg Bond, Ann Caldwell, Betty Diener, Sherri DuFloq, Mary Jane England, Mary Fifield, Betsy Fitter, Ellen Friedman, Jennifer Hicks, Sheryl Marshall, Alana Murphy, Carol Nadelson, Janis Pryor, Virginia Pfifer, and Marie Sheehan. Brandeis students Carol Lue and Tammy Pels, along with Northeastern Law School students Alyson Robbins and Jessica Copeland, spent endless hours researching discrimination cases and federal statistics. Joan Bok, Clare Dalton, Harold Meyerson, Shelby Scott, and Faith Zwemke provided important data or resources. Ellen Goodman, Hamilton Jordan, and John Laub gave me timely and sage advice about the process of publishing.

EEOC lawyers, plaintiff's bar attorneys, expert witnesses, court monitors, and others involved in discrimination cases provided valuable materials and insights about discrimination cases. I am particularly indebted to Marc Bendick, William Bielby, Stephanie Bornstein, Noelle Brennan, Barry Goldstein, Donna Harper, Nancy Kreiter, Peter Laura, Adele Rapport, Larry Schaeffer, Gary Shultz, and Debra Smith.

Arlene Ash, Tracey Hurd, Sandy Jones, Elizabeth Marks, Marsha Mirkin, Phyllis Mutschler, Cheri Ostroff, Eleanor Shore, Janet Swim, Rhoda Unger, Robin Vann-Ricca, Nancy Wecker, and Lisa Wuennenberg generously gave their time to help me understand how their professional disciplines bear on wage discrimination.

I want especially to acknowledge the amazing women who volunteered to be interviewed. Some even gave permission to use their names. I offer my personal gratitude and hope everyone who reads this book appreciates their courage. Their voices add credibility and speak for many others who related their experiences but felt that if I used their names they might jeopardize their current jobs or future careers. I understand well that the latter must earn a living and respect their need for anonymity.

To Vikki Pryor I owe a special debt. For years, Vikki urged me and encouraged me not to speak through numbers and data but rather to interpret and draw conclusions from what I found in the facts. She helped me "find my voice" for this work.

When I first met Jill Kneerim, she said to me, "I want to be your agent because I believe in this book." She is a treasure—a trusted friend as well as literary agent. Without her guidance, advice, and help, this book simply would not exist. My heartfelt thanks to her hardly seem adequate.

E.J. Graff is a brilliant journalist who told me, "I'll write this book the way you speak, rather than the way you write." She did that and much, much more. In the spirited collaboration we developed during the last two years, E.J.'s ideas and insights became interwoven with mine throughout the book. I will be forever grateful for her singular contribution to this work. Her amazing research assistant Kelly Kinneen pitched in wonderfully at the last minute. Her writing group of Suzanne Berne, Madeline Drexler, and Laura Zimmerman contributed hours of editing and feedback, for which there can never be thanks enough.

Doris Cooper, a first-class editor, deserves enormous gratitude for her skill in stretching my thinking. She inspired me to explain more about the research I had gathered, in ways that greatly enhanced the final product. Peter Karanjia's superb legal advice sharpened the book's accuracy and punch. Of all the sympathetic men who want to help women get even, I am indebted most to publisher Mark Gompertz for his support and keen desire to see this book find its audience.

To those whose contributions I have not acknowledged through sheer oversight or failure of memory, please accept my apologies along with my gratitude.

While this book springs from a vast, ardent collaboration, I alone am responsible for any errors that slipped through the fact checking, for any misinterpretations of the advice given by those who reviewed various chapters, and for all the conclusions. Most of those who read the manuscript or early versions did not see my final conclusions. While all were sympathetic to my arguments, I make no claim that they agree entirely with the contents of this book.

Finally, my deepest appreciation goes to Jacque Friedman, to whom this book is dedicated, for her wholehearted support and belief in this work every step along the way. More than anyone, she has always encouraged me to pursue my dreams.

Evelyn Murphy
Brookline, Massachusetts
December 2004

Index

academia, *see* education
Adams, Lisa, 56–57
adolescents, 44, 65, 222
  sexual harassment and, 109–17,
    119–21, 132
Advantage Staffing, Inc., 43, 58, 60–61,
    150
advertising industry, 167–68, 173,
    177
AFL-CIO, 24
African Americans, 14, 43, 153, 276,
    294
age, aging, 5, 210
  and attempts to end sex
    discrimination, 244–45
  discrimination based on, 43, 48–49,
    51, 91, 262, 295, 303, 308
  everyday discrimination and, 175–76,
    190, 193
  and excuses for not dealing with wage
    gap, 219–20

and personal costs of wage gap, 26–28,
    30–33
  workplace sex segregation and, 149,
    163, 169–70
airlines:
  lawsuits and, 44, 46, 71–72, 81, 84, 92,
    136, 139
  workplace sex segregation at, 145,
    173
*Althea Rapier, et al., v. Ford Motor
    Company,* 123–24
Amaranth, Karel, 166, 172
American Bar Association, 206
American Express Financial Advisors,
    Inc., 43, 70, 94
American Federation of State, County,
    and Municipal Employees
    (AFSCME), 93
Antilla, Susan, 125
Arango, Gabriella, 105
Ashe, R. Lawrence, Jr., 67–68

assaults, 40, 43
  sexual harassment and, 105–7,
    114–16, 126, 132, 134–35
Atkins, Carol, 61

Bailey v. Scott-Gallaher, Inc., 194
Baker & McKenzie, 116
Baton Rouge, La., 58, 78–79
Bean Lumber Company, 43, 84, 199
Bendick, Marc, 296
Benn, Laquinta, 56
Berge Ford, 81, 84
Bergland, Linda, 261
Berry, Anne, 142
Bielby, William, 248, 294–95
Birgenau, Bob, 242, 244, 246, 248–49
Blagojevich, Rod, 201–3
Blank, Arthur, 63–64, 66–67, 151
blatant sex discrimination, 51–99, 125,
    175, 217, 303
  costs to women of, 52, 54–55, 57, 76,
    86, 93, 95–96
  firings and, 51, 53, 55, 81–85, 87–96
  hiring practices and, 51–53, 55–66,
    73–75, 78, 85, 98–99
  lawsuits and, 51, 53–55, 57–61, 63–67,
    69–73, 75–81, 83–99
  pregnancy and, 53–55, 77, 81–86, 93
  promotions and, 51–55, 58–59, 61–78,
    84, 87, 90, 95–97, 186
  statistics on, 57, 60, 73
  wage gap and, 52, 55, 60, 63–64, 66,
    68–69, 71–87, 90, 92–96, 98–99
  why employers do not fix it, 96–99
  workplace sex segregation and, 149,
    155, 158–60, 164–65
Boies, Schiller & Flexner, 43, 70, 94
Boise State University, 72, 77
bonuses, 177, 236
  and discrimination against mothers,
    200, 204, 206, 209
  and working from top down, 287–89

bookkeepers, 30, 33, 84, 187
  workplace sex segregation and, 146,
    164–65
Brackey, Harriet Johnson, 105
Brennan, Noelle, 133–34, 256–57, 260
Bridges, William, 270
Brigham and Women's Hospital,
    250–52, 264, 289–90
Brown, Bob, 245–46
Brummell, Vera, 143
Built from Scratch (Blank and Marcus),
    64, 66–67
bus drivers, 118, 122, 191
Byrd, Alton, 142

California, 153–54, 180
Capitol, U.S., 78, 81, 227
car dealerships, 43–44, 104, 109–10,
    119, 122, 136–38
Carley, Richard, 127
cars, *see* transportation, travel
Carter, Barbara, 143
cashiers, 227
  blatant sex discrimination and, 53,
    63–65, 68
  sexual harassment and, 114, 116, 119,
    122
  workplace sex segregation and, 146,
    151, 164–65
Catalyst, 101
Caterpillar, Inc., 51, 90
CBS Broadcasting, Inc., 70, 94
Census Bureau, U.S., 9, 25–26
Chicago Women in Trades, 148, 155
chief executive officers (CEOs), 45, 47,
    225
  and attempts to end sex
    discrimination, 243, 245–46, 253
  blatant sex discrimination and, 97–98
  motivation of, 286–89
  outside pressure and, 299, 301–3,
    305

sexual harassment and, 106–7, 110,
    112–13, 141
in sketch of solution to wage gap,
    234–37
and working from inside up, 267–69,
    275, 281–82
and working from top down, 281,
    284–98
workplace sex segregation and, 171,
    173, 285
children, child care, 14, 261
blatant sex discrimination and, 62, 82,
    86
and discrimination against mothers,
    194–97, 200–203, 205–9, 211–12
everyday discrimination and, 187–90,
    193
and excuses for not dealing with wage
    gap, 220, 222–23, 225
and personal costs of wage gap, 22–32
sexual harassment and, 106, 123
workplace sex segregation and, 149,
    152, 154, 162–63, 169
see also adolescents
Chronicle of Higher Education, The, 75
Chrysler Corporation, 253–54
Civil Rights Act (1964), Title VII of the,
    9, 13, 21, 52, 83, 304
and sexual harassment, 101–3, 254
and workplace sex segregation,
    146–47
Civil Rights Act (1991), 52, 93
clerks, clerical workers, 6, 17, 48, 199
and attempts to end sex
    discrimination, 261, 263
blatant sex discrimination and, 80, 84
everyday discrimination and, 187, 191
sexual harassment and, 107, 113, 116,
    120, 122
workplace sex segregation and, 146,
    150, 163–65, 169, 173
Coachmen Automotive, 136, 142

collaborating, 286, 301
in working from inside up, 266,
    273–77, 280–83
college graduates, 17–20, 128, 172
blatant sex discrimination and, 73, 86
everyday discrimination and, 190–91
of 1991, 18–20
and personal costs of wage gap, 26,
    30–31
see also professional school graduates
computer workers, 6, 47, 63–64, 91
Congress, U.S., 13, 93, 140, 254
outside pressure and, 299, 301–7
Conley, Michele, 56
consent decrees:
and attempts to end sex
    discrimination, 252–54, 256–57,
    259, 287
blatant sex discrimination and, 58–59,
    70–71
sexual harassment and, 110–11, 113,
    117, 119–20, 122, 136–37, 144
and working from top down, 287,
    291
Consolidated Freightways, 94
construction industry, 6, 65, 137, 187,
    227
workplace sex segregation and, 146,
    148, 150–56, 173
corporate cultures, 235
and attempts to end sex
    discrimination, 250, 257, 259
blatant sex discrimination and, 53,
    63–65, 67, 74, 98
sexual harassment and, 140–41
and working from inside up, 275,
    278
and working from top down, 285, 287,
    292, 297–98
Corrections Department, D.C., 48, 140,
    143
credit card debts, 28–29, 31

Criminal Justice Division, N.J., 127, 138, 149
Crittenden, Ann, 26

David, Lori, 51
Davis, Barbara, 127, 149
DeCoster Farms, 116, 118, 140
Defense Department, U.S., 140
Del Laboratories, 106–7
demotions, 48, 161, 195
  blatant sex discrimination and, 54, 74, 82–85, 89–90, 92–94
  sexual harassment and, 125, 130
DeRossett, Julie, 142
Dial Corporation, 144, 227
  sexual harassment at, 128–36, 149, 154–55, 164
Diamond Star Motors, 289
  attempt to close wage gap at, 257–58, 260
  sexual harassment at, 253–54, 260
discrimination:
  age-based, 43, 48–49, 51, 91, 262, 295, 303, 308
  race-based, 43, 45–47, 57, 59, 61, 92, 95, 103, 261–62, 276, 293–94, 303, 307–8
diversity, diversity consulting, 49, 156
  blatant sex discrimination and, 66, 89
  failure of, 233–34
  and working from top down, 295–96
divorces, 86, 226, 261
  and discrimination against mothers, 195, 211
  and personal costs of wage gap, 28–29, 31–32
  sexual harassment and, 109, 116–22
doctors, 6
  and attempts to end sex discrimination, 250–51
  blatant sex discrimination and, 73, 93

and discrimination against mothers, 196–98, 210
everyday discrimination and, 182–83
and excuses for not dealing with wage gap, 222, 224
sexual harassment and, 110, 113, 119
workplace sex segregation and, 146, 168–69, 173
Dukes v. Wal-Mart, 69
DuPont:
  blatant sex discrimination at, 87–93, 149, 155
  lawsuits against, 88–89

Eddy, Dan, 56
education, 4–6, 9, 16–20, 73, 199, 261, 271, 289
  attempt to end sex discrimination in, 237–50, 256, 263, 269–70, 272, 276, 279, 281
  blatant sex discrimination and, 54, 59, 70, 72–78, 92–93
  everyday discrimination and, 176, 182, 184, 190–92
  and excuses for not dealing with wage gap, 224, 226–27, 229–31
  lawsuits and, 43, 45, 47, 58–59, 70, 72–73, 75–80, 91–93, 110, 112–13, 117, 120
  and personal costs of wage gap, 26, 29–32
  sexual harassment and, 107, 110, 112–13, 117, 120–22, 132, 135
  working from inside up in, 238–43, 269–70, 272, 276, 279, 281
  working from top down in, 244–47, 286, 288, 290, 294, 296
  workplace sex segregation and, 146, 156, 164–66, 169–70, 285
  see also college graduates; professional school graduates; tenure

employers, 12–13, 234
  attempts to end sex discrimination by,
    237–65, 275, 281, 285, 287,
    289–90, 292, 296–97, 302
  blatant sex discrimination and, 51–61,
    63–67, 69–99
  and discrimination against mothers,
    194, 212
  and excuses for not dealing with wage
    gap, 224, 226–29
  lawsuits against, 38–51, 53–54, 56–61,
    63–67, 69–73, 75–78, 81, 83–99,
    110–13, 117–22, 136–39, 141
  outside pressure and, 299, 305
  and personal costs of wage gap, 23, 27
  sexual harassment and, 105–8,
    110–13, 124
  and working from inside up, 266–68,
    271, 283
  workplace sex segregation and, 147,
    156
Engineering Department,
  Bloomingdale, Ill., 122, 143
engineers, engineering, 17–20, 24
  and attempts to end sex
    discrimination, 245–46, 248
  everyday discrimination and, 177, 181
  working from inside up in, 276,
    280–81
  workplace sex segregation and, 146,
    166–67
Equal Employment Opportunity
  Commission (EEOC), 7, 38,
  41–42, 150, 228, 236, 275
  and attempts to end sex
    discrimination, 252–54, 256,
    258–60, 287
  blatant sex discrimination and, 57, 61,
    75–76, 79, 81, 89
  and discrimination against mothers,
    195, 200, 205
  outside pressure and, 303–4

sexual harassment and, 100, 104, 106,
    108–9, 115–16, 121, 123, 133, 135,
    143–44, 253–54, 256
  and working from top down, 287,
    293
Equal Pay Act, 21, 52
Equal Rights Advocates, 153
everyday discrimination, 174–93, 217,
    230
  costs to women of, 175, 179, 182–83,
    186–87, 190, 193
  double standards in, 184–87
  exclusions in, 181–84, 186
  expectations of others in, 177–79
  state employee's story on, 190–93
  visibility in, 180–81
  Wilkinson's story on, 187–90
executives, 14, 27, 233–35
  and attempts to end sex
    discrimination, 240–51, 253,
    256–64
  blatant sex discrimination and, 56–57,
    63–67, 90–92, 97–98
  and discrimination against mothers,
    204–5
  everyday discrimination and, 174, 182,
    185, 191
  and excuses for not dealing with wage
    gap, 218, 224–27
  outside pressure and, 299–306
  sexual harassment and, 100, 106–7,
    110–13, 121, 124, 141–42
  in sketch of solution to wage gap,
    234–35
  and working from inside up, 267–70,
    273–77, 281–82
  workplace sex segregation and, 145,
    166, 171, 173, 285
  see also chief executive officers

Fair Pay Act, 305
family-friendly policies, 233–34

financial services firms, 10, 17, 40, 43,
    45–46, 49, 253, 293
  blatant sex discrimination and, 54,
    70–71, 79, 84, 91, 94
  everyday discrimination and, 182, 185
  and excuses for not dealing with wage
    gap, 228, 230
  sexual harassment and, 101, 103–4,
    120–21, 125–27, 136–39, 144
Fire Department, Atlanta, Ga., 69–70
Fire Department, Muskogee, Okla.,
    157–62, 230
firefighters, 296
  blatant sex discrimination and, 69–70,
    92
  and excuses for not dealing with wage
    gap, 224, 230
  sexual harassment and, 104, 122, 140
  workplace sex segregation and, 146,
    156–62
firing, firings, 40, 191, 230, 288
  blatant sex discrimination and, 51, 53,
    55, 81–85, 87–96
  and discrimination against mothers,
    194–96, 199–200
  lawsuits and, 43–48, 88–96
  sexual harassment and, 105, 107,
    125–26, 130–31, 134, 143–44
Flying Horse Woodworks, 282
Forcier, Sandra, 156–57
Ford Motor Company, 300
  lawsuits against, 44–45, 118, 123–24,
    137
  sexual harassment at, 123–24, 137,
    154
fund-raising jobs, 170–71

gender wage gap:
  and attempts to end sex
    discrimination, 237, 250–52,
    260–65, 285, 289–90
  author's interest in, 4–6
  causes of, 4–5, 7, 9–11, 16–17, 147
  costs to women of, 22–33, 273, 277
  definition of, 5
  excuses for not dealing with, 217–31
  failures in dealing with, 232–34
  in future, 7–8, 32–33, 218, 221–22,
    230–31, 275, 307
  groups impacted by, 14
  narrowing of, 5, 17–18
  in past, 4–5, 18
  prevalence of, 3, 5–6
  solutions to, 8, 11–15, 234–37
  statistics on, 3–5, 8–10, 14, 16–20,
    23–32, 60, 73, 165, 169, 210–11,
    221–24, 229–31, 236, 263–65, 305
  as status quo, 42
  urgency of, 4
  widening of, 4–5, 17–21, 37
General Motors (GM), 118, 137, 142
Gilligan, Rich, 258
Glorious Food, 57–59
Goldberg, Carol, 217–18
Goldstein, Barry, 95, 102
Goodyear Tire & Rubber, 72, 79
Grace Culinary Systems, 135, 137
Gray, Doug, 108
Greenstein, Martin, 116
Gretzinger, Norman, 144

Hartford, Inc., The, 201
Hartmann, Heidi, 21
Hay job evaluation system, 261–62
health, health care, health insurance,
    44–45, 47–48, 218
  attempt to close wage gap in, 250–52,
    264, 289–90
  blatant sex discrimination and, 73, 77,
    79, 85, 90
  and discrimination against mothers,
    204–5, 208
  everyday discrimination and, 182,
    188–90

and personal costs of wage gap, 23–24, 29–30, 32

sexual harassment and, 101, 110–13, 115, 117, 119, 122, 133, 135, 137–38, 140, 143

workplace sex segregation and, 155, 161, 285

see also doctors; nurses; nurse's aides

help-wanted ads, sex-segregated, 55

high school graduates, 20, 26, 135, 156

hiring practices, 233

and attempts to end sex discrimination, 237, 246, 249–53, 296

blatant sex discrimination and, 51–53, 55–66, 73–75, 78, 85, 98–99

everyday discrimination and, 175, 178, 186

and excuses for not dealing with wage gap, 226–28

lawsuits and, 43–46, 48, 51–61, 98–99

sexual harassment and, 125, 134–41, 143

and working from inside up, 269, 275–76

and working from top down, 288, 293–98

workplace sex segregation and, 150–51, 153, 156, 165, 172

Hispanics, 14, 45–46

sexual harassment of, 135–40

Hockfield, Susan, 249

Home Depot (HD), 151

attempt to end sex discrimination at, 237, 253

blatant sex discrimination at, 63–69, 71, 73, 82, 164, 186

lawsuits against, 64–67, 71, 91, 95, 227, 294

working from top down at, 294–95

Hopkins, Nancy, 168, 238–50, 269, 272–74, 279

hostile environment, 47

blatant sex discrimination and, 88–89, 92

sexual harassment and, 101–2, 123–42, 182

House of Delegates, Va., 48, 107, 113

housing inspectors, 163–65

Hyde, Alan, 127

Hyundai Semiconductor America, Inc., 58, 61, 276

immigrants, 135–40, 150

information technology (IT) industry, 167, 173

Ingles Markets, 62, 71, 95, 227

Institute for Women's Policy Research, 21, 25–26

insurance, insurance industry, 7, 161, 201, 251

everyday discrimination and, 188–89

and personal costs of wage gap, 22, 24, 30

investments, 32–33

Jackson, Jesse, 254

janitors, 14, 46, 227

blatant sex discrimination and, 58, 78–81, 85

sexual harassment and, 117, 121, 134, 139

workplace sex segregation and, 147, 163–64, 285

Joe's Stone Crab, 58, 60

Joint Apprenticeship and Training Committee (JATC), 153

Josephthal, 127, 138

Joyner, Cheryl, 194

Joyner, Samuel E., 194, 200

J.P. Morgan Chase, 144, 228

"Jury Hits Mazda Hard in Sex-Harassment Case" (Brackey), 105

Karraker, Michael, 56
Klein, Freada, 116
Klein, Lydia, 125–26
Kornegay, Alison, 123
Kreiter, Nancy, 144, 254–56, 258–60

Labor and Industries Department,
    Wash., 144
Labor Department, U.S., 58, 164, 303
Lawrence, Robin, 94
Lawrence Livermore Labs, 77, 91,
    294
lawsuits, 9–10, 12, 14, 38–67, 236
    and attempts to end sex
        discrimination, 245, 248, 252–55,
        259, 261–62, 264
    awards and settlements in, 38–49, 51,
        57–60, 66–67, 69–72, 76–81,
        84–85, 90–96, 102–5, 107–8,
        110–13, 115, 117–22, 125, 127,
        133, 135–40, 142, 252, 254, 270,
        292, 305
    blatant sex discrimination and, 51,
        53–55, 57–61, 63–67, 69–73,
        75–81, 83–99
    class action, 42–49, 58–59, 64, 69, 71,
        80, 84, 86, 94–95, 133, 144, 248,
        253
    costs to women of, 10, 41, 53–54, 76,
        86, 93–94, 96, 98, 103–4, 108, 126,
        133–34, 142–43, 200, 220, 252,
        254
    and discrimination against mothers,
        194–96, 199–201, 205
    everyday discrimination and, 174–76,
        186–87, 192
    and excuses for not dealing with wage
        gap, 218, 220, 227–28
    firings and, 43–48, 88–96
    hiring practices and, 43–46, 48,
        51–61, 98–99
    outside pressure and, 303–5

    reluctance of women to participate in,
        94–95, 98, 133, 142–43, 192, 200,
        220, 252
    sexual harassment and, 43–49,
        100–113, 115–27, 132–44, 160,
        253–54, 259, 292
    and working from inside up, 266, 268,
        270–71, 275
    and working from top down, 285, 287,
        289, 292, 294
    workplace sex segregation and, 147,
        153, 160, 162, 165
lawyers, 43, 46
    blatant sex discrimination and, 55, 70,
        91, 94
    and discrimination against mothers,
        199, 201, 206–10, 212
    everyday discrimination and,
        180–81
    and excuses for not dealing with wage
        gap, 224, 229–30
    sexual harassment and, 112, 116,
        127
    workplace sex segregation and, 146,
        168, 170
Ledbetter, Lilly M., 72
Legalizing Gender Inequality (Nelson
    and Bridges), 270
Levin, Diane, 185
light industrial jobs:
    working from top down in, 293–94
    workplace sex segregation and,
        150–51, 173
Lynn Public Schools, 78, 80

McFarland, Linda, 142
McKinney, Amy, 157–62, 230
McKinney, Tom, 157–62
Magnenti, Tom, 246
Maine, 305
managers, management, 6, 43–45,
    233–35, 300

Index 335

and attempts to end sex discrimination, 246, 253, 255–56, 258, 260

blatant sex discrimination and, 53, 56, 61–69, 73–74, 79–82, 88–89, 91–92, 97

and discrimination against mothers, 195, 197–98, 200–201, 203–4, 210, 212

everyday discrimination and, 174, 176, 180–83, 185–86, 188–93

and excuses for not dealing with wage gap, 220, 224–28

and personal costs of wage gap, 23–25

senior, *see* executives

sexual harassment and, 104, 107–24, 126, 128–36, 141–44

in sketch of solution to wage gap, 234–35

and working from inside up, 270, 275–76, 280–81

and working from top down, 291, 294–98

workplace sex segregation and, 148, 150, 156, 162–65, 169–70, 172–73

Manor, Tammie, 60–61

manufacturing industry, 6

attempts to end sex discrimination in, 237, 252–60, 263, 287, 289, 292, 297

blatant sex discrimination and, 57, 59, 70–71, 79–80, 84, 90

everyday discrimination and, 187–88

sexual harassment and, 113, 116–18, 120, 123–24, 128–39, 141, 144, 253–56, 258–60, 292, 297

workplace sex segregation and, 148, 151, 173, 285

Marcus, Bernard, 63–64, 66–67, 151

marriages, 142

blatant sex discrimination and, 82, 94

and discrimination against mothers, 195–97

everyday discrimination and, 179, 187, 189, 192

and personal costs of wage gap, 28–29, 31

Massachusetts Institute of Technology (MIT), 8, 168

attempt to end sex discrimination at, 237–50, 256, 263

lesson to take from, 249–50

outside pressure and, 247–49

working from inside up at, 238–43, 270, 272–74, 276, 281

working from top down at, 244–47, 286, 288, 290, 296

maternity leaves, 19, 48, 233, 291

blatant sex discrimination and, 84–85

and discrimination against mothers, 194–95, 199–200, 205, 207, 211

Mazda North America, 105, 120

media, 39–42, 160, 176

and attempts to end sex discrimination, 247, 254, 257

blatant sex discrimination and, 51–52, 55, 75, 81–83

and discrimination against mothers, 195, 199, 202–3, 222

and excuses for not dealing with wage gap, 219, 222

outside pressure and, 301, 306

sexual harassment and, 101, 105, 107, 111–13, 116, 127, 134, 140, 142

and working from inside up, 267–68, 271, 274–75, 283

and working from top down, 286–88

Mehringer, Shelly, 143

merit gap, 4–5, 16–18

Meritor Savings Bank v. Vinson, 103

Merrill Lynch, 10
  lawsuits against, 40, 71, 138
  sexual harassment at, 126–27, 138
Mike Shannon's Restaurants, 59–60
Mikva, Abner, 254
Miller, Jessica, 280
Miller, Lee, 280
Milwaukee, Wis., 45, 107, 112
Minnesota, 80, 90, 113, 147
  attempt to close wage gap in, 237,
    260–65, 275, 281, 285, 289–90, 302
Mitsubishi Motor Manufacturing of
    America, Inc. (MMMA):
  attempt to end sex discrimination at,
    237, 252–60, 263
  commitment from top at, 256–60,
    287, 292, 297
  outside pressure and, 252–57,
    259–60
  sexual harassment at, 138, 144,
    253–56, 258–60, 292, 297
Mobil, 128, 144
Monkmeyer, James, 143
Moore v. Alabama State University, 199
mothers, discrimination against, 13–14,
    27, 194–213, 217
  and blatant sex discrimination, 82,
    86
  costs to women of, 194–96, 198,
    200–201, 203, 209–13, 222–23
  and performance evaluations, 200,
    203–4, 207
  and promotions, 10–11, 13, 195,
    197–202, 206–7, 209–12, 223
  and raises, 10, 198, 200, 202–4, 223
  and stereotyping, 196, 199–212
  and wage gap, 204, 206, 210–13
mothers, motherhood, 4–6, 11, 176
  blatant sex discrimination and, 54,
    67–68
  sexual harassment and, 109–14
  stay-at-home, 4–5, 19

mothers, working, 37, 62
  cycle of, 28–29
  everyday discrimination and, 174,
    187–90
  and excuses for not dealing with wage
    gap, 220, 222–24, 226
  1991 college graduates and, 18–20
  and personal costs of wage gap,
    22–27
  sexual harassment and, 109, 116–22
  single, 22, 25, 28–29, 31, 94, 109,
    116–22, 188–90, 203–4, 211, 220,
    226, 261
  workplace sex segregation and,
    149–50, 152, 154, 162–63, 169

Nadelson, Carol, 250–51
Nakashima, Masaki, 105
Namgyal, Palden Gyuimed, 144
National Association for Female
    Executives (NAFE), 233
National Center for Women and
    Policing, 252
National Organization for Women, 55,
    254
Navy, U.S., 47, 121, 140
negotiating, 221, 231
  and attempts to end sex
    discrimination, 243, 251
  in working from inside up, 266, 271,
    275–83
Nelson, Robert, 270
New England Serum Co., Inc., 45, 120,
    135–40
New York City, 45, 91, 120, 159, 166
  blatant sex discrimination in, 57–59
New York Times, The, 127, 247
New York Times Magazine, The, 195
nonprofit sector, 182, 206, 277, 306
  workplace sex segregation and, 166,
    170–73, 285
Norquist, John, 107

Nuesse, Barbara, 93
nurses, 37, 44
    workplace sex segregation and, 146,
        162, 164–65, 170, 285
nurse's aides, 106, 117, 261

O'Connor, Sandra Day, 55
Office of Federal Contract Compliance
        Programs (OFCCP), 75, 303
    lawsuits and, 58–59, 79–81
Olympia, Wash., 150
Oney, Genevieve, 68
Operation PUSH, 254
Ostroff, Cheri, 169–70
outside pressure, 12, 299–308
    and attempts to end sex
        discrimination, 247–49, 252–57,
        259–60, 262, 265
    from every one of us, 299, 305–8
    Fortune 100 companies and,
        299–301
    from president and Congress, 299,
        301–7
    in sketch of solution to wage gap, 234,
        236–37
    and working from top down, 287–88
overtime, 135, 160
    blatant sex discrimination and, 70,
        82–86
    and discrimination against mothers,
        205, 212

part-time jobs, 4, 82, 191, 233
    and discrimination against mothers,
        195, 197–98, 200, 206–8, 222
    workplace sex segregation and, 162,
        168
Paycheck Fairness Act, 305
pay pattern audits, 290–91
Peckinpaugh, Janet, 51
pensions, see retirement, retirement
    plans

performance, performance evaluations,
        226
    and attempts to end sex
        discrimination, 261–62
    blatant sex discrimination and, 69, 72,
        82, 90
    and discrimination against mothers,
        200, 203–4, 207
    everyday discrimination and, 177–78,
        184–86, 189
    sexual harassment and, 100, 126,
        130–31
    and working from inside up, 271,
        280
    and working from top down, 287–90,
        293–95
    workplace sex segregation and, 154,
        158–59
Perpich, Rudy, 262–63
Peterson, Iver, 127
Pickler, Marylyn, 81, 199
Pizza Hut, 109–16, 120, 132
Police Department, Santa Barbara,
        Calif., 46, 48, 71, 227–28
police officers, 252
    blatant sex discrimination and, 58,
        70–71, 80, 82–87, 90–92
    and discrimination against mothers,
        200, 205
    and excuses for not dealing with wage
        gap, 224, 227–28, 230
    lawsuits and, 45–48, 58, 70–71, 80, 84,
        90–92, 110–12, 117–18, 120–21,
        136–39
    sexual harassment and, 104,
        110–12, 117–18, 120–22, 124,
        136–39
    workplace sex segregation and, 146,
        156
Pollard, Sharon, 87–93, 149, 155
Porter, Bonnie, 94
poverty, 14, 29, 31–33, 190, 193

pregnancy, 40, 43–49, 125, 224, 291
  blatant sex discrimination and, 53–55,
    77, 81–86, 93
  and discrimination against mothers,
    195, 199–200, 205–6, 211
Pregnancy Discrimination Act, 83
pressure triangle, see outside pressure;
    working from inside up; working
    from top down
professional school graduates, 20, 127
  blatant sex discrimination and, 55, 73
  and discrimination against mothers,
    206–8
  everyday discrimination and, 179,
    191–92
  and excuses for not dealing with wage
    gap, 225, 229
  and personal costs of wage gap, 26, 30
  workplace sex segregation and, 168,
    172
promotions, 6, 37, 41
  and attempts to end sex
    discrimination, 237, 246, 250,
    252–53
  blatant sex discrimination and, 51–55,
    58–59, 61–78, 84, 87, 90, 92,
    95–97, 186
  and discrimination against mothers,
    10–11, 13, 195, 197–202, 206–7,
    209–12, 223
  everyday discrimination and, 175–79,
    183–86, 190–91, 193
  and excuses for not dealing with wage
    gap, 219, 221, 223, 225–26
  lawsuits and, 43, 46, 48–49, 58–59,
    61–67, 69–72, 77, 84, 90, 92
  sexual harassment and, 101, 107, 125,
    128, 131–32, 135, 141, 143
  in sketch of solution to wage gap,
    235–36
  and working from inside up, 269, 275,
    277, 279–80, 282–83

  and working from top down, 291,
    293–96
  workplace sex segregation and,
    164–65, 168
Publix Super Markets, Inc., 227
  blatant sex discrimination at, 61,
    67–69, 71, 73, 164, 186
  lawsuit against, 61, 71, 95

Quality Art, LLC, 138, 140
quitting:
  and discrimination against mothers,
    204–5
  and excuses for not dealing with wage
    gap, 220, 226
  sexual harassment and, 106, 108,
    115–16
  and working from inside up, 269, 282
  workplace sex segregation and,
    161–62

Rainbow Coalition, 254
raises, 17, 19, 24, 172
  and attempts to end sex
    discrimination, 242–43, 263–64
  blatant sex discrimination and, 68, 74,
    76–77, 95
  and discrimination against mothers,
    10, 198, 200, 202–4, 223
  everyday discrimination and, 177–78,
    184, 187–88, 191–93
  and excuses for not dealing with wage
    gap, 219, 223
  sexual harassment and, 100–101,
    106–7, 125, 130, 132, 141
  and working from inside up, 277,
    279–80, 282–83
  and working from top down, 289–90,
    293, 296
Rapier, Althea, 123–24
Rapport, Adele, 61, 104, 109, 116–22,
    143–44

Raytheon, 69, 71
Rent-A-Center, Inc. (RAC), 253
  blatant sex discrimination at, 56–57,
    63
  lawsuits against, 46, 48, 56–57, 92,
    100, 108, 123, 205
  sexual harassment at, 100, 108, 123,
    149
  and working from inside up, 275–76
Reskin, Barbara, 149
restaurants, 43–44, 85
  blatant sex discrimination and, 57–60,
    93
  sexual harassment at, 108–21, 132,
    136–37
retail industry, 46
  blatant sex discrimination in, 54, 61,
    63–69
  sexual harassment and, 121, 139,
    143–44
retaliation, 160, 292
  blatant sex discrimination and, 51, 70,
    77, 79–80, 85, 90–93
  lawsuits and, 43–48, 70, 77, 79–80, 85,
    90–93
  sexual harassment and, 100, 132, 142,
    259
retirement, retirement plans, 5–6, 41
  blatant sex discrimination and, 73, 76,
    85, 96
  and discrimination against mothers,
    198, 205
  everyday discrimination and, 180, 188,
    190, 192–93
  and personal costs of wage gap, 22–24,
    26–27, 29, 31–32
  sexual harassment and, 135, 144
  workplace sex segregation and, 161,
    172
Richards, Cindy, 202–3
Rothchild, Nina, 261–65
Rowland, Ginger, 199

Ruggiero, Mary, 156
Rustic Inn Crabhouse, 93

Sacramento Kings, 46, 121, 142
Sadler, Norma, 72
salespeople, 44
  blatant sex discrimination and, 63–64,
    66, 80, 90–91
  everyday discrimination and, 183, 187
  and excuses for not dealing with wage
    gap, 224, 227
  sexual harassment and, 111, 118–19
  workplace sex segregation and, 146,
    151
Salomon Smith Barney, 46, 49, 101,
    125–27, 138–39
San Francisco Bay Bridge, 154
Santiago, Monica, 108
Schaeffer, Larry, 94–95
Schroeder, Patricia, 254
science, scientists:
  and attempts to end sex
    discrimination, 238–49
  and working from inside up, 238–43,
    273–74
  and working from top down, 293–94
  workplace sex segregation and,
    166–68
Sears, 46, 121, 143–44
second jobs, 161–62
secretaries, 24, 184, 230, 239, 243
  blatant sex discrimination and, 80,
    84
  sexual harassment and, 111–13, 116,
    120, 122, 143
  workplace sex segregation and,
    146–47, 163–65, 170
Securities and Exchange Commission
    (SEC), 126, 304–5
security guards, 72, 117, 163
  blatant sex discrimination and, 51, 72,
    90

sex discrimination:
  as default behavior, 41–42
  definitions of, 13–14
  documenting incidences of, 10,
    234–37, 243, 245, 247, 255–56,
    260, 262, 265–66, 268–71, 277,
    283, 286, 305
  as illegal, 13, 51–52, 54, 60, 62, 67,
    228, 230, 233, 277, 281, 284–85,
    288, 303–4
  in past, 238
  prevalence of, 40–42, 217
  statistics on, 40, 42–49, 228
  wage gap as measurement of, 37–38,
    40–49
sexual harassment, 14, 217, 230, 269,
  297
  activities associated with, 101–3,
    105–15, 123–27, 129–34, 143–44,
    253, 259
  and attempts to end sex
    discrimination, 253–56, 258–60
  blatant sex discrimination and, 84,
    88–93, 95
  causes of, 140–41
  costs to women of, 101, 104, 125–26,
    130–42
  everyday discrimination and, 175, 182
  by few bad people, 108–23
  large-scale, 123–42, 144
  lawsuits and, 43–49, 100–113, 115–27,
    132–44, 160, 253–54, 259, 292
  by one bad person, 105–8, 110–13
  in past, 102–3
  prevalence of, 102–3, 135, 141
  serial, 47, 116, 124, 130
  wage discrimination by, 100–144
  why it continues, 141–42
  workplace sex segregation and,
    148–49, 154–56, 158, 164
Shain, Sidney, 73
Shearson Lehman, 125–27

Shultz, Gary, 257–59, 287, 289
Siler-Khodr, Theresa, 73, 76
Simat Helliesen & Eichner (SH&E),
  107, 113
skilled trades, 151–54
Smith, Debra, 153–55
Smith, Larry, 140
socializing, 53, 212, 268
  everyday discrimination and, 182–83,
    186
Social Security, 22, 24, 27, 32
Sprenger + Lang, 94
Stearn, Jamey, 81, 199
Steinberg, Ronnie, 262
stereotypes, stereotyping:
  and attempts to end sex
    discrimination, 246, 248, 251
  and discrimination against mothers,
    196, 199–212
  everyday discrimination and, 178–79,
    181, 183, 185–86
  for working fathers, 10, 201–4, 210
  and working from inside up, 271,
    279
  and working from top down, 285–86,
    293–95, 298
  workplace sex segregation and,
    148–49, 152–53, 164–65,
    169
Stop & Shop Supermarket Companies,
  218
Sugerman, Lauren, 148, 155–56
Summers, Liz, 69
Supreme Court, U.S., 52, 89, 103
Swift, Jane, 201

Tailhook convention, 140
Tales from the Boom-Boom Room
  (Antilla), 125
Talley, Ernest, 56–57, 63
Technicolor Videocassette, Inc., 47,
  139–40

tenure, 43, 269, 294
  and attempts to end sex
    discrimination, 239, 242, 244, 249
  blatant sex discrimination and, 74–77
Texas, University of, 48, 73, 77
Thomas, Clarence, 89
tokenism, 297–98
trades, 151–54, 293–94
  see also construction industry
transfers, 69, 82, 85, 87
transportation, travel, 83, 151, 178, 227,
    272
  and discrimination against mothers,
    195, 205
  and personal costs of wage gap, 22–24,
    29–32
  sexual harassment and, 109–14
truck drivers, truck riders, 44, 46, 263,
    285
  blatant sex discrimination and, 57–59,
    92
  sexual harassment and, 120, 138

unions, 24, 191
  and attempts to end sex
    discrimination, 253–55
  workplace sex segregation and, 153,
    155, 157–58, 160
unpaid leaves, 82, 84

Vest, Charles, 8, 241–49, 256, 270, 276,
    281, 286, 288
Virginia, 46, 48, 107, 113, 194
volunteerism, 166, 170

waitresses, 44
  blatant sex discrimination and, 57–60,
    93
  sexual harassment and, 110, 112, 117,
    119, 121
  workplace sex segregation and, 146,
    164, 285

Waldron, Sandra, 156–57
Wal-Mart, 10, 48–49, 122, 199
  blatant sex discrimination at, 69, 81,
    85
warehouse workers, 58–61, 80
Washington, 150–51, 261
Washington Post, The, 107, 116
Wassong, Dan, 106–7
Weddington, Pennie, 62
Weeks, Rena, 116
WFSB-TV, 51, 93
widows, 31–32
Wilfong et al., and EEOC v. Rent-a-
    Center, Inc., 100, 108, 123
Wilkins, S. Vance, Jr., 107
Wilkinson, B. J., 187–90, 282
Williams, Joan, 178, 198–200, 295
Winston-Salem, N.C., 156–57
Woman's Guide to Successful
    Negotiation, A (Miller and Miller),
    280
women:
  alleged deficiencies of, 9–11, 27,
    52–53, 55, 62, 64–65, 68–69,
    146
  ambitions of, 4–5, 27, 78, 82, 86, 128,
    132, 191, 224–26
  pragmatism, 25
  self-blame of, 55
  statistics on, 16, 28–29, 31, 54, 146,
    153
Women Are Getting Even (WAGE)
    Clubs, 267–68, 270, 272, 274, 278,
    282–83
Women Are Getting Even (WAGE)
    Project, 43, 237
  outside pressure and, 300–301
  and working from inside up, 267–68,
    270–72, 275, 283
  and working from top down, 286–87,
    289–90
Women in the Fire Service, 156

woodworkers, 7, 22, 119, 153, 224, 282
  and discrimination against mothers,
    205, 210
  everyday discrimination and, 174,
    187–90
working from inside up, 265–83
  and attempts to end sex
    discrimination, 238–43, 245, 247,
    250, 255–56, 260, 262, 265
  celebrating in, 266, 268, 282–83
  collaboration in, 266, 273–77, 280–83
  documentation in, 266, 268–71, 277,
    283
  negotiating in, 266, 271, 275–83
  research in, 266, 271–73, 277, 280,
    282–83
  in sketch of solution to wage gap,
    234–37
  talking to boss in, 280–82
working from outside in, see outside
  pressure
working from top down:
  to adjust pay scales throughout
    companies, 289–91
  and attempts to end sex
    discrimination, 244–47, 256–60
  and CEOs, 281, 284–98
  and hiring practices, 288, 293–98
  insisting on roughly equal numbers in,
    297–98

insisting on zero tolerance for overt
  discrimination in, 291–93
monitoring and measuring progress
  in, 296–97
and promotions, 291, 293–96
and raises, 289–90, 293, 296
in sketch of solution to wage gap,
  234–37
workplace sex segregation, 14, 145–73,
  175, 217, 302
causes of, 146–47
construction trades and, 146, 148,
  150–56, 173
costs to women of, 147, 154, 162
firefighters and, 156–62
girls keep out mentality in, 148–51,
  157, 167
lawsuits and, 147, 153, 160, 162, 165
nonprofit sector and, 166, 170–73,
  285
skilled trades and, 151–54
statistics on, 146, 153, 156–57, 165,
  169
wage gap and, 147–48, 162–73
white-collar, 166–70
World Health Organization (WHO), 145
www.salary.com, 271, 282
www.wageproject.org, 43, 187, 267, 273

Zwemke, Faith, 263–65, 290

About the Authors

EVELYN MURPHY was the Lieutenant Governor of Massachusetts from 1987 to 1991. She was the first woman in the state's history to hold statewide office. She has been an executive vice president of Blue Cross & Blue Shield of Massachusetts and is a corporate director of SBLI USA Mutual Life Insurance Company, Inc. She is the founder and president of The WAGE (Women Are Getting Even) Project Inc., which is dedicated to closing the wage gap in every American workplace. Visit her at wageproject.org.

E.J. GRAFF, a senior correspondent for *The American Prospect*, has written for such publications as *The New York Times, The New Republic, The Boston Globe,* the *Los Angeles Times,* and Salon.com. She is the author of *What Is Marriage For? The Strange Social History of Our Most Intimate Institution.*